THE LAW OF HUMANITY PROJECT

This book provides the first comprehensive introduction to the role of humanity in international law, offering a fresh perspective to a discussion with global implications. The 1990s and the first decade of the twenty-first century witnessed the sporadic emergence of a new vision of global law. Although the vision has taken many different forms, all instances of it have been uniform in their attempt to radically alter how we understand international law, by seeking to posit the human as the primary subject of the international legal order and humanity as its main source of legitimacy. Together, this book calls these instances 'the law of humanity project'. In so doing, it also paints a picture of and critically assesses a particular moment in the history of international law – a moment which may have already come to a sudden end as a consequence of the current populist backlash in world politics, but during which it seemed inevitable that the law of humanity vision would come to play an increasingly important role in world affairs.

Volume 82 in the series Studies in International Law

Studies in International Law

Recent titles in this series

Allocating International Responsibility Between Member States and International Organisations
Nikolaos Voulgaris

Predictability and Flexibility in the Law of Maritime Delimitation, 2nd edition
Yoshifumi Tanaka

Feminist Engagement with International Criminal Law: Norm Transfer, Complementarity, Rape and Consent
Eithne Dowds

Asylum Control and Access to Protection: Admission, Readmission and Human Rights
Mariagiulia Giuffré

Intertemporal Linguistics in International Law: Beyond Contemporaneous and Evolutionary Treaty Interpretation
Julian Wyatt

The Responsibility to Protect and the Failures of the United Nations Security Council
P M Butchard

The Role of Multilateral Environmental Agreements: A Reconciliatory Approach to Environmental Protection in Armed Conflict
Britta Sjostedt

Prosecutorial Discretion at the International Criminal Court
Anni Pues

Judicial Deference in International Adjudication: A Comparative Analysis
Johannes Hendrik Fahner

Human Rights Commitments of Islamic States: Sharia, Treaties and Consensus
Paul McDonough

Intervention in Civil Wars: Effectiveness, Legitimacy, and Human Rights
Chiara Redaelli

General Principles as a Source of International Law: Art 38(1)(c) of the Statute of the International Court of Justice
Imogen Saunders

For a complete list of titles in this series, see www.bloomsburyprofessional.com/uk/series/studies-in-international-law

The Law of Humanity Project

A Story of International Law Reform and State-making

Ukri Soirila

•HART•

OXFORD • LONDON • NEW YORK • NEW DELHI • SYDNEY

HART PUBLISHING
Bloomsbury Publishing Plc
Kemp House, Chawley Park, Cumnor Hill, Oxford, OX2 9PH, UK
1385 Broadway, New York, NY 10018, USA
29 Earlsfort Terrace, Dublin 2, Ireland

HART PUBLISHING, the Hart/Stag logo, BLOOMSBURY and the Diana logo are trademarks of Bloomsbury Publishing Plc

First published in Great Britain 2021

A catalogue record for this book is available from the British Library.

Library of Congress Cataloging-in-Publication data

Names: Soirila, Ukri, author.

Title: The law of humanity project : a story of international law reform and state-making / Ukri Soirila.

Description: Oxford, UK ; New York, NY : Hart Publishing, an imprint of Bloomsbury Publishing, 2021. | Series: Studies in international law ; volume 82 | Includes bibliographical references and index.

Identifiers: LCCN 2021004288 (print) | LCCN 2021004289 (ebook) | ISBN 9781509938919 (hardback) | ISBN 9781509950065 (paperback) | ISBN 9781509938933 (pdf) | ISBN 9781509938926 (Epub)

Subjects: LCSH: International law and human rights.

Classification: LCC KZ1266 .S65 2021 (print) | LCC KZ1266 (ebook) | DDC 341.4/8—dc23

LC record available at https://lccn.loc.gov/2021004288

LC ebook record available at https://lccn.loc.gov/2021004289

ISBN: HB: 978-1-50993-891-9
ePDF: 978-1-50993-893-3
ePub: 978-1-50993-892-6

Typeset by Compuscript Ltd, Shannon

To find out more about our authors and books visit www.hartpublishing.co.uk. Here you will find extracts, author information, details of forthcoming events and the option to sign up for our newsletters.

Acknowledgements

THIS BOOK STARTED its life as a doctoral thesis. My greatest debt goes to my supervisor Martti Koskenniemi, who both encouraged and constructively challenged me throughout the writing process of the book. I am also grateful to my doctoral examination opponent, Samuel Moyn, and pre-examiners, Susan Marks and Pål Wrange, for their insightful comments that greatly helped to transform the thesis into a book.

I have been privileged to have Jan Klabbers, Jarna Petman, Pamela Slotte, Miia Halme-Tuomisaari and Samuli Hurri as my mentors during my doctoral studies and the first years of my postdoctoral life. I owe a great deal to all of them, as well to Guilherme Vasconcelos Vilaça, David Scott, Luca Bonadiman and Susanna Lindroos-Hovinheimo, all of whom read the entire manuscript – in some cases more than once – and provided important comments. Furthermore, Elina Almila, Janis Grzybowski, Ville Kari, Margareta Klabbers, Laura Kirvesniemi, Tero Kivinen, Daria Krivonos, Tero Lundstedt, Ketino Minashvili, Sanna Mustasaari Kati Nieminen, Outi Penttilä, Eliška Pírková, Santtu Raitasuo, Sahib Singh, Milka Sormunen and Kangle Zhang have been important fellow travellers on this journey.

The Faculty of Law at the University of Helsinki and the Erik Castén Institute have provided a safe and inspiring home for writing this book. I have benefited from conversations with and support from Paolo Amorosa, Maria José Belmonte Sanchez, Martin Björklund, Anja Blank, Mónica Garcia-Salmones, Dorota Gozdecka, Lauri Hannikainen, Miikka Hiltunen, Ari Hirvonen, Manuel Jimenez Fonseca, Jukka Kekkonen, Magdalena Kmak, Katja Kreutz, Ida Koivisto, Paavo Kotiaho, Visa Kurki, Veronica Lankinen, Luíza Leão Soares Pereira, Päivi Leino-Sandberg, Pia Letto-Vanamo, Sakari Melander, Parvathi Menon, Panu Minkkinen, Pekka Niemelä, Liisa Nieminen, Kimmo Nuotio, Tuomas Ojanen, Anne Orford, Darina Petrova, Anne-Sophie Rapp, Diliana Stoyanova, Nicole Stybnarova, Immi Tallgren, Nadia Tapia, Paul Tiensuu, Tuomas Tiittala, Reetta Toivanen, Kaius Tuori, Taina Tuori, Anna-Kaisa Tuovinen, Lauri Uusi-Hakala, Anna Van der Velde, Freek Van der Vet, Sanna Villikka and Sam Wrigley.

Writing this book would not have been possible without generous finding from the Doctoral School Law in a Changing World, the University of Helsinki Research Foundation, the Finnish Cultural Foundation, the Finnish Lawyers' Association and the Kone Foundation. I am also grateful to Anna Liski and Linda Sydänmaanlakka for their tremendous research assistance during the editing phase of the book, and to Sinead Moloney, Sasha Jawed and others at Hart Publishing for guiding this book to publication.

Finally, I wish to thank my family: my mother Eliisa, my father Ari and my brother Pauno. This book is for you.

Contents

List of Cases

International Court of Justice

International Criminal Tribunal for the Former Yugoslavia

European Court of Human Rights

Canada

France

Germany

Israel

South-Africa

UN Documents

1

Introduction

THE 1990S AND the first years of the twenty-first century witnessed the sporadic emergence of a new vision of global law. In a moment of history when the Berlin Wall had fallen, globalisation was producing both new threats and novel opportunities, and human rights seemed the 'last utopia',[1] it was possible to argue that international law was undergoing a dramatic structural, substantive and ideological transformation. For many, the emerging global legal order was becoming significantly different from the 'old' international law, built around states and deriving its legitimacy from their sovereign consent. In contrast to that old system, observers envisioned a global order that ranged far beyond interstate relations in that it would be based on the human individual and aimed at the protection of the interests of 'humanity'.[2] Although this vision has taken many forms, from descriptive to normative, they all share the aim of radically altering how international law is perceived and understood. The vision is spelled out rather explicitly in some academic works, hinted at in others and emerges in different forms in international legal practice and global governance.

This book calls these collective instances 'the law of humanity project'. By the term *law of humanity*, I refer to a vision of a radically altered, 'humanised' version of international law. International law has traditionally been defined as a discipline that deals with the rights and obligations existing between states. After its separation from natural law, the law of nations became – according to the common narrative – positive interstate law, uninterested in individuals and instead treating the state as its primary juridical entity, with a will separable from that of its members.[3] And while that approach was softened towards the end of the twentieth century – as it became generally accepted that individuals

[1] S Moyn, *The Last Utopia: Human Rights in History* (Cambridge, MA, Belknap Press of Harvard University Press, 2012).

[2] R Teitel, *Humanity's Law* (New York, Oxford University Press, 2011); R Domingo, *The New Global Law*, reprint edn (Cambridge, Cambridge University Press, 2011); A Peters, 'Humanity as the A and Ω of Sovereignty' (2009) 20 *European Journal of International Law* 513; J Waldron, 'Are Sovereigns Entitled to the Benefit of the International Rule of Law?' (2011) 22 *European Journal of International Law* 315; E Benvenisti, 'Sovereigns as Trustees of Humanity: On the Accountability of States to Foreign Stakeholders' (2013) 107 *American Journal of International Law* 295; EJ Criddle and E Fox-Decent, *Fiduciaries of Humanity: How International Law Constitutes Authority* (Oxford, Oxford University Press, 2016).

[3] JE Nijman, *The Concept of International Legal Personality: An Inquiry into the History and Theory of International Law* (The Hague, Asser Press, 2004) 83; K Parlett, *The Individual in the*

are beneficiaries or even partial subjects of international law, to the extent that they possess rights and duties deriving from treaties and customary international law[4] – states continued to be perceived as the primary subjects of international law.[5] The law of humanity project, by contrast, seeks to change international law more radically by positing the human as the primary subject, not only a beneficiary, of the legal order and by making the interests of humanity its guiding principle. In the process, the role of the state is to be either diminished or radically altered to that of a trustee, fiduciary or official of humanity.

By the term *project*, the book tries to capture a collection of academic literature describing or advocating for a shift to the law of humanity – sometimes explicitly, other times as a side product of other academic endeavours – as well as the use and circulation of these ideas in the practice of international law and global governance. Together these form a loosely bordered project, or at least a cluster of different projects, with both academic and professional manifestations. With events in the practice of international law and global governance providing material for theories, and theories motivating innovation in practice, the project is perpetually on the move, while always remaining an aspiration. In other words, the project is in a constant state of *becoming*. It is, in Deleuzian terms, *virtual* in the sense that it is *real*, yet not *actual*, and has concrete effects in shaping social reality.[6]

The book provides a story of the rise, fall and potential rebirth of the law of humanity project; a story of ideas, and the use of those ideas in action. At the level of theory, the book analyses academic works which describe, prophesise or demand a change from international law to law of humanity. Although these theories range from descriptive to normative and differ in their substance, theoretical inspiration and observations, they nevertheless form a somewhat unified discourse, with certain key elements, underlying assumptions and ideas. At the level of practice, the book analyses how and with what outcomes have the key concepts of the law of humanity theories been used in global governance, in such diverse fields as human rights law, international criminal law, foreign investment, international territorial administration, global security law and war on terrorism, and humanitarian governance of refugees.

In providing this analysis, the book also paints a picture of a specific moment in the history of international law. During that moment, it seemed inevitable

International Legal System: Continuity and Change in International Law, reprint edn (Cambridge, Cambridge University Press, 2013) 11–14. See, eg E de Vattel, *The Law of Nations* (Indianapolis, Liberty Fund, 2008).

[4] Parlett, *The Individual in the International Legal System*, 353–54.

[5] For an analysis of the international legal personality of the individual under positive international law, as well as the main theoretical positions to it, see A Kjeldgaard-Pedersen, *The International Legal Personality of the Individual* (Oxford, Oxford University Press, 2018).

[6] On the concept of 'virtuality', as it is employed here, see G Deleuze, *Bergsonism*, reissue edn (Cambridge, MA, MIT Press, 1991) 96–98.

that international law would move steadily in a law of humanity direction. Yet, the moment may have already come to a sudden end. During the past decade or so, there has been a turn towards right-wing, populist politics at the domestic level, and consequently a backlash against international law, international institutions and international cooperation.[7] This has been a significant setback for the law of humanity project. Although the core of the liberal international order – including treaties and other methods of facilitating reciprocal relations, state responsibility and diplomacy – are unlikely to be shaken,[8] the law of humanity project has thrived from precisely those developments that have taken the largest blow, such as human rights, global governance, multilateralism and 'universal' community values.

The aim of this book is twofold. On the one hand, it identifies and introduces the law of humanity project, and in so doing connects familiar texts, events and practices in a new way. In particular, the book is interested in how the acclaimed shift towards a humanised international law is represented and what kind of discourse it produces. On the other hand, the book provides an imminent critique of the project. In so doing, it focuses especially on how the language of humanity is employed and on the law of humanity concepts put into practice beyond the law of humanity theories. By comparing these uses to the stated aims of the project, the book argues that some of the uses of the language have been inimical to the aims of the law of humanity theorists, and connects these uses to forms of power and ways of thinking that have been prevalent in the world during the past few decades.

Although the law of humanity project may be less powerful now than it was a decade or two ago, there is much to be gained from its critical assessment. Whilst the project cannot be blamed for the populist backlash, nor is it its direct target, analysing the past 30 years from the perspective of the law of humanity project provides new points of view to some of the developments that the backlashers react to, on complex relations between different mindsets and ways of thinking, on structural forces that have constrained the realisation of different ideas and on developments in international law more generally. As such, the analysis provides a different window into some of the shortcomings of global governance during the past decades, but also outlines possible methods of resistance in the current political climate. Indeed, some of the underlying values and sensibilities of the law of humanity project may provide a valuable counterforce to the prevailing right-wing populist mindset. Hence, although this book seeks to unveil some of the weaknesses and blind spots of the project, and argues that

[7] J Crawford, 'The Current Political Discourse Concerning International Law' (2018) 81 *MLR* 1; M Koskenniemi, 'Enchanted by the Tools? An Enlightenment Perspective' (2019) 35 *American University International Law Review* 397; A Orford, 'International Law and the Populist Moment: A Comment on Martti Koskenniemi's Enchanted by the Tools? International Law and Enlightenment' (2019) 35 *American University International Law Review* 427.

[8] Crawford, 'The Current Political Discourse'.

some of the underlying assumptions of the project are actively counter-productive, it does so in the hope of making the project more politically relevant in the challenging times we live in. In particular, in seeking to understand the ways in which the project has by necessity been embedded in power relations and mindsets which are to some extent inimical to it, the book is primarily seeking to find ways for the project to break free from these connections and become a force of resistance against competing projects which have been dominant in global governance during the past few decades.

I. THE POST-COLD WAR WORLD AND THE HUMANISATION OF INTERNATIONAL LAW

Since its beginning, international law has had a liberal, cosmopolitan pull.[9] Generations of international lawyers have 'attacked sovereignty and re-imagined diplomacy – especially multilateral diplomacy – as the administration of a world society'.[10] For many of them, the individual has also been the true international legal person,[11] even if this has been rarely reflected in international legal practice.[12] In this sense, it would be quite possible to argue that the law of humanity project is nothing new under the sun of international law.

However, what was unprecedented in the first two decades after the Cold War – which is where I place the beginning of the law of humanity project – was the intensity and extent of humanity discourse.[13] By the early 1990s, the world had started to seem like one unit of action as a consequence of the fall of the Berlin wall, ever-closer linkages between national economies, development in information and communication technology, and the rise of the globalisation discourse. The United Nations Security Council was reinvigorated, and took an active role, first in Iraq, soon after in Somalia and then in Libya, Angola, Haiti, the former Yugoslavia and elsewhere. Transnational social movements and international organisations mushroomed,[14] while talk about the retreat or hollowing

[9] M Koskenniemi, *The Gentle Civilizer of Nations: The Rise and Fall of International Law, 1870–1960* (Cambridge, Cambridge University Press, 2002).

[10] M Koskenniemi, 'Global Governance and Public International Law' (2004) 37 *Kritische Justiz* 241, 245–46.

[11] Nijman, *The Concept of International Legal Personality*, ch 3; A Peters, *Beyond Human Rights: The Legal Status of the Individual in International Law* (J Huston trans, Cambridge, Cambridge University Press, 2016) 18–19.

[12] R Portmann, *Legal Personality in International Law* (Cambridge, Cambridge University Press, 2010) 126–72; Parlett (n 3) 13–16. For an alternative reading of the history of international legal personality of the individual, see Kjeldgaard-Pedersen, *The International Legal Personality*.

[13] E Jouannet, *The Liberal-Welfarist Law of Nations: A History of International Law* (C Sutcliffe trans, Cambridge, Cambridge University Press, 2012) 208–09.

[14] ME Keck and K Sikkink, *Activists beyond Borders: Advocacy Networks in International Politics* (Ithaca, Cornell University Press, 1998).

out of the state increased.[15] Following the collapse of both communism and the new international economic order, liberalism seemed like the only option and human rights was the 'last utopia',[16] while authors such as Thomas Franck announced the emergence of individualism and the 'empowered self'.[17]

Yet that sense of euphoria fails to tell the whole truth of the post-1989 moment. Amidst great changes, discontent about international law was growing amongst practitioners and commentators. Instead of beginning to govern the world, international law 'was revealed as part of an old world – part of the problem, not of its solution'.[18] Too formalistic, it was deemed to be too often in the way of doing 'the right thing'. According to the prevailing vision of efficiency and problem-solving, institutions had to be empowered to deal with the unknown by strengthening the executive branch.[19] The space for the clumsy, tiresome rule of international law was consequently shrinking, as it was increasingly seen to be in the way of progress.

The period was also one of uncertainty and instability in many parts of the world. States were crumbling not only in the ruins of the former Soviet Union, but across the globe. What emerged was an increasing number of smaller, less powerful states, which were disintegrating under the pressure of global economic forces, separatist movements and ethnic conflicts. Several states were also either fragmented into two or more pieces, such as the Soviet Union, Yugoslavia and Czechoslovakia, or were declared as failed states or states of insecurity, such as Somalia, Ethiopia, Afghanistan, Sierra Leone, Liberia, Rwanda, Congo and Sudan. In this fragile condition, states were quickly losing power to transnational and international authorities at the same time as they were outsourcing many of their formerly public functions to private companies. Structural adjustment and shock therapy programmes constrained political participation and self-determination by making it impossible for the people of the target states to determine their economic and political system, and limited states' ability to ensure that their populations had access to food, health, education, social security or employment. This produced marginalisation, created conditions where serious violations of civil and political rights were more likely, and increased discontent on the position of foreign investors in comparison to local populations.[20] Even the UN Secretary-General Kofi Annan declared in 1998 that the most optimistic interpretations of globalisation were little more than 'utterly wishful thinking',

[15] S Strange, *The Retreat of the State: The Diffusion of Power in the World Economy* (Cambridge, Cambridge University Press, 1996); K Ohmae, *The End of the Nation State: The Rise of Regional Economies* (New York, Free Press, 1996); RAW Rhodes, *Network Governance and the Differentiated Polity, Selected Essays*, vol 1 (Oxford, Oxford University Press, 2017) ch 8.

[16] Moyn, *The Last Utopia*.

[17] TM Franck, *The Empowered Self: Law and Society in an Age of Individualism* (Oxford, Oxford University Press, 1999).

[18] Koskenniemi, 'Global Governance and Public International Law', 248.

[19] A Somek, *The Cosmopolitan Constitution* (Oxford, Oxford University Press, 2014) 216.

[20] A Orford, 'Contesting Globalization: A Feminist Perspective on the Future of Human Rights' (1998) 8 *Transnational Law & Contemporary Problems* 171, 178–82.

drawing attention to the fact that 'the belief in the ability of markets to resolve all divisions neglected the reality of differences of interest and outlook'.[21] In stark contrast to the promises of capitalism, the combination of globalisation and the shutting down of traditional domestic defence mechanisms threatened to leave the losers of global capitalism completely without shelter against the worst social effects of global economic forces.[22] Conflicts increased, and fragility, combined with globalisation, provided fertile ground for the circulation of drugs, weapons and even nuclear material, and gave birth to ever more complex terrorist and criminal networks.[23]

These events in world politics, economics, culture and technology were reflected also in developments in international law. Novel possibilities and increasing global cooperation stimulated the creation of new rules and the reinterpretation of old ones, whereas the sense of new threats and a rapidly changing world filled international lawyers with a sense of urgency and provoked claims that international law had to adapt to be able respond to the challenges of globalisation. Many of the ensuing developments were of crucial importance for the birth of the law of humanity theories. Most importantly, new rules and judicial decisions inspired claims about the 'humanisation of international law', and thus provided material for the law of humanity theorists to argue that international law was undergoing a radical structural shift. The new theories again stimulated new developments in practice, producing a kind of mutually reinforcing loop between scholars and practitioners. Indeed, a key feature of the law of humanity project, as this book tries to present it, is that it is built around a co-productive relation between practice and theory, practice feeding academic arguments and academic arguments inspiring and guiding practice. Thus, the project has both theoretical and practical manifestations, but is not reducible to either.

Perhaps the most important development prompting arguments about the humanisation of international law was the final breakthrough of human rights. Not only did international human rights law gain in importance, but, even more crucially, human rights were also claimed to produce ripple effects throughout international law. As the argument now goes, the success story of human rights has solidified the position of the individual as a (perhaps still passive) subject of international law[24] and has saturated all fields of international law with human rights considerations.[25]

[21] K Annan, 'The Politics of Globalisation' (1998), academy.wcfia.harvard.edu/politics-globalization-hon-kofi-annan.

[22] E Hobsbawm, *Age of Extremes: The Short Twentieth Century, 1914–1991*, new edn (London, Abacus, 1995) ch 19.

[23] The Commission on Global Governance, Global Governance: Our Global Neighbourhood, 'Chapter 1: A New World', www.gdrc.org/u-gov/global-neighbourhood/.

[24] VP Tzevelekos, 'Revisiting the Humanisation of International Law: Limits and Potential. Obligations Erga Omnes, Hierarchy of Rules and the Principle of Due Diligence as the Basis for Further Humanisation' (2013) 6 *Erasmus Law Review* 62, 66.

[25] T Meron, *The Humanization of International Law* (Leiden, Brill Academic Publishers, 2006); AA Cançado Trindade, *International Law for Humankind* (Leiden, Brill Academic Publishers, 2010). See also Tzevelekos, 'Revisiting the Humanisation'.

Another development that has produced ripple effects throughout international law is the mainstreaming of the concept of human security in world politics. Human security is commonly defined as a people-centred approach to security, based on the idea that the human individual, rather than the state, should be the referent object of security.[26] Within international law, the human security approach is reflected in the responsibility to protect concept. According to the formulation of the International Commission on Intervention and State Sovereignty (ICISS), the responsibility to protect concept entails that when a state manifestly fails to protect its population from grave human rights violations, the responsibility to do so falls on the international community.[27] While responsibility to protect has failed to crystallise as a rule of customary international law, it has nevertheless shaped in important ways how we perceive many aspects of international law and international relations.[28]

Among the ripple effects produced by human rights and human security are crucial changes in international humanitarian law.[29] According to commentators, human rights and human security considerations have broadened the scope of protection under humanitarian law, both spatially and in terms of the persons entitled to protection.[30] The influence of human rights and human security considerations is said to be visible, for example, in the strict prohibition of reprisals against civilian targets,[31] in the changing nature of the law of occupation,[32] in the re-emergence of international criminal liability[33] and in the discussion surrounding immunities.[34]

Another area where the position of the individual is claimed to have increased significantly has been international investment law. Under the International Centre for Settlement of Investment Disputes (ICSID) Convention, private investors from the parties to the Convention can make arbitration claims against other state parties in which they have made investments. According to Anne Peters, this is 'a genuine, autonomous procedural right of the investor under international law'.[35] Furthermore, secondary claims arising from investment

[26] S Alkire, 'A Conceptual Framework for Human Security', Working Paper 2 (Oxford, CRISE, 2003) 3; L Axworthy, 'Human Security and Global Governance: Putting People First' (2001) 7 *Global Governance* 19; G Oberlietner, 'Human Security: A Challenge to International Law' (2005) 11 *Global Governance* 185; B von Tigerstrom, *Human Security and International Law: Prospects and Problems* (Oxford, Hart Publishing, 2007) 16–17.

[27] Human security and responsibility to protect will be discussed more extensively in ch 5.

[28] J Bartelson, *Sovereignty as Symbolic Form* (Abingdon, Routledge, 2014) 84.

[29] Teitel, *Humanity's Law*, 9; Meron, *The Humanization of International Law*, 3–4.

[30] T Meron, 'The Humanization of Humanitarian Law' (2000) 94 *American Journal of International Law* 239.

[31] ibid 247–50.

[32] E Benvenisti, *The International Law of Occupation*, 2nd edn (Oxford, Oxford University Press, 2012); GH Fox, *Humanitarian Occupation* (Cambridge, Cambridge University Press, 2008).

[33] For discussion, see Peters, *Beyond Human Rights*, 122–23. Peters believes that individuals do have criminal responsibility under general international law.

[34] A Bianchi, 'Immunity versus Human Rights: The Pinochet Case' (1999) 10 *European Journal of International Law* 237, 246–47.

[35] Peters (n 11) 285; see also Parlett (n 3) 106.

disputes 'belong almost indisputably to the investors' and host states have international legal responsibility towards those investors.[36]

It has also been claimed that the humanisation process has reached such traditional areas of international law as consular law, diplomatic protection, law of treaties and state responsibility. According to the traditional approach, Article 36(1) of the Vienna Convention on Consular Relations granted rights to the contracting states. According to a more contemporary approach, however, consular assistance is also an individual right of citizens located abroad.[37] Similarly, although it is still unclear under existing international law whether the state exercising diplomatic protection asserts its own right, the right of its nationals or both, it has been claimed that courts and other international actors are at least increasingly open to the idea that the right holder could be the individual.[38] Moreover, it seems to be also fairly well accepted that the ability of an individual to exercise her rights is not affected by the fact that the remedy is sought by the state.[39] When it comes to law of treaties, the discussion has been mostly focused on reservations, following the European Court of Human Rights' (ECtHR) *Loizidou* case, in which the Court found Turkey's reservation to the European Convention on Human Rights to be against its object and purpose.[40]

Finally, in the context of state responsibility, evidence of humanisation is found in the International Law Commission's (ILC) work on the Articles on the Responsibility of States for Internationally Wrongful Acts (ARSIWA).[41] Article 33(2) states that anything written in the ARSIWA about obligations to other states is without prejudice to possible responsibility towards non-state actors, such as human persons. Article 48 of the ARSIWA also confirms that, in the case of a breach of *erga omnes* or *erga omnes partes* obligations, a state may invoke the responsibility of another state in the interest of the beneficiaries of the obligation breached – those beneficiaries including individuals.[42] Indeed, according to Tzevelekos, *erga omnes* obligations are transforming the previously state-centric international order, based on bilateral relations and reciprocity, towards the idea of a community. Whilst *erga omnes* obligations may have been included into positive international law through a rather 'revolutionary obiter dictum',[43] it has, according to Tzevelekos, become an integral

[36] Peters (n 11) 346.

[37] ibid 349.

[38] ibid 406–07.

[39] G Gaja, 'The Position of Individuals in International Law: An ILC Perspective' (2010) 21 *European Journal of International Law* 11, 13–14.

[40] *Loizidou v Turkey* (Preliminary Objections) Series A no 310 (1995) 20 EHRR 99.

[41] ILC, 'Draft Articles on Responsibility of States for Internationally Wrongful Acts' (2001) 53rd Session, Supplement no 10 (A/56/10), ch IV.E.1.

[42] Gaja, 'The Position of Individuals', 11–12.

[43] Tzevelekos refers to *Barcelona Traction, Light and Power Company, Limited (Belgium v Spain)* (Second Phase, Preliminary Objections) [1970] ICJ Rep 3, paras 33–35.

part of international law. This, again, may allow even further mainstreaming of common values such as human rights and human dignity in international law. As Tzevelekos writes,

> obligations *erga omnes* may have far-reaching implications, allowing for change in a number of areas of international law … and do have the potential to fertilise the legal order with a series of innovative elements that affect the very essence of its systemic structure.[44]

In light of these developments, it would indeed seem rather uncontroversial that individuals, as well as 'humanity' at large, have an increasingly important place in international law – at least at the level of discourse. Nevertheless, it is worth pointing out that there have also been important countertrends to the process of humanisation. The ECtHR's 'activist' stance on reservations in *Loizidou* caused wide debate on the special nature of human rights law, the President of the International Court of Justice (ICJ), for example, blaming the ECtHR for the fragmentation of international law,[45] and the ILC also took the view that what counts is state will.[46] Similarly, both the ICJ and the ECtHR have been remarkably tolerant towards immunities, even when human rights are at stake.[47] Tzevelekos also points out the glaring contrast between the initial progressive vision of Special Rapporteur John Dugard and the ILC and the final result of the ILC project with regard to diplomatic protection. The ILC and Dugard defended the view that 'states should be obliged to resort to diplomatic protection in case of *jus cogens* violations'.[48] Yet, such a vision has 'either entirely disappeared or been downgraded to spineless form of recommendation',[49] inviting states merely to 'give due consideration'[50] to the possibility of exercising diplomatic protection. And most recently, of course, there has been a populist backlash against various forms of international cooperation and international institutions.[51]

According to Tzevelekos, these instances demonstrate 'that the humanisation of international law has proven to have limits'.[52] Kate Parlett, too, takes a rather cautious stance after analysing in detail the position of the individual in

[44] Tzevelekos (n 24) 67.
[45] 'The Proliferation of International Judicial Bodies: The Outlook for the International Legal Order', speech by his Excellency Judge Gilbert Guillaume, President of the International Court of Justice, to the Sixth Committee of the General Assembly of the United Nations, 27 October 2000, www.icj cij.org/court/.
[46] ILC, 'Guide to Practice on Reservations to Treaties' (2011), 63rd session (A/66/10), Art 4.5.3(4).
[47] *Jurisdictional Immunities of the State (Germany v Italy, Greece intervening)* [2012] ICJ Rep 3, paras 93 et seq; *Al-Adsani v The United Kingdom* (2002) 34 EHRR 273, para 54.
[48] Tzevelekos (n 24) 65. See ILC, 'First Report on Diplomatic Protection by Mr John R Dugard, Special Rapporteur' (2000), 52nd Session (A/CN 4/506) Art 4, paras 75 et seq.
[49] ibid.
[50] ILC, 'Draft Articles on Diplomatic Protection' (2006), 61st Session, Supplement no 10 (A/61/10), Art 19(4).
[51] Crawford (n 7).
[52] Tzevelekos (n 24) 65.

international law. Although she agrees that international law is less state-centric and gives more prominence to the individual than its nineteenth-century variant, she argues that states still have a dominant role in it, whereas the capacities of individuals remain rather limited and their protection is contextual.[53]

In the absence of any objective yardsticks on which to measure the humanisation of international law, then, it seems that the process, or lack of it, is in the eye of the beholder. This book does not seek to make a claim in either direction. Rather, the developments referred to as humanisation are introduced here because they form an essential building block for the law of humanity theories. As will be discussed in more detail in chapter two, different theorists I connect to the law of humanity project emphasise rather different aspects of humanisation of international law and globalisation. While most theorists are optimistic, reading globalisation and increased interconnections in positive light, others focus more on the novel threats posed by globalisation – such as unfettered capitalism, increasing trafficking of persons, weapons and drugs, cultural conflicts provoked by increasing cultural homogenization, and climate change – in making a more normative claim for the need of law of humanity as a response to these global threats.[54] Furthermore, the authors seek to participate in rather different theoretical discussions, ranging from constitutionalisation[55] and fragmentation[56] of international law to global law.[57] But almost all of them nevertheless base their empirical or normative arguments on the aforementioned developments.

II. CONTRIBUTIONS AND ARGUMENTS

Instead of making a case for or against humanisation of international law, this book is interested in how that humanisation is represented in academic works, what kind of discourse those works form and how the humanity language has been used in the practice of global governance. The book seeks to make three main contributions. First, in analysing, synthesising and combining familiar works, events and practices in a new way, the book identifies and introduces what it calls the law of humanity project. Although those connections have not been made before and the authors that I associate with the project likely perceive themselves as participating in different discussions and having their own individual projects, I contend that identifying and analysing the law of humanity

[53] Parlett (n 3) 371–72.

[54] Domingo, *The New Global Law*, xiii.

[55] A Peters, 'The Merits of Global Constitutionalism' (2009) 16 *Indiana Journal of Global Legal Studies* 397.

[56] R Howse and R Teitel, 'Does Humanity-Law Require (or Imply) a Progressive Theory or History? (And Other Questions for Martti Koskenniemi)' (2013) 27 *Temple International & Comparative Law Journal* 377.

[57] Domingo (n 2).

project is important, for it reveals a mindset that has played an important ideological role in international legal discourse and global governance since the 1990s and continues to do so in a slightly weakened form even today, despite some recent setbacks.

Although the law of humanity theories form a diverse cluster of works, with important differences, I argue that they nevertheless share certain key aspects which make them a loosely connected project. For one, they represent themselves as seeking to posit the human at the centre of international law, or at least make the empirical claim that such a process is ongoing. Moreover, the theories make the claim that that process is diminishing or at least radically altering the role of the state. And finally, all of the theories have concepts, rather than, say, new rules, as their central tools: it is assumed by law of humanity theorists that the increased relevance of certain fundamental concepts of law of humanity will eventually change the way international law is perceived, shifting it in the direction of the law of humanity, and replacing the state with the human at the centre of the legal order. Three such concepts are particularly important, according to my reading, namely human rights, human security and human dignity. Although other concepts also play a role in the project, they are usually derived from, and thus rely on, one of the aforementioned three.

The second contribution of the book is to provide an immanent critique of the project, focusing especially on its blind spots. In so doing, it measures the success of the law of humanity project not against external standards, but rather against how the project presents itself. What differentiates the approach from mere internal critique, however, is that the book goes beyond demonstrating discrepancies between the theory of the law of humanity and the use of humanity rhetoric in action: in turning the internal critique into an immanent one, the book focuses especially on the forms of power and power relations behind these discrepancies. In so doing, the book adds a more large-scale social and structural component to the analysis.[58]

At the heart of the critique presented in this book is the observation that, in the law of humanity mindset, concepts have a clear meaning and produce outcomes that are aligned with that meaning. Thus, for the proponents of the project, increased use of concepts such as human rights, human security and human dignity is a victory in itself and a sign of social progress. This book challenges that way of thinking. According to a basic premise of the book, the meaning of a concept in the social world is not about its reference but its *use*,[59] and hence the meaning of concepts is in constant fluctuation as both situational and long-term struggles are waged over their ownership.[60] As the

[58] C Browne, 'The End of Immanent Critique?' (2008) 11 *European Journal of Social Theory* 5, 8.

[59] F Kratochwil, 'Has the "Rule of Law" Become a "Rule of Lawyers"? An Inquiry into the Use and Abuse of an Ancient Topos in Contemporary Debates' in G Palombella and N Walker (eds), *Relocating the Rule of Law* (Oxford, Hart Publishing, 2009) 195.

[60] K Palonen, 'An Application of Conceptual History to Itself: From Method to Theory in Reinhart Kosellecks's Begriffsgeschifte' (1997) 1 *Finnish Yearbook of Political Thought* 36.

chapters of the book demonstrate, the key concepts of the law of humanity project have been used by a very wide range of actors, with somewhat different aims, from non-governmental organisations to governments, from churches to international organisations and from social movements to powerful economic actors, such as multinational corporations and the World Bank. Thus, the starting point of my critique towards the law of humanity project is that it should learn to pay more attention to what its key concepts do in the practice of global governance – or, rather, what is done with them in the global architecture of power – and with what outcomes. Consequently, the project's narrative of progress also has to be rejected, for that narrative has more to do with the presuppositions of the humanity discourse 'than with the empirical proof of an "evolution" brought about either by conscious design or working itself out behind the backs of the actors'.[61]

One of the key arguments of the book is that perhaps the most tangible outcome of the use of the humanity language in global governance has been the disciplining of the state. From international human rights law to international investment law, and from international territorial administration missions to humanitarian governance of refugees, humanity language has been used to convince or coerce states into adopting very specific policies, laws and institutions, and to enable deeply penetrating interventions into the core functions of the state. This is partly in line with the aims of the law of humanity project, one of those aims being to replace the state or alter its role as the leading actor in international law. Yet, this book argues that the outcomes of this disciplining are not, in fact, in line with the more fundamental aim of the project, namely increased human welfare and empowerment. As is demonstrated in chapter four, the most fundamental forces in the 'battle for the state',[62] fought through, among other things, humanity language, have been the managerialist and neoliberal projects, which have a very specific, limited function for the state and are highly suspicious of mass politics.[63] As I argue, the ensuing outcomes of the disciplining of the state, including privatisation, the extension of the market logic to all

[61] F Kratochwil, 'Leaving Sovereignty Behind? An Inquiry into the Politics of Post-Modernity' in R Falk, M Juergensmeyer and V Popovski (eds), *Legality and Legitimacy in Global Affairs* (Oxford, Oxford University Press, 2012) 131.

[62] A Orford, 'Food Security, Free Trade, and the Battle for the State' (2015) 11 *Journal of International Law & International Relations* 1.

[63] Q Slobodian, *Globalists: The End of Empire and the Birth of Neoliberalism* (Cambridge, MA, Harvard University Press, 2018); J Whyte, *The Morals of the Market: Human Rights and the Rise of Neoliberalism* (London, Verso, 2019); W Brown, *Undoing the Demos: Neoliberalism's Stealth Revolution*, reprint edn (Cambridge, MA, Zone Books – MIT Press, 2017); W Brown, *In the Ruins of Neoliberalism* (New York, Columbia University Press, 2019); A Orford, 'Book Review Article: International Territorial Administration and the Management of Decolonization' (2010) 59 *International & Comparative Law Quarterly* 227; M Koskenniemi, 'Human Rights Mainstreaming as a Strategy for Institutional Power' (2010) 1 *Humanity: An International Journal of Human Rights, Humanitarianism, and Development* 47.

aspects of society and priority being given to a certain conception of property rights, are inimical to the aims of the law of humanity project, and have also played a role in the populist backlash that is threatening the law of humanity project but has left neoliberalism mostly unscathed.

The final contribution of the book, then, is to rethink some of the assumptions of the law of humanity project and consider possible paths ahead in a moment of history dominated by neoliberalism, managerialism and the populist backlash. In particular, the aim is to make the project politically savvy, more resilient to competing projects that try to hijack its concepts and more attuned to addressing the economic inequalities that are (alongside climate change) the most pressing issues of our time. With this aim in mind – and starting from the premise that some of the key values of the law of humanity project can provide a valuable counterforce to the right-wing, nationalistic and even authoritarian mindset – the book proposes that the project should: become more sensitive to the ways in which concepts are tools of power; resist depoliticisation of human rights and related concepts by engaging in concrete political struggles at the grassroot level; adopt a more heterogeneous, situated and localised approach to law of humanity concepts, while keeping in mind structural and global issues; increase its willingness to engage in detailed discussions within fields dominated by different experts languages; rethink its contribution to the battle for the state; and be more willing to grasp and wield power where possible.

III. OUTLINE

The rest of the book is structured as follows. Chapter two provides an overview and an analysis of law of humanity theories. On the one hand, the chapter seeks to demonstrate that the project is by no means uniform but consists of separate approaches with important differences. In this sense, it seeks to do justice to the manifoldness and complexity of the project. On the other hand, the chapter stresses certain key similarities which nevertheless justify placing these approaches under the common umbrella of the 'law of humanity project'. The observations made in this regard set the tone for the following chapters and include, among other things, the ways in which the theories represent themselves as positing the human individual at the centre of international law, their interest in altering the role of the state and their reliance and focus on concepts such as human rights, human security and human dignity as a tool for structural change.

Moving from description and analysis to critique, chapter three challenges the assumption that the increased relevance of the key concepts of the law of humanity project would necessarily lead to the outcomes its proponents desire. Drawing from the methodological tools available to critical scholars – such as the use of binaries in order to unearth the moments of conscious or subliminal decisions between two equally valid ways of interpreting concepts in concrete situations[64] – the chapter demonstrates the analytical indeterminacy of the concepts of human rights, human security and human dignity, and suggests that they may lead in practice to very different outcomes than those assumed by the law of humanity theorists.

Chapter four takes an almost opposite – but, in my opinion, complementary – approach to the previous chapter and asks what has happened to the law of humanity concepts when they have been put into practice in the muddy waters of global governance. At the background of the chapter is the assumption that our possibilities and realities are always shaped by 'limits and pressures, tendencies and orientations, over-determination and determination'.[65] The implication is that even though concepts might be analytically indeterminate and lead to arbitrary results in theory, they might not do so in practice, as their use and outcomes are determined at least to some extent by existing power relations, structures and ideologies. Chapters three and four should therefore be read together to demonstrate that the outcomes of the increased circulation of the humanity rhetoric might not be what the narrative of an emerging law of humanity effectively leads us to believe, and thus opens space for hopefully more sombre analyses of those outcomes.

In collecting together prevalent uses of the humanity language in action, chapter four draws from a wide range of studies touching on international human rights law, international criminal law, international investment law, international territorial administration, responsibility to protect, anti-terrorism measures and humanitarian governance of refugees. My contribution to the topic is to bring these works together and make observations on general trends. Three observations are particularly important from the perspective of the law of humanity project. First, although the humanity rhetoric has been ubiquitous in global governance, it is not clear that it would have increased the well-being of individuals or empowered them – indeed, in some cases, the opposite might be true. Second, where the rhetoric has clearly made an impact is in relativising state sovereignty and allowing deep-penetrating interventions into what goes on within states and how they are organised. Finally, in many of the analysed instances, humanity rhetoric has been captured and used to justify economic transformations, broadly aligning with the neoliberal mindset.

Chapter five discusses the recent populist backlash in international law and its impact on the law of humanity project. The chapter studies the root causes of the backlash and analyses the ways in which the law of humanity is by necessity embedded in a web of power relations and ways of thinking that are partly responsible for the backlash. Holding that there are nevertheless many aspects in

[64] M Koskenniemi, *From Apology to Utopia: The Structure of International Legal Argument* (Cambridge, Cambridge University Press, 2005); D Kennedy, *International Legal Structures* (Baden-Baden, Nomos Publishers, 1987).

[65] S Marks, 'False Contingency' (2009) 62 *Current Legal Problems* 1, 10.

the law of humanity project that are worth defending and that it may provide a valuable counterforce to the right-wing populist mindset, the chapter concludes by outlining four issues that the project should rethink in order to become more politically savvy, more resilient and more impactful in our complex political, economic and ideological moment of history. Chapter six concludes the book by drawing together its main findings.

2

Visions of Law of Humanity

WHAT THIS BOOK calls the law of humanity project is certainly not a uniform movement, although it is united by some key ideas. Indeed, the authors writing on the topic, or the practitioners employing the language and notions of humanity, most likely do not even see themselves as participants in some unified 'project'. By contrast, many theorists this book associates with the law of humanity project have written their work as interventions to other theoretical discussions, such as those dealing with global law,[1] constitutionalisation of international law[2] or fragmentation of international law.[3] This chapter thus seeks to provide a more nuanced picture of the law of humanity project by mapping and distinguishing between different theories and accounts of it. I hope to give an appreciation of the complexity of the project, but also aim for conceptual clarity. In particular, I seek to understand how the claim of or call for humanisation of international law is represented in international legal theory, what kind of discourse it forms and through what means the theories pursue the change towards a law of humanity.

I. DIFFERENT APPROACHES TO THE LAW OF HUMANITY

In mapping the different theories of the law of humanity, I take inspiration from Neil Walker's taxonomy of different approaches to global law, which, much like the law of humanity, is also in a fragile, disaggregated state of becoming.[4] According to Walker, there are two main visions of global law, both of which seek to give a 'legal shape to the world',[5] but which imagine that world differently. The first vision of global law seeks to 'encourage a general dynamic of legal convergence',[6] while the second is concerned with accommodating that of

[1] R Domingo, *The New Global Law*, reprint edn (Cambridge, Cambridge University Press, 2011).

[2] A Peters, 'The Merits of Global Constitutionalism' (2009) 16 *Indiana Journal of Global Legal Studies* 397.

[3] R Howse and R Teitel, 'Does Humanity-Law Require (or Imply) a Progressive Theory or History? (And Other Questions for Martti Koskenniemi)' (2013) 27 *Temple International & Comparative Law Journal* 377.

[4] Neil Walker, *Intimations of Global Law* (Cambridge, Cambridge University Press, 2014).

[5] ibid 56.

[6] ibid 55.

legal divergence. Furthermore, Walker divides both the convergent and divergent approaches into subcategories.

The specifics of these categories and subcategories are not relevant for this chapter. However, there are two important observations that can be made from Walker's work. First, many works I associate with the law of humanity project are distributed across Walker's taxonomy, which suggests that there are important differences between them. Second, most of the theories – such as the works of Anne Peters, Jeremy Waldron and Ruti Teitel – fall into hard-to-define hybrid categories of the taxonomy, suggesting that there are aspects to them that are difficult to include within its parameters. Whereas Walker is interested in structurally different ways of imagining global law, I am interested here in one very particular, more tangible vision, characterised most of all by its substance rather than its form. Indeed, I treat the different works discussed in this book as a somewhat united project because they all share a sufficiently narrow and tangible normative goal, namely that of making humanity and the human individual the reference point and primary subject of international law – or the law of humanity. These accounts therefore imagine a rather radical transformation of the international legal order, whereas much of the global law movement 'takes for granted existing legal forms and their defining criteria and merely supplements or modifies them as circumstantially appropriate with reference to the notion of a "universal or otherwise global-in-general warrant"'.[7]

Taking these points into account, I have, for the purposes of this chapter, decided to divide the visions of law of humanity into four categories, and selected at least one key author to represent each of them. The first vision imagines a completely new global law of humanity, as represented in Rafael Domingo's *New Global Law*.[8] The second vision, by contrast, does not necessarily seek to replace the traditional system of international law with a completely new system; rather, it aims at the humanisation of international law by shifting the system's fundamental source of the legitimacy to humanity and the human person. This vision is clearly articulated in Anne Peters's recent work.[9] Third, there is a kind of hybrid of the aforementioned two visions, which sees something called 'humanity law' emerging from within both international and domestic legal practice and eventually replacing the old system of international law. This vision is represented in Ruti Teitel's *Humanity's Law*.[10] Finally, the chapter also briefly introduces a few other theories that are on the fringes of the law of humanity project, such as different versions of the 'international community school' and Mireille Delmas-Marty's pluralistic humanisation of globalisation.

[7] ibid 19.

[8] Domingo, *The New Global Law*.

[9] A Peters, 'Humanity as the A and Ω of Sovereignty' (2009) 20 *European Journal of International Law* 513; A Peters, *Beyond Human Rights: The Legal Status of the Individual in International Law* (J Huston trans, Cambridge, Cambridge University Press, 2016).

[10] R Teitel, *Humanity's Law* (Oxford, Oxford University Press, 2011).

There are several omissions in this list that are worth clarifying. In selecting theories to represent the law of humanity project, I have, first of all, included only theories dealing with international law. Thus, I have ruled out not only political theorists, philosophers and economists, but also legal scholars writing, for example, through the lenses of private international law, transnational law, European Union law and so on. Second, I have included only works published after the end of the Cold War, for I see the 1990s as having ignited – or at least set free – a specific way of looking at international law.[11] Finally, I have focused on authors who envision a radical change in the global legal order, from international law to what is here called the 'law of humanity'. I do not therefore discuss those authors who mostly describe and analyse the humanisation of international law, take a black-letter law approach to it or use the concept of humanity without envisioning a radical project for transforming the existing system of international law.[12]

A. The New Global Law of Humanity as a System of Systems

The first approach to law of humanity theory imagines a more-or-less-new global law of humanity as a system of systems, built around the human person. This approach is represented in its most detailed form in Rafael Domingo's *New Global Law*.

Like many authors writing about global law, Domingo tells his narrative against the background of profound change, occurring at dizzying speed. Globalisation and the emergence of new technologies have brought new possibilities, but also new threats, such as terrorism, human and arms trafficking and climate change, as well as the destructive effects of global capitalism. This change has made global law a necessity. As Domingo writes:

> Faced with this reality, which is as certain as our existence, we jurists cannot and should not turn a blind eye, thereby allowing the law of the jungle to take over in this age of globalisation because of lack of foresight, consistency, or imagination.[13]

Domingo's project is therefore not one of tracking changes in the global sphere of law. Rather, it is one of actively changing the world in the face of new threats. International law must be changed, or else it might become 'hostage to outmoded,

[11] See the Introduction.

[12] T Meron, *The Humanization of International Law* (Leiden, Brill Academic Publishers, 2006); VP Tzevelekos, 'Revisiting the Humanisation of International Law: Limits and Potential: Obligations Erga Omnes, Hierarchy of Rules and the Principle of Due Diligence as the Basis for Further Humanisation' (2013) 6 *Erasmus Law Review* 62; C Le Bris, *L'humanité saisie par le droit international public* (Paris, LGDJ Lextenso éditions, 2012); A Kjeldgaard-Pedersen, *The International Legal Personality of the Individual* (Oxford, Oxford University Press, 2018). Cancado Trinade's work is on the threshold. See AA Cançado Trindade, *International Law for Humankind* (Leiden, Brill Academic Publishers, 2010).

[13] Domingo (n 1) xiii.

transient paragons'. This is, for Domingo, 'a moral obligation', which can be accomplished only by creating a system of global law,[14] since sovereign nations – which, Domingo admits, were once useful – have become incapable of taking care of the needs of humanity. Not only are states too large for some issues and too small for others, and thus unable to govern effectively, but they cannot have de facto equality as they lack the inherent dignity of human persons.[15]

According to Domingo, then, international law is facing a crisis which stems from its very core structure and basic concepts, most importantly those of sovereignty, territoriality and the nation state.[16] As Domingo writes, 'each historical era begets a unique juridical system embedded with its own idiosyncrasies', and the time of nation states and international law has been ended by the intensification of globalisation. Being tied to notions of sovereignty, territory and the nation state, international law has lost its relevance in the new globalised world.[17]

Only global law, then, is adequate in the world of globalisation, according to Domingo. Now that the most important problems threaten the whole of humanity, 'we need imagination and creativity to create a global law that unites the whole [of] humanity, not just nation-states'.[18] Domingo defines global law as 'a world legal order that governs the ambit of justice as it affects humanity as a whole'. This new order will eventually grow out of the model of nation states and 'employ a legal metalanguage in response to the new challenges of globalisation in all its permutations'. Global law would not, however, be only a collection of rules. Rather, it would be a system of systems, the purpose of which Domingo compares to that of the sun in the solar system, circulated by planets, each representing a legal tradition on which various legal systems depend. In the words of Domingo, 'global law would be like the sun's nucleus, which radiates energy by thermonuclear reactions, whereas global jurisdiction would be the gravitational force that attracts them'.[19]

Most important about the new global law would be, however, that it would be built around the human person. The worst sin of international law is, according to Domingo, that 'it places at the centre of the system something that actually should take second place to the person'. As he continues, 'the world's nearly 200 states are effectively the primary subjects of international relations because they possess plenary legal capacity', whereas individuals 'are nothing more than "objects" of such capacity subject to their power'.[20] It has been this 'personification of the state' which has caused 'the dehumanisation of the person, its

[14] ibid xiv.
[15] ibid 62–64.
[16] ibid 54.
[17] ibid 4.
[18] ibid xv.
[19] ibid xvii.
[20] ibid 58–60.

objectification and stripping of the special properties of human dignity'.[21] Admittedly, the emergence of human rights law has made persons more central in international law, but in Domingo's mind even human rights law remains too tied to the state, for nationality still links individual persons to specific states, even though 'there should be no significant difference between being part of a national community and being a member of an international collectivity'. Human persons should be subjects – *the* subjects – of international law without any intermediate means.[22] If sovereignty was the foundation of international law, the person is the foundation of global law.

Many of these ideas are echoed by Christopher Barbara. Like Domingo, Barbara starts from the notion of globalisation. Unlike Domingo, however, he does not focus on the threats created by globalisation but, rather, on the possibilities it enables. In particular, Barbara emphasises the new possibilities to communicate – globalisation being in fact a result of 'Man's [*sic*] innate interest in interacting with other human beings'.[23] Despite this difference, Barbara arrives at the same conclusion as Domingo, namely that an international law based on the state can no longer adequately defend the interests of humanity. If the existence of states was justified in a time when it was necessary to concentrate communication through certain state officials, this is no longer the case in an age of emails, smartphones and social media.[24] There is therefore no reason to base the international legal order on the state. 'In safeguarding its position,' Barbara writes, 'the state is motivated out of self-interest rather than concern for the well-being of mankind.'[25]

Barbara, too, is agonised by the fact that international law is based on a legal fiction – the state – rather than the natural – human – person[26] who is 'the *only* true element in any and every social construction'. Consequently, building a system based on the human being is 'an obvious and relevant basis around which to order the discipline of international law'.[27] Barbara does not, however, have a clear plan on what the new law of humanity would look like. Instead, his approach focuses on completely reconstructing the concepts of international legal personality so that it can be made to fit the human being instead of the state. This reconstruction, Barbara argues, would change the way we understand international law and 're-align the international system with the "first principles" of law: safeguarding the well-being of Mankind [*sic*]'.[28]

[21] ibid xxi.
[22] ibid 58–60.
[23] C Barbara, 'International Legal Personality: Panacea or Pandemonium? Theorizing about the Individual and the State in the Era of Globalization' (2007) 12 *Austrian Review of International and European Law* 17, 55. See also 38–44.
[24] ibid 45.
[25] ibid 25.
[26] ibid 45, 47.
[27] ibid 37.
[28] ibid 55.

Domingo, by contrast, has a much more detailed blueprint for his new global law. At the centre of his legal order would be the concept of human dignity, which he sees as an attribute that is common and unique to persons.[29] According to Domingo, the human person is the subject of global law by virtue of the dignity of that person.[30] As he writes, dignity is 'a metalegal but not legally irrelevant concept, much less a paralegal or antilegal one, for it plays a dispositive role in the law … Without the person, there is no dignity, and without dignity, there is no law'. Attacking the legal positivist tradition, Domingo argues that through human dignity, 'the law makes contact with ethics, morality, anthropology, and the other sciences of man, retrieving these from the ivory tower in which Kelsen tried to keep them isolated'.[31] Indeed, even though Domingo insists that global law would not involve natural law (though it would remain open to it), he still argues that the crisis of modern international law is partly a result of its separation from that tradition.[32] The normative formalism of international law leads necessarily into the rule of the most powerful, whereas global law's focus on human dignity opens a window onto transcendence. The latter is, then, a system of justice.[33]

From a legal perspective, human dignity is defined by Domingo as 'the right of every person to be treated in accordance with justice, especially in accordance with those rights that are inherent: human rights'. Human rights therefore derive from human dignity, but are also further specified by it.[34] They are of fundamental importance to global law, but not its raison d'être. Human rights have been a crucially important step in the change of international law towards global law. Yet they are, according to Domingo, only a point of departure, a new beginning. In the transition to global law, human rights must be separated from all their ties to sovereign states. Because globalisation affects all of us directly, writes Domingo, our human rights cannot be dependent on the state tasked with protecting them, nor can they have links to the concepts of sovereignty and territoriality. Rather, the task of protecting human rights must be the task of the international community and its institutions since persons are equal rights-bearing global citizens.[35]

Starting from these premises, Domingo moves to outline his system of global law in more detail. The key part in the governance of the world would be played by global institutions. The International Court of Jutice, the International Criminal Court and other global and regional institutions are already a good start in this direction, according to Domingo, but the decision-making power of

[29] Domingo (n 1) 99.
[30] ibid 196.
[31] ibid 134–35.
[32] ibid 49.
[33] ibid 134–35.
[34] ibid 139.
[35] ibid 142–44.

these institutions would have to be increased significantly. In particular, jurisdiction would be separated from sovereignty, and would belong in each case to that actor that is best suited to solving humanity's problems.[36] Instead of 'exaggerated' self-determination, the global legal system would be guided by solidarity, 'making it possible to build an energetic and determined global consensus capable of responding in a timely and efficient manner to any attack on human rights'.[37]

The old institutions of international law would not, however, be enough to govern the world under global law. This is so especially because those institutions are so tied to the old world of nation states. Most importantly, the United Nations would have to be replaced with a new world organisation called the United Humanity. The legitimacy of the institution would be drawn from the fact that globalisation has turned humanity into a supreme community, not governed by anyone per se, but in great need of finding solutions to the global problems that affect us all. However, this legitimacy would be improved by creating a Global Parliament to lead the United Humanity. In this sense, then, Domingo takes a leap further than Thomas Franck, who called, at the turn of the millennium, for a 'cosmopolitan democratic model', based on the direct participation of individuals in a global parliamentary system, but acknowledged that such a change 'would have to take into account the continuing reality of state pre-eminence'.[38] According to Domingo, United Humanity 'would be composed of a network of global institutions that, distributed throughout the world and given jurisdiction based on subject matter, concern themselves with those issues that affect humanity as a whole, especially in whatever concerns human rights'.[39] Arbitration and other alternative dispute settlement methods would play an important role, for in arbitration 'the parties are the true actors in judicial actions, unlike in state law where the state becomes the protagonist'.[40] Finally, citizens of the world community would have a global passport,[41] and United Humanity would have its own military academy, army and global institutions to permit swift action when humanity is threatened.[42]

Yet, even though Domingo believes that the world has to be ordered through global institutions, he is against the idea of a world state. As Domingo writes, it is unlikely that democracy could survive in such a state. Instead, the result would be tyranny. Global law would be less totalising than the law of a world state, claims Domingo. The global order would not eliminate local, national

[36] ibid 76–81.

[37] ibid 86.

[38] TM Franck, *The Empowered Self: Law and Society in an Age of Individualism* (Oxford, Oxford University Press, 1999) 37.

[39] Domingo (n 1) 118–19.

[40] ibid 111–12.

[41] ibid 108.

[42] ibid 92.

or supranational ones. Rather, it would harmonise them, without appealing to any higher level of sovereignty.[43] Drawing from Hart's theory of law, Domingo argues that 'the global order, unlike international law, should be formed by primary rules or rules of conduct and by secondary rules – that is, rules for the recognition, change, and adjudication of primary rules'. The global order would form a harmonious order, characterised by a pyramid, and forming a synthesis with domestic orders. As Domingo writes,

> If they accept global law, these orders must integrate it in their own *ordo iuris* … The global order, on the other hand, creates a legal structure of interrelation and complementarity. In this way, each order would be represented figuratively by a communicating vessel; it would be perfectly identifiable, having its own existence. These orders would all be connected by global law. Control of the valve that communicates the various vessels – that is, the various national orders – does not belong to the states but to the global order.[44]

In this way, then, all legal orders would be interconnected, with the human person at the centre. According to Domingo, Kelsen's big mistake was to place a norm at the top of his pyramid, instead of starting from the person. In Domingo's pyramid, by contrast, the human person is at the top, and between the top and the base there are countless institutions aiming for the development of humanity, from parliaments to families and sports communities. This pyramid would therefore not be about norms; instead, it would be 'personal, social, and human'.[45]

Global law would be universal, but not total or all-encompassing, as it would regulate only those issues that interest humanity as a whole or are related to the protection of persons and human dignity.[46] It would be guided by principles, but it would be not just a set of principles, but an order of principles. As such, it would be a *sui generis* order, centred on the person. For Domingo, this new global law must 'integrate the highest values of different legal traditions while acknowledging the living synthesis of diverse and often disparate cultures'.[47] As such, it is most of all about a new mentality, not about an exact set of rules.[48]

B. Humanised International Law – A Radical Take

In contrast to the first one presented, the second version of law humanity theory does not necessarily seek to replace the traditional system of international law with a completely new system. Rather, it argues that the existing international

[43] ibid 122.
[44] ibid 122–23.
[45] ibid 148–49.
[46] ibid 189.
[47] ibid xv.
[48] ibid 100–02.

law is being humanised as a consequence of the system's fundamental source of legitimacy having become the protection of the human person. This approach is reflected to some extent in some rather rule-oriented descriptions of how considerations of humanity have slowly started to penetrate international legal thinking and jurisprudence, most notably as a corollary to the human rights revolution. Theodor Meron, for example, in his *The Humanization of International Law*,[49] aims to demonstrate how the radiation effect of human rights and humanitarian law has slowly transformed international law to the extent that most of its fields are now saturated by human rights considerations. In this section, however, I am interested in more radical versions of this humanisation of international law argument – arguments which hope to make the human person not only *a* subject, but *the* subject of international law.

An author whose work is very much attached to the practice of international law, but whose vision nevertheless shares a closer affinity to that discussed here than Meron's, is Cançado Trindade. In his *International Law for Humankind*, Cançado Trindade argues that the purely interstate dimension of international law belongs to the past as international legal personality has expanded so as to also encompass 'individuals – the human person – as true subjects (and not only "actors") of International Law'.[50] According to Cançado Trindade, there are four developments that have made it impossible to think of international law as catering mainly for state interests: the emergence of areas of international law devoted entirely to the safeguarding of human beings; the invocation of humankind in multiple treaties; the establishment of tribunals taking account of the concerns of individuals and the humankind; and the practice of states 'bearing witness to the needs and aspirations of human beings, of peoples, and of humankind as a whole'.[51] These developments have brought about the humanisation of international law, which now 'comes to occupy itself more directly with the realization of common superior goals', and is increasingly 'independent of the will of its subjects of law'. As Cançado Trindade writes, the new international law 'ultimately stems from human conscience, and is erected upon ethical foundations incorporating basic human values, shared by the entire international community and humankind as a whole',[52] perhaps the most important of such values being human dignity.[53] The new international law has 'placed peoples and human beings at the centre of international concerns, not only to meet their basic needs, but also to foster their empowerment'.[54]

However, Cançado Trindade does not explain in much detail what the humanisation of international law would mean on a structural level. Instead,

[49] Meron, *The Humanization of International Law*.
[50] Cançado Trindade, *International Law for Humankind*, 3. See also 280, 639–40.
[51] ibid 4.
[52] ibid 637.
[53] ibid 638.
[54] ibid 645.

he focuses more on legal interpretation and general principles. Other scholars have, however, taken on this task by focusing on the changing role of the state. One such author is Jeremy Waldron. Waldron approaches the issue from a somewhat curious angle by asking whether sovereign states are entitled to benefit from the international rule of law. Waldron starts this inquiry with the structure of international law. Does the fact that there is no overarching sovereign at the international level affect the way the rule of law applies? At issue here is the Hobbesian problem of subjugating the sovereign to her own laws. While Waldron argues that many Hobbesian problems do not arise at all on the international level, and in fact questions whether they exist even at the national level, he nevertheless admits that some relics of the problem may occur. Some have raised concerns about the power of the UN Security Council, but Waldron focuses particularly on states. As he writes, problems may arise from the fact that states are the main sources of international law, while at the same time being its main enforcers. Thus, some of them may be able to free themselves from subjection to the norms that do not appeal to them.[55]

Waldron's analysis starts to gain a strong normative push – and moves towards the issue of humanisation of international law – when he takes a detour to ask whether rule of law is needed at all in international law. Here, Waldron takes for granted that the raison d'être of rule of law is to 'protect individual values, like liberty, dignity etc'. Hence, he wonders whether rule of law is unnecessary in international law, considering that states are not vulnerable to attacks on dignity or exercise of power in the same way as natural individuals are.[56] Waldron's answer to this question is, however, a resounding 'no', for the rule of law need not protect only the formal subjects of international law. By contrast, the real concern of international law and international rule of law is 'to improve the lives of real individuals, billions of them – men, women, and children – in the world'. As Waldron continues, states are no longer the bearers of ultimate value. Rather, they exist for the sake of human individuals, whose well-being is the ultimate end of international law.[57]

Waldron argues, therefore, that international lawyers should change the way we perceive international law. The traditional view has been that states at the international level are equated to individuals at the national level. This is a mistake, according to Waldron. As he writes, states are law-constituted entities and their sovereignty 'is not given as a matter of the intrinsic value of its individuality but determined by the rules of the international order'. The state should not therefore be considered so much a subject of international law as a source and an official of it.[58] In this sense, Waldron is not too far from Anne-Marie

[55] J Waldron, 'Are Sovereigns Entitled to the Benefit of the International Rule of Law?' (2011) 22 *European Journal of International Law* 315, 317–19.

[56] ibid 322–23.

[57] ibid 325–26.

[58] ibid 328–30.

Slaughter, according to whom we should stop thinking about a world of states and start thinking about a world of disaggregated governments, networked together in complex ways in order to effectively govern contemporary issues touching the whole of humanity.[59] Hence, the rule of law should apply to them 'for the same reason it always does': for the sake of the well-being, liberty and dignity of individuals. As Waldron writes:

> Those values are as much at stake when the state acts externally as they are when it acts internally: the main difference is that many more individuals may be affected by the state's external action than by its internal action.[60]

The idea of states as 'officials' of international law, with no direct independent value of their own, is also developed by other authors. For Eyal Benvenisti, states should be seen as 'trustees of humanity'. Benvenisti notes that we are increasingly confronted with issues which go beyond the jurisdiction of any single sovereign. In a world of increased interdependency and interconnection, the concept of sovereignty should therefore be adapted to the realities of our world in the sense that states should, as trustees of humanity, be bound to take certain other-regarding considerations of humanity into account even if they are not bound by specific treaties or custom.[61] Somewhat similarly, Evan J Criddle and Evan Fox-Decent have recently introduced the idea of sovereigns as 'fiduciaries of humanity'.[62] As Criddle and Fox-Decent write, 'the time has come to retire the traditional, but increasingly embattled, conception of state sovereignty as exclusive jurisdiction'. State sovereignty is therefore not a prerogative of the state but emanates from 'a fiduciary relationship between states and the people subject to their jurisdiction'. In practice, this means that a state's sovereignty and autonomy 'is derived from, and wholly dependent upon', the fulfilment of its fiduciary duties.[63]

It is, however, Anne Peters who takes this argument the furthest. Peters's main argument is that 'sovereignty has been ousted from its position as the *Letztbegründung* (first principle) of international law' and replaced by humanity.[64] Unlike Domingo, Peters does not want to get rid of the concept of state sovereignty but notes that it will remain relevant in a historical or

[59] A-M Slaughter, *A New World Order*, new edn (Princeton, Princeton University Press, 2005).

[60] Waldron, 'Are Sovereigns Entitled', 341.

[61] E Benvenisti, 'Sovereigns as Trustees of Humanity: On the Accountability of States to Foreign Stakeholders' (2013) 107 *The American Journal of International Law* 295, 300.

[62] EJ Criddle and E Fox-Decent, *Fiduciaries of Humanity: How International Law Constitutes Authority* (Oxford, Oxford University Press, 2016). On the fiduciary turn in law, see PB Miller and AS Gold (eds), *Contract, Status, and Fiduciary Law* (Oxford, Oxford University Press, 2016); EJ Leib and SR Galoob, 'Fiduciary Political Theory: A Critique Essay' (2015) 125 *Yale Law Journal* 1820; AS Gold and PB Miller (eds), *Philosophical Foundations of Fiduciary Law* (Oxford, Oxford University Press, 2014); DT Rave, 'Politicians as Fiduciaries' (2012) 126 *Harvard Law Review* 671.

[63] Criddle and Fox-Decent, *Fiduciaries of Humanity*, 3.

[64] Peters, 'Humanity as the A and Ω of Sovereignty', 513.

ontological sense. Yet she does argue that the normative status of sovereignty is now 'derived from humanity, understood as the legal principle that human rights, interests, needs, and security must be respected and promoted, and that this humanistic principle is also the telos of the international legal system'. As Peters declares, humanity is now 'the A and Ω of sovereignty', meaning that:

> State sovereignty is not only – as in the meanwhile canonical view – limited by human rights, but is from the outset determined and qualified by humanity, and has a legal value only to the extent that it respects human rights, interests, and needs. Sovereignty, and with it international law, has therefore been humanized.[65]

Peters's argument is at the same time empirical, conceptual and normative. Much of the article seeks to prove empirically that a shift to a humanised international law is underway. A big step in this direction was already taken after World War II, with the codification of human rights. However, the true shift in international law occurred, according to Peters, with the emergence of the responsibility to protect concept, which not only solidified the notion of sovereignty as responsibility, but also made it clear that the interests of humanity ultimately take precedence over state sovereignty.[66]

At the same time, Peters's approach is also conceptual. In order to justify her claim that humanity is becoming, or at least should become, the basis of sovereignty, Peters engages in a conversation on what sovereignty actually means and entails. First, she defines sovereignty as a legal status 'from which certain legal consequences, in particular rights, but also obligations, are derived'. Second, she links internal and external sovereignty, making the latter dependent on the former. As she argues, the notion of sovereignty as responsibility to protect has infused external sovereignty with internal sovereignty, which requires the legitimacy of power.[67] Hence,

> a government's exercise of (delegated) sovereign powers enjoys both input and output legitimacy when it takes into account the concerned natural persons' voice (ie is based on popular sovereignty) and fulfils certain overlapping functions (as valued by the affected individuals themselves), namely to protect human rights, to create and preserve a space for individual and collective self-fulfilment, to enable and host political participation, and to provide a point of reference and identification.[68]

All of this has two consequences. First, sovereignty is no longer an all-or-nothing status, like in traditional positive international law, but a matter of degree – although this has not yet been translated into binding international documents. Sovereignty requires fulfilment of certain functions, such as the protection of human rights, and can be enjoyed more or less depending on how well these

[65] ibid 514.
[66] ibid.
[67] ibid 515–18.
[68] ibid 519.

functions are performed. Second, and consequently, what matters is 'not only the willingness, but also the capability, of a government to guarantee human security and so on'. The legitimacy – and hence sovereignty – of a government is, in other words, dependent also on its factual powers.[69] This is not, however, against the sovereign equality of states, according to Peters, because 'Justice requires proportional equality'. Formally differentiated treatment is therefore permissible 'as long as this is necessary and adequate to fulfil objectives enshrined in international law'. This is especially the case when it comes to dealing with basic human rights. As Peters writes, 'A concern for humanity (ie for human rights, interests, needs, and security) is fully engrained in international human rights law and in other parts of international law, and may therefore outweigh the interest in observing formal equality'.[70]

Finally, Peters's approach is strongly normative. Even though Peters aims to support her arguments with conceptual analysis and empirical material, many of her arguments are nevertheless very much *lex ferenda*. In other words, she sees the humanisation of sovereignty and international law as a dynamic, ongoing project which she tries to push forward.[71] The shift from absolute sovereignty to sovereignty as responsibility produces, according to Peters, a larger 'humanization' or 'individualization' of international law. As she writes, the 'ongoing process of humanizing sovereignty is the cornerstone of the current transformation of international law into a system centered on individuals'.[72]

The end result of this humanisation process, for Peters, would be a constitutionalised international legal system.[73] According to Peters, the fact that the normative status of sovereignty is now derived from humanity is precisely because of the principle that certain community values, such as the protection of human rights and human security, have become constitutional globally. Consequently, they have become a matter of the international community, not only of single states.[74]

Peters's constitutionalised international legal system is one centred on individuals, whom states and international organisations serve. Indeed, constitutionalisation is further linked to law of humanity in breaking the distinction between 'full' and 'derivative' international legal subjects. Once international law has its constitution, 'it no longer makes sense to speak of "original" legal subjects, because all subjects have been transformed into *pouvoirs constitués*'. Although different actors might still have different rights and obligations, 'there

[69] ibid.

[70] ibid 529.

[71] ibid 543.

[72] Peters, 'The Merits of Global Constitutionalism' (n 2) 398–99.

[73] For a discussion on the link between humanisation of international law and constitutionalisation of international law, see VP Tzevelekos and L Lixinski, 'Towards a Humanized International "Constitution"?' (2016) 29 *Leiden Journal of International Law* 343; Tzevelekos 'Revisiting the Humanisation of International Law'.

[74] Peters, 'The Merits of Global Constitutionalism' (n 2) 398–99.

is no categorical distinction between states and all others'.[75] In Peters's constitutionalised law of humanity, individuals are no longer mere beneficiaries of international law. Instead, they are full – and, indeed, primary – international legal persons, who enjoy 'international individual rights', encompassing not only human rights, but more broadly the individual's political right to participate in the production of international law and her access to courts and other judicial proceedings.[76]

Similar views are shared by other important continental international legal scholars. For example, Janne Nijman writes that granting international legal personality to individuals 'can help us turn the fundamental relationship between the individual, the state and the international community around'. According to Nijman, legal personality is necessary for a humane life, for it guarantees the possibility to participate in common political life. As such, it is a natural right of every human being.[77] As a consequence of globalisation, however, the political is as much international as national. Hence, the human person has to be a 'citizen' of the international community as well, meaning that she must be granted international legal personality. If states fail to protect this right of an individual, then the international community must take responsibility and 'transform him back from thing to person'.[78]

C. Emergent Humanity's Law

Third, there is a sort of hybrid of the previous two approaches – one that starts from empirically observable trends in current international and domestic law and interprets them as forming a new, spontaneously created global law. This vision is developed in Ruti Teitel's *Humanity's Law*. As Teitel writes, 'a vital vision is emerging, which depends on a threshold consensus on the need to guarantee the humane treatment of persons and peoples, and ensure their preservation'.[79] This vision is, according to Teitel, that of humanity's law (referred to sometimes simply as 'humanity law', without the genitive), which can be defined quite simply as 'the law of persons and peoples'.[80] In other words, humanity law entails a shift away from international law, dominated by state-centric, territorialised rule of law values, and towards a global legal vision focused on the protection of persons and peoples.

[75] J Klabbers, A Peters and G Ulfstein, *The Constitutionalization of International Law* (Oxford, Oxford University Press, 2011) 155. These quotes are from Peters's part of the book and do not necessarily entirely reflect the views of its other two authors.

[76] Peters, *Beyond Human Rights* (n 9).

[77] JE Nijman, *The Concept of International Legal Personality: An Inquiry into the History and Theory of International Law* (The Hague, Asser Press, 2004) 467.

[78] ibid 468.

[79] Teitel, *Humanity's Law*, 17.

[80] ibid x.

Teitel constructs her narrative over simultaneous progress and the emergence of new threats. The end of the Cold War, with its polarised geopolitics, has allowed interventions in the name of 'humanity', while at the same time the increasing number of fragile states and the interlinked phenomena of religious fundamentalism and terrorism pose new dangers.[81] It is in this context that Teitel sees the new humanity law emerging. Humanity law is not, however, constituted, as is the case with Domingo's global law, but emerges spontaneously in myriad practices at both the international and the domestic level, with different strands coming together to form a paradigm shift from state security-based international order to a human security-based global one. The key word in Teitel's account is therefore 'dynamic', for she is most of all interested in tracing the logic of humanity law on various platforms, with a strong focus on how law shapes and is shaped by politics. Teitel's humanity law is therefore flexible but fragile, always in the process of change.

Despite its dynamic nature, humanity law still has some fixed key features. Teitel herself identifies three. First, humanity law is the product of multiple traditions 'which converge in a distinctive subjectivity', deriving from 'the recognition of individual agency and individuals' capacity and responsibility for action in the international sphere'. In other words, it operates largely on human persons, granting them rights, but also giving them obligations. Second, humanity law 'implies a standard of treatment that is based on humanity as both the subject and object of action'. Finally, 'humanity law's orientation or telos is the preservation of humanity'.[82]

However, for the purposes of this chapter, it might be beneficial to point out three other, more practically oriented characteristics of Teitel's vision. First, Teitel, like Peters, starts from existing rules of international law. The starting point is humane treatment of the body, which Teitel sees enshrined, for example, in Article 7 of the International Covenant on Civil and Political Rights, Article 3 of the European Convention on Human Rights and Common Article 3 of the Geneva Conventions. On top of this, humanity law generates new rules, deriving from the emerging regulation of other issues related to human survival, such as economic interdependence, diseases and environmental threats. The enforcement of these rules depends, furthermore, on existing enforcement processes, review mechanisms and other rule of law issues.

Humanity law starts from these already existing rules, yet it needs to push further. This leads to its second practical characteristic, namely emphasis on interpretation. As Teitel writes, humanity law 'simply cannot be framed in terms of the application of a rule that is based on the divination of the common will of states that consented to that rule'. Rather, the meaning of those rules must be determined 'by interpretative practices ex post their "original" articulation

[81] ibid 3–4.
[82] ibid 19.

in positive legal instruments'.[83] This is so because, starting from the concrete needs of human persons, humanity law is always applied in a particular context. As such, the normativity of humanity law transcends the state and relativises sovereignty.[84] Indeed, for Teitel, humanity law is primarily about interpretation, guided by the principle of preservation of humanity. According to Teitel, this focus on interpretation makes humanity law particularly fit to respond to contemporary problems of global law, such as the diversity of normative sources, the increased amount of political and moral conflicts, fragmentation of international law, and the complexity of globalisation and global governance. To quote Teitel:

> In the presence of different cultures and traditions, humanity-law-based interpretation offers the possibility of a ground of shared meaning. Humanity law, as an interpretative lens, navigates the narrow strait between the Scylla of difference and the Charybdis of universalism. But since practice arises in real cases of individual rights, steering this path is not about defining a static ideal; rather, it concerns the continuing evolution of a norm that will help to guide and manage conflict.[85]

This connects to the third characteristic of humanity law. Just like for Domingo, for Teitel the 'ambit of humanity law is intrinsically global'.[86] By basing protection on common characteristics of humanity, humanity law 'gives persons and peoples a legal and ethical status that is not entirely dependent on their membership in a particular political community'.[87] Human beings are protected simply by virtue of them being human. While dependent on the particular situation of these people, humanity law simultaneously 'implies a measure of universalizability across situation and regimes'. Yet, humanity law should, according to Teitel, be distinguished from natural law by the fact that it does not have an a priori view of the norms we all share. Although it makes reference to universal absolutes, it comes into being dynamically through evolving and contextually bound practice.[88]

If Domingo's work on law of humanity intervenes in discussions on global law and Peters's contributes to the constitutionalisation of international discourse, Teitel's work is written against the background of the fragmentation of international law. According to Teitel, her 'humanity's law' is not only particularly capable of operating in the context of fragmentation, but also enabled and powered by it. As she writes, fragmentation entails that 'the exercise of adjudication or dispute settlement simply cannot be framed in terms of the application of a rule that is based on the divination of the common will of the states that consented to that rule', for the meaning of rules is 'significantly deterred by

[83] ibid 169–70.
[84] ibid 58.
[85] ibid 169–70.
[86] ibid 193.
[87] ibid 195.
[88] ibid 203.

the interpretative practices ex post their "original" articulation in positive legal instruments'. This is, however, not a problem for humanity law, which is made to operate in the context of normative pluralism. Because humanity law is dynamic and evolving, it will learn from fragmentation and adapt to 'guide and manage conflict'.[89] Thus, fragmentation may in fact help in disseminating and increasing the importance of humanity law-based normativity, interpretation and decision-making.[90] This can perhaps be seen as an Anglo-Saxon approach to the law of humanity, made compatible with the pluralistic liberal tradition, whilst maintaining a strong policy orientation, in promoting a certain vision of the world based on human rights, democracy and global civil society.[91]

What, then, would be the consequences of this shift to humanity law, accelerated by the fragmentation of international law? According to Teitel, humanity law creates 'a greatly expanded juridical-philosophical landscape',[92] and partly transforms the prevailing content and sources of international law.[93] Upon close reading, at least five key changes emerge from Teitel's vision. First, the shift to humanity law changes what we see as authoritative sources of law. Different international bodies gain more legislative power and the role of state-to-state treaties diminishes. By the same token, customary international law both becomes more important and changes its key characteristics. According to Teitel, *opinio juris* becomes privileged over state practice under humanity law. Further, *opinio juris* no longer refers necessarily to the intentions of states, but becomes equally dependent on other actors, most importantly the judiciary. Indeed, in Teitel's reading, the *Oil Platforms*[94] and *Nuclear Weapons*[95] cases demonstrate that courts are already willing to simply declare the existence of rules of customary international law without much attention to state practice or traditional *opinio juris*.[96]

Second, then, the emergence of humanity law also changes the way we understand sovereignty. Unlike in the old system of international law, states are no longer bound only to the rules they consent to but are also automatically bound by different humanity norms. This shift does not mean sovereignty disappears; but it does mean that the sovereign is no longer she who decides on the exception but, rather, she who protects.[97] Even though sovereignty still exists, it is no longer the foundation of international law, which is now 'constructed more along humanity law lines'. To give an example, use of force becomes focused 'on

[89] Teitel (n 10) 170.
[90] Howse and Teitel, 'Does Humanity-Law Require', 393.
[91] See E Jouannet, *The Liberal-Welfarist Law of Nations: A History of International Law* (C Sutcliffe trans, Cambridge, Cambridge University Press, 2012) 211–13.
[92] Teitel (n 10) 14.
[93] ibid 4–5.
[94] *Oil Platforms (Islamic Republic of Iran v United States of America)* [2003] ICJ Rep 161.
[95] *Legality of the Threat or Use of Nuclear Weapons* (Advisory Opinion) [1996] ICJ Rep 226.
[96] Teitel (n 10) 172–74.
[97] ibid 108.

the rights and claims of persons and peoples rather than on the interests and prerogatives of states as such'.[98]

Third, non-state actors play an increasingly important role in setting and enforcing humanity law. As Teitel writes, 'one can see a new standard of political legitimacy emerging, where across the state/nonstate divide a variety of groups and actors now struggle for authority'. Non-state actors are therefore no longer mere recipients of governance but actually practice governance in framing rights.[99]

Fourth, the emergence of humanity law entails the collapse of some 'outdated' distinctions. Combining human rights law with humanitarian law means blurring war and peace. And humanity law also traverses the distinction between public and private power, as courts are more willing to extend their jurisdiction to address claims against corporate and other private entities suspected of violations of humanity law.[100]

Fifth, and finally, humanity redefines security and shifts its focus from states to human beings. The normative starting point of humanity law is the survival of humanity, at both the individual and the group level. Hence, it 'pursues a range of normative aims, traditionally reflected in different international legal regimes', guided by the concept of human security.[101] As Teitel writes, humanity law operates in an exceptionally fragmented world with an increased number of weak and failed states and a heightened number of conflicts – a world of interconnection without integration. To this world, humanity law 'affords a language and a framework that are capable of recognizing the claims and interests of multiple actors in preservation and security'. Furthermore, it provides global law with a foundation derived from humanitarian values and ensures the protection of human security.[102]

D. Other and Alternative Approaches

The previous three sections have highlighted those academic works which I find most explicit in their use of the humanity language and which clearly attempt to change the structure of international law. Nevertheless, many of the ideas discussed above are reflected in one form or another in other works which envision an international or global law with an emphasis on the interests of humanity as a whole, in contrast to reciprocal state-to-state relations based on matching rights and obligations. Hence, although many of these works might be less overt in their use of humanity language, they nevertheless have similar inclinations to those discussed above.

[98] ibid 8–10.
[99] ibid 214.
[100] ibid 180, 220.
[101] ibid 163.
[102] ibid 212.

Whilst I cannot go into much more detail here, it is at least worth mentioning the so-called 'international community school' as a general umbrella term in this respect. This school is characterised by its emphasis on norms rather than institutions as a structuring force in international law, the argument being that normative developments help to produce a genuine international community and facilitate its ever-deeper integration.[103] There are obvious cultural as well as more subtle differences existing within the international community school. It is characteristic for the German tradition to treat international law as an almost complete system, with treaties as its 'laws', and to approach it through the teachings and principles of public law. Hence, the German approach to the international community – and law of humanity, as reflected in Peters's work – tends to focus on the verticalisation and constitutionalisation of international law.[104] Drawing from the principle of rule of law, the German tradition envisions a global legal system based on a clear hierarchy of rules and guided by overarching principles which guide their interpretation. Alternatively, the Manhattan-shaped Global Administrative Law school approaches global governance through administrative law principles and practices.[105]

In contrast to their German colleagues, French international lawyers have traditionally shied away from firm theoretical commitments.[106] Hence Catherine Le Bris,[107] for example, seeks to analyse the concept of humanity in international law from a 'neutral' perspective.[108] Not only are theoretical views often hidden behind the posture of neutrality,[109] but French theoretical thinking has also commonly been channelled from questions of foundation to the question of 'how international law operates'.[110] This discussion is often presented as one between voluntarists and solidarists. It is the latter group that is interesting here. According to the French solidarists, 'international law is moving toward the realization of a genuine international community – one that is integrated and ordered around common values that go beyond taking only states into account'.[111] This

[103] A Bianchi, *International Law Theories: An Inquiry into Different Ways of Thinking* (Oxford, Oxford University Press, 2016) 49.

[104] M Koskenniemi, 'Between Coordination and Constitution: International Law as a German Discipline' (2011) 15 *Redescriptions: Political Thought, Conceptual History and Feminist Theory* 45, 63–64; Bianchi, *International Law Theories*, 44–45.

[105] See, eg B Kingsbury, N Krisch and RB Stewart, 'The Emergence of Global Administrative Law' (2005) 68 *Law and Contemporary Problems* 15; B Kingsbury, 'The Concept of "Law" in Global Administrative Law' (2009) 20 *European Journal of International Law* 23; C Harlow, 'Global Administrative Law: The Quest for Principles and Values' (2006) 17 *European Journal of International Law* 187; S Cassese, *Research Handbook on Global Administrative Law* (Cheltenham, Edward Elgar Publishing, 2017).

[106] E Jouannet, 'A Century of French International Law Scholarship' (2009) 61 *Maine Law Review* 83, 102.

[107] Le Bris, *L'humanité saisie*.

[108] P-M Dupuy's Avant-Propos in ibid xv.

[109] Jouannet, 'A Century of French International Law Scholarship', 109–10.

[110] ibid 116.

[111] ibid 118.

descriptive argument is usually combined with a normative one, for most of the solidarists also hold that the common values must be promoted because 'they are the ramparts against state arbitrariness and selfishness'.[112] The common values are reflected, for example, in *jus cogens* norms and *erga omnes* obligations, which international law scholars have actively made a 'part and parcel of the fabric of the international law discourse'.[113]

Although French international lawyers are careful to avoid mentioning natural law, they nevertheless call upon principles of international law, in particular those reflected in human rights and criminal justice, to 'counter domestic law' and 'renew the international legal experience and practice'.[114] Pierre-Marie Dupuy, for example, argues that international law includes a set of rules which provide it with not only formal, but also substantial unity. These rules include those 'prohibiting the use of force, outlawing genocide, and establishing non-intervention, the rights of people, and the basic rights of the human person', as well as 'the essential rights of the human being' which have been developed in international criminal law.[115] According to Dupuy, international courts should take an increasingly large role in identifying these rules for the international community. Consequently, the International Court of Justice's (ICJ's) judges, inter alia, should be willing to share 'a legal philosophy according to which there is some kind of international legal order that should be respected, under any circumstances, by each and every subject of that law'.[116] Similarly, Dupuy sees and welcomes a clear ideology behind the UN Charter which would guide further integration of the international community[117] and defends the recourse to universal values.[118]

It should be emphasised that the German and French approaches cannot be distinguished too clearly in the sense that constitutionalisation and the integration of the international community through universal values go together. This is clear in Erika de Wet's work on an international constitutional order, for example. The order de Wet envisions is hierarchical, but layered and based

[112] ibid.

[113] A Bianchi, 'Human Rights and the Magic of Jus Cogens' (2008) 19 *European Journal of International Law* 491, 494; see also S Villalpando, 'The Legal Dimension of the International Community: How Community Interests Are Protected in International Law' (2010) 21 *European Journal of International Law* 387.

[114] Jouannet (n 106) 131.

[115] P-M Dupuy, 'The Danger of Fragmentation or Unification of the International Legal System and the International Court of Justice Symposium Issue: The Proliferation of International Tribunals: Piecing Together the Puzzle' (1998) 31 *New York University Journal of International Law and Politics* 791, 794–95. See also P-M Dupuy, '2000–2020: Twenty Years Later, Where Are We in Terms of the Unity of International Law?' (2020) 9 *Cambridge International Law Journal* 6.

[116] Dupuy, 'The Danger of Fragmentation', 806.

[117] P-M Dupuy, 'The Constitutional Dimension of the Charter of the United Nations Revisited' (1997) 1 *Max Planck Yearbook of United Nations Law Online*, www.booksandjournals.brillonline.com/content/journals/10.1163/187574197x00038.

[118] P-M Dupuy, 'Some Reflections on Contemporary International Law and the Appeal to Universal Values: A Response to Martti Koskenniemi' (2005) 16 *European Journal of International Law* 131.

on global values with 'superior legal standing and ethical force'. These values include those enshrined in *jus cogens* norms and *erga omnes* obligations which 'constitute a fundamental yardstick for post-national decision-making'.[119] As such, de Wet's order shifts power 'away from the nation State towards international actors', thus eroding the idea of sovereignty as 'a total or exclusive constitution'.[120]

Some contributions to the international community school take substantively more specific forms. One such example is the international criminal law project. The Preamble of the Rome Statute emphasises that 'all peoples are united by common bonds' and raises concern that the common interests of the international community can be jeopardised by core crimes. Particularly important in this respect is the crime against humanity, which produces the subject 'humanity', which can be seen as a somewhat unified whole, represented by the 'international community', which, again, is represented by the International Criminal Court (ICC).[121] As the argument goes, crimes against humanity are crimes which attack humanity itself and affect the international community as a whole. As Macleod writes, 'an action is a crime against humanity if and only if it is a crime that damages humankind'.[122] Others further emphasise the 'political' nature of crimes against humanity, arguing that the crimes are a concern of the entire international community because 'they strike at the core of the human condition, by shattering the political realm'.[123] As van der Wilt writes, for example, crimes against humanity bereave 'people of a vital capacity and simultaneously arouses the concern of all humanity, because the essential destruction of the political realm reflects upon all of us'.[124] In this mindset, the ICC plays a crucial role by giving a 'determinate and effective institutional form' to the 'moral idea of a human community'.[125]

Some scholars have used international criminal law as a springboard to a more overarching theory of international law. For example, the late Antonio Cassese imagined a global community grounded in human rights – one in which

[119] E de Wet, 'The International Constitutional Order' (2006) 55 *International and Comparative Law Quarterly* 51, 57.

[120] ibid 75.

[121] L Corrias, 'The Inhuman Stain: Representing Humanity in International Criminal Law' in B van Beers, L Corrias and WG Werner (eds), *Humanity across International Law and Biolaw* (Cambridge, Cambridge University Press, 2014) 77; A Duff, 'Authority and Responsibility in International Criminal Law' in S Besson and J Tasioulas (eds), *The Philosophy of International Law* (Oxford, Oxford University Press, 2010) 600.

[122] C Macleod, 'Towards a Philosophical Account of Crimes against Humanity' (2010) 21 *European Journal of International Law* 281, 295.

[123] H van der Wilt, 'Crimes against Humanity: A Category Hors Concours in (International) Criminal Law?' in van Beers et al, *Humanity across International Law and Biolaw*, 34.

[124] ibid 35; see also D Luban, 'A Theory of Crimes against Humanity' (2004) 29 *Yale Journal of International Law* 85.

[125] Duff, 'Authority and Responsibility', 600.

universal human rights are actually followed and enforced, unlike in today's world.[126] Cassese's approach is one of critical positivism, somewhere in between natural law and doctrinal constructivism. Although critical positivism gives a more important role to existing international law than natural law does, it still 'openly engages in teleological interpretation and allows room for non-legal considerations to inform interpretation and construction of the law'.[127] This approach is reflected in Cassese's approach to *jus cogens*. As Ruiz-Fabri writes, Cassese does not seem to even doubt that an enhanced role for *jus cogens* is a desired goal of action. Hence, Cassese's work on *jus cogens* reflects a very clear agenda, founded on his 'belief that law can bring about change in the world'.[128] Indeed, Cassese's global community of human rights is to be achieved, he argues, by distinguishing between core human rights, which should have the status of *jus cogens* and be followed universally without exception, and other human rights, the precise application of which may vary from one legal culture to another. This distinction, he suggests, should make human rights enforcement more feasible and thus more efficient. But, even more importantly, the gradual expansion of *jus cogens* norms 'might eventually lead in the future to the formation of a global community where all the basic norms of human rights must be equally respected by everyone in any part of the planet'.[129] In order to give teeth to the global human rights system, Cassese advocates for the establishment of fact-finding commissions, an increased role for the ICC, reliance on universal jurisdiction and the mobilisation of civil society.[130] In particular, the ICC and other international (and domestic) courts should take a larger role in deciding whether a rule has gained the status of *jus cogens*, and all disputes concerning possible *jus cogens* norms should be subjected to the compulsory jurisdiction of the ICJ.[131] As Milanovic comments, Cassese's project is therefore 'a manifesto for judge-made law', one in which states cannot be trusted but it is for international courts to develop the norms of the international community.[132]

Finally, it should be mentioned that there are also alternative versions of the humanisation of international law that emphasise plurality over unity. One such example is Mireille Delmas-Marty's recent work on 'humanization of globalization'.[133] Situating Delmas-Marty in relation to the law of humanity project

[126] M Milanovic, 'On Realistic Utopias and Other Oxymorons: An Essay on Antonio Cassese's Last Book' (2012) 23 *European Journal of International Law* 1033.

[127] I Feichtner, 'Realizing Utopia through the Practice of International Law' (2012) 23 *European Journal of International Law* 1143, 1150–51.

[128] H Ruiz Fabri, 'Enhancing the Rhetoric of Jus Cogens' (2012) 23 *European Journal of International Law* 1049, 1053–54.

[129] A Cassese, *Realizing Utopia: The Future of International Law* (Oxford, Oxford University Press, 2012) 140.

[130] ibid 142–43.

[131] Milanovic, 'On Realistic Utopias', 1041–43; Ruiz Fabri, 'Enhancing the Rhetoric of Jus Cogens', 1055.

[132] Milanovic (n 126) 1041–42; see also Ruiz Fabri (n 128) 1056.

[133] See especially M Delmas-Marty, *Résister, responsabiliser, anticiper: ou comment humaniser la mondialisation* (Paris, Le Seuil, 2013); M Delmas-Marty, *Aux quatre vents du monde. Petit guide de navigation sur l'océan de la mondialisation* (Paris, Le Seuil, 2016).

is tricky: she both criticises and defends the humanist tradition, and is rather suspicious of universal projects. Nevertheless, I find it important to briefly address her work here since she shares the impulse of humanising the global legal order and urges us to imagine international law differently.[134]

A key factor of motivation behind Delmas-Marty's work is her concern of some of the disastrous effects of globalisation, emphasising in particular the contradiction in states promoting free movement in trade and upholding the language of human rights while at the same time closing their borders to human beings in need and using the language of human rights for neo-imperial purposes.[135] She does not, however, want to discard the project of humanism, but rather to strengthen it by replacing the old, static versions of humanism with a new, dynamic and interactive 'reciprocal humanization'.[136] Her method is to start from the contradictions of globalisation in order to achieve a threefold objective: to resist dehumanisation, to hold decision-makers responsible and to anticipate future risks.[137]

Delmas-Marty accordingly shares with the law of humanity project the vision of humanising the world. In Delmas-Marty's view, however, this humanisation cannot be achieved through sudden structural changes and not even through an emergent humanity's law. Whilst she does hold that increasing entanglements between national and international law could lead to the birth of some kind of global law, she is of the opinion that such a global law would, without history or territory, be inevitably too fragmented to work as a functional system of law.[138] Delmas-Marty's project of reciprocal humanisation is therefore not one of creating a new system but of humanising globalisation through cross-cultural dialogue. Hers is a predominantly pluralistic vision, which nevertheless welcomes increasing harmonisation. As Delmas-Marty explains, humanisation is a cultural process which has to do with the ethical construction of humanity. At its heart is cultural diversity and cultural dialogue and their delicate balance with harmonisation: as Delmas-Marty warns, too much coherence and integration might damage cohesion and hence our resistance to the worst aspects of globalisation.[139] At the same time, however, processes such as fragmentation might damage the universality of such key concepts as human rights.[140]

[134] M Delmas-Marty, 'The Imaginative Forces of Law' (2003) 2 *Chinese Journal of International Law* 623.

[135] Delmas-Marty, *Résister, responsabiliser, anticiper*, 8–10.

[136] For an earlier, slightly different take on these issues, see M Delmas-Marty, *Towards a Truly Common Law: Europe as a Laboratory for Legal Pluralism* (N Norberg trans, Cambridge, Cambridge University Press, 2002) 199–220.

[137] Delmas-Marty, *Résister, responsabiliser, anticiper* (n 133) 11.

[138] ibid 7.

[139] Delmas-Marty, *Aux quatre vents du monde*, 71–73. On the themes of pluralism and harmonisation, see also M Delmas-Marty, *Ordering Pluralism: A Conceptual Framework for Understanding the Transnational Legal World* (N Norberg trans, Oxford, Hart Publishing, 2009); Delmas-Marty, *Towards a Truly Common Law*.

[140] Delmas-Marty, *Ordering Pluralism*, 99–100.

Thus, humanisation has to always respect plurality and diversity in seeking to find common understandings and reciprocal transformation. Delmas-Marty therefore rejects the idea of a new political framework, preferring 'orderly pluralism',[141] based on 'a modest vision of the law' and the tinkering of national and international laws through myriad interactions and dynamic processes.[142]

In particular, humanisation of globalisation may, according to Delmas-Marty, occur by way of identifying and promoting those practices which are beneficial to humanity, whilst trying to curb unbeneficial ones. Some of these beneficial practices include the promotion of non-derogable human rights, increased corporate and state responsibility for social justice,[143] anti-impunity and anti-amnesty measures,[144] as well as responsibility sharing between state and non-state actors. Furthermore, in her most recent work, Delmas-Marty suggests that a key role in the humanisation of globalisation is played by fear. Fear may divide, leading us to exclude and dehumanise, as has happened in the anti-terrorist campaign; but it may also produce solidarity in uniting us against common dangers, such as climate change.[145] Thus, reciprocal humanisation can also be thought of as curbing 'fear-exclusion' and promoting 'fear-solidarity'. An important role in this process is played by the concept of human dignity, which is inherent and absolute, and 'constitutes an act of faith in the value of the human person'.[146] The concept of human dignity guides us to resist exclusive and dehumanising practices and to embrace those that protect humanity and diversity.

All in all, then, Delmas-Marty does not promote a large-scale structural change in international law – such as the diminution of the role of the state, for example – but nevertheless shares with the law of humanity project the trust in the power of imagining a different kind of world, leading potentially, through a long process, to mutations in the way we perceive the legal order.[147] She draws attention to 'the most innovative forms of international law … that have given legal life to the universal', mentioning the Universal Declaration of Human Rights, legal recognition of crimes against humanity and common heritage of mankind as examples. Whilst she cannot promise that these developments ever produce 'a common language, a common wisdom', she nevertheless holds that 'we must more than ever hope for it, without dissipating the imaginative forces of law'.[148] Furthermore, she shares the trust in the potential of concepts such as

[141] See Delmas-Marty, *Ordering Pluralism* (n 139).

[142] M Delmas-Marty, *Etudes juridiques comparatives et internationalisation du droit, Cours au Collège de France, Un pluralisme ordonné, available at* www.college-de-france.fr/media/mireille-delmas-marty/UPL12910_r_sum_cours0405.pdf.

[143] Delmas-Marty, *Résister, responsabiliser, anticiper* (n 133) 143.

[144] ibid 167.

[145] Delmas-Marty, *Aux quatre vents du monde* (n 133) 54.

[146] ibid 85–86.

[147] Delmas-Marty, 'The Imaginative Forces of Law', 623.

[148] ibid 623–24.

human dignity and human rights to shape the way we approach law and guide it to a more human-centred direction.

II. KEY CHARACTERISTICS OF THE LAW OF HUMANITY THEORIES

As the above analysis demonstrates, the law of humanity theories are by no means uniform. Yet, the analysis also reveals that the theories nevertheless share certain key ideas which make it meaningful to treat them as a loosely connected cluster. These relate in particular to how the theorists of law of humanity present their projects and what kind of discourse is formed. There are at least three key elements that keep repeating in the theories. The first two are closely linked and mutually reinforcing. The first is that the individual and humanity at large are becoming or should become (these two seem to be often mixed together) the centre of international law (or the law of humanity), whereas the second is the idea that the increasing role of the individual and humanity require the diminishing role of the previous protagonist of international law, namely the state. Finally, the third key characteristic of the law of humanity discourse is that it is dominated by concepts.

A. The Central Roles of the Individual and Humanity

The idea of the increasingly central role of individuals and humanity seems to take at least two forms in the discourse. The first is a change in international legal personality. International legal personality is generally used in international law to refer to 'the capacity to be the bearer of rights and duties under international law',[149] or to competences attributed to designated actors within a systemic legal order.[150] As Jan Klabbers writes,

> international legal personality is thought to be a *conditio sine qua non* for the possibility of acting within a given legal situation. Personality is considered to be a threshold which must be crossed. Without legal personality, those entities do not exist in law.[151]

At least according to the mainstream narrative, (full) international legal personality was the exclusive prerogative of sovereign states from the birth of modern international law until the late twentieth century. By the end of the nineteenth century, it was commonly held that individuals are under no circumstances

[149] JR Crawford, *The Creation of States in International Law*, 2nd edn (Oxford, Oxford University Press, 2007) 28.
[150] M Craven, 'Statehood, Self-Determination, and Recognition' in M Evans (ed), *International Law*, 4th edn (Oxford, Oxford University Press, 2014) 215.
[151] J Klabbers, 'The Concept of Legal Personality' (2005) 11 *Jus Gentium* 35, 37.

subjects, but only objects under international law, comparable to, for example, territories, and that the only link between international law and individuals was through nationality, in that states could *choose* to protect the interests of its nationals abroad – but by no means had the duty to do so.[152] This approach remained more or less the same in the early twentieth century and in the inter-war period. Whilst first Brierly, Kelsen and Scelle,[153] and later Lauterpacht and some of his contemporaries,[154] held the individual to be the ultimate international legal person, capable of holding rights and obligations, such views remained somewhat marginal when it came to international legal practice.[155] According to the so-called 'object theory', individuals could not be right holders under international law, but enjoyed only benefits deriving from the rights and obligations of states.[156]

Much changed in international legal theory at the end of the twentieth century and the beginning of the twenty-first. It has since been generally accepted that 'to the extent that entities other than states "directly possess" rights, powers and duties in international law' they can be regarded as subjects of international law.[157] Furthermore, these rights and obligations are now endowed to individuals under human rights law, humanitarian law and international criminal law, and to different entities under international investment law, international organisations law and international environmental law. Thus, it is sometimes suggested that the old subjects/objects distinction within international law has collapsed, as it has been accepted that international legal persons are not identical, but rather form a spectrum, starting from the state as a full subject of international law and leading to non-governmental organisations, which are recognised as subjects by some intergovernmental organisations.

Nonetheless, there remains much disagreement amongst international legal scholars about how international legal personality should be perceived.[158] Some have argued that what should matter is the actual capacity of an entity to engage in the international legal system in a given context, and that we should therefore get rid of the problematic notion of legal personhood altogether.[159] According to the New Haven School, for example, there are no subjects and objects of

[152] K Parlett, *The Individual in the International Legal System: Continuity and Change in International Law*, reprint edn (Cambridge, Cambridge University Press, 2013) 13–16.

[153] Nijman, *The Concept of International Legal Personality*, ch 3; Peters, *Beyond Human Rights* (n 9) 18–19.

[154] Nijman (n 77) ch 4.4; Peters, *Beyond Human Rights* (n 9) 20–21.

[155] See further R Portmann, *Legal Personality in International Law* (Cambridge, Cambridge University Press, 2010) 126–72.

[156] G Manner, 'The Object Theory of the Individual in International Law' (1952) 46 *American Journal of International Law* 428.

[157] Parlett, *The Individual in the International Legal System*, 353–54.

[158] For an overview, see Portmann, *Legal Personality in International Law*, especially pt II. Kjeldgaard-Pedersen *The International Legal Personality*, ch 2.

[159] R Higgins, *Problems and Process: International Law and How We Use It*, new edn (Oxford, Oxford University Press, 1995) 50.

international law, but only participants to it, including individuals.[160] Others, drawing from Kelsen's conception of legal personhood as a 'personified unity of a set of legal norms', have argued that anyone can be a person, for personhood is acquired whenever an international norm is addressed to an entity.[161] Still others argue that human rights and humanitarian law have changed the interpretation of international law so that it now recognises individuals as legal persons.[162]

The law of humanity project has intervened radically in this discussion, arguing for the primary international legal personality of the human individual. Indeed, while Anne Peters has drawn from the aforementioned attempts to rethink international legal personality, she has also clearly distinguished her position. As Peters writes, all of the aforementioned attempts to rethink international legal personhood are flawed in that they have trouble recognising the individual as a full international legal person. If international legal personality is taken to be enjoyed by those entities that enjoy an adequate *number or density* of rights to give them a certain freedom of action under international law, then individuals would fall into a grey area: they might not yet have enough rights to meet the threshold of freedom, but such rights are rapidly increasing. If, on the other hand, international legal personality were to require rights which have the right *substance*, such as the right to conclude treaties or join international organisations, then individuals would not qualify at all. The same would be true if international legal personality were to require certain capacities, as individuals do not at the moment have the same capacities as states do under international law.[163] Similarly, Christopher Barbara argues that graduated international legal personality and international capacity rely on state action and hence 'differ mainly on nomenclature and on where to draw the line between being an international legal person and everything else'.[164] While individuals and other non-state actors might be argued to enjoy international legal personality of some sort in that they may, for example, appear in certain international courts such as human rights courts,[165] these are, according to Barbara, 'secondary grants of circumscribed ILP [international legal personality] and not equivalent to the "full" ILP exercised by States'.[166] Hence, 'if individuals were granted full and formal ILP on the same hierarchical level as the state, it would have to be one specially adapted for them – in other words, a new type of ILP'.[167] What unites at least most – if not all – of the law of humanity theorists, then,

[160] See MS McDougal, HD Lasswell and L Chen, *Human Rights and World Public Order: The Basic Policies of an International Law of Human Dignity* (New Haven, Yale University Press, 1977).
[161] Kjeldgaard-Pedersen (n 12); see also Portmann (n 155) pt III.
[162] Cançado Trindade (n 12); Meron (n 12); A Cassese, *International Law*, 2nd edn (Oxford, Oxford University Press, 2003) 165–66.
[163] Peters, *Beyond Human Rights* (n 9) 36–38.
[164] Barbara, 'International Legal Personality', 25.
[165] ibid 23.
[166] ibid 23–24.
[167] ibid 29.

is the idea that the individual should not only have personhood under international law; she should be *the* primary international legal person, the foundation of the system.

The second way in which the idea of the increasing roles of the individual and humanity occupies the centre of the law of humanity discourse has less to do with formal rules of international law. Instead of international legal personality, it deals with interpretation and legitimacy. According to Peters, humanity should be the 'new normative foundation of international law'.[168] Similarly, Domingo also declares that the human person would be the normative foundation of his global law,[169] and Teitel writes that, 'Reaching beyond the state and the prevailing international system', humanity's law 'offers a new basis legitimation and interpretation'.[170] In a way, then, the law of humanity theorists wants to change the structure of the international legal argument.

In *From Apology to Utopia*, Martti Koskenniemi has shown that the international legal argument has, since the birth of liberal international law, oscillated between two patterns of argument: a descending one and an ascending one. This oscillation does not derive only from the indeterminacy of language, however, as Koskenniemi is sometimes misread, but more fundamentally from the very contradictory foundation of the liberal international legal system, focused on the freedom and equality of states. In seeking to be practical rather than theoretical, the liberal tradition insists that international law must be based on the free will of sovereign states, but that it must at the same time be binding on all states equally.[171] Hence, any argument is necessarily based on two patterns of argument: one ascending from the sovereign will of states and the other descending from some objective, communal basis. Yet both are vulnerable to criticism from the opposite perspective, descending arguments seeming all too much like utopian natural law and ascending arguments like apologia for the strongest. Moreover, when pushed further, the descending argument also starts to seem apologist (for without any objective criteria it is ultimately those who get to decide what the universal rules are) and the ascending argument starts to seem utopian (for it is obvious that states are not equal or fully sovereign in practice). Hence, any legal case can oscillate endlessly between apology and utopia, or ascending and descending arguments,[172] and decisions necessarily depend on the structural bias of the decision-making institution.[173]

[168] Peters, 'Humanity as the A and Ω of Sovereignty' (n 9) 514.
[169] Domingo (n 1) xvi.
[170] Teitel (n 10) 15.
[171] Martti Koskenniemi, *From Apology to Utopia the Structure of International Legal Argument* (Cambridge, Cambridge University Press 2005) 16–23, 74–94.
[172] ibid 59–60, 83–89.
[173] ibid 606–07. Structural bias means that the institution 'de facto prefers some outcomes or distributive choices to other outcomes or choices'.

The law of humanity discourse seems to suggest that all of this is changing. When states are no longer seen as autonomous, equal 'individuals', as relatively sovereign officials of the law of humanity serving the fundamental core of the system, that is, the protection of human life, the old system of binaries would – so it is assumed – collapse. Any decision would always be tilted in favour of 'humanity', 'human rights' or 'human dignity'. There would be no oscillation, but decisions would be made with humanity in mind, irrespective of whether the decision would go against the will of a state or not. As Anne Peters writes,

> conflicts between state sovereignty and human rights should not be approached in a balancing process in which the former is played off against the latter on an equal footing, but should be tackled on the basis of a presumption in favour of humanity.[174]

B. The Diminishing Role of the State

The second, closely interlinked, key element of the law of humanity theories is the idea that the increasing role of the individual and humanity require the diminishing role of the previous protagonist of international law, namely the state. The project's critique of the state comes in both sociological and ethical form, often mixed together, but summarised in a helpful way by Koskenniemi.[175] According to sociological critique, the state is withering away because of factual developments in the (globalising) world. As the argument goes, states are no longer able to handle problems such as increasing poverty, the global climate crisis or the refugee crisis. Consequently, sovereignty has become a mere illusion in the globalised world and the management of global problems requires surpassing the obstacles posed by statehood.[176] As Benvenisti argues, for example:

> We live in a shrinking world where interdependence between countries and communities is increasing. These changes also affect – as they should – the concept of sovereignty. In past decades the predominant conception of sovereignty was akin to owning a large estate separated from other properties by rivers or deserts. By contrast, today's reality is more analogous to owning a small apartment in one densely packed high-rise that is home to two hundred separate families. The sense of interdependency is heightened when we recognize the absence of any alternative to this shared home, of any exit from this global high-rise. The privilege of bygone days of opting out, of retreating into splendid isolation, of adopting mercantilist policies or erecting iron curtains is no longer realistically available.[177]

[174] Peters, 'Humanity as the A and Ω of Sovereignty' (n 9) 514.
[175] M Koskenniemi, 'The Wonderful Artificiality of States' (1994) 88 *American Society of International Law Proceedings* 22.
[176] ibid 23.
[177] Benvenisti, 'Sovereigns as Trustees of Humanity', 295.

Similarly, Domingo writes that:

> The state has proven too small for global issues, yet too large for local ones. The most important decisions of our day – such as global security, the elimination of poverty, defence of the environment, education of the masses, or the reduction and nonprofileration of nuclear arms – should be dealt with by structures that transcend the material and conceptual borders of the state which is ultimately incapable of providing practical solutions.[178]

The ethical critique, by contrast, views statehood as 'morally indefensible egotism'. Drawing from cosmopolitanism, the critique 'sees all people united in a Kantian community of independent individuals equally entitled to human rights and fundamental freedoms, regardless of which passport they happen to carry'.[179] According to this view, statehood is a mere historical accident and has little or no value, often simply preventing the realisation of universal human rights. In its communitarian version, it posits that humanity is a unity separated artificially through state borders; in its individualistic version, it stresses the priority of the individual over the state and the ways in which states have, since their birth, abused their power and violated human rights.[180] The ethical view is advocated in some form by most, if not all, law of humanity theorists. For Barbara, the greatest problem of the international legal system is that the pre-eminent role is reserved for a legal fiction, the state, rather than the human person.[181] In Barbara's mind, it is 'extremely problematic to have at the centre of our legal order something which amounts to nothing more than a figment of our imagination'.[182] Similarly, Domingo writes that, the 'state worship that characterises international law hobbles its development and hinders proper analysis and critique of its institutions, for it places at the center of the system something that actually should take second place to the person'.[183] Furthermore, according to Teitel, humanity law's normativity 'clearly transcends the state and relativizes sovereignty'.[184] And almost all of the law of humanity theorists seem to see the state as an obstacle to the realisation of human rights.

Nevertheless, it is worth pointing out that none of the authors studied in this chapter want to do without states altogether. It is quite obvious that states would still be key actors in Waldron's and Peters's humanised international law, as well as in Delmas-Marty's reciprocal humanisation. For Peters, the key change is that

[178] Domingo (n 1) 62.
[179] Koskenniemi, 'The Wonderful Artificiality of States' 23. Kant did not, however, advocate for free borders or free migration, but only for a right of visit. See I Kant, *Toward Perpetual Peace and Other Writings on Politics, Peace, and History* (P Kleingeld ed, DL Colclasure trans, New Haven, Yale University Press, 2006) 82–85.
[180] Koskenniemi (n 175) 23.
[181] Barbara (n 23) 45.
[182] ibid 47.
[183] Domingo (n 1) 58.
[184] Teitel (n 10) 58.

state sovereignty is now made dependent on protection of humanity, whereas Waldron advocates for altering the role of the state from a subject of international law to its official, and Delmas-Marty's project aims at increased cultural dialogue and harmonisation, not at the withering of the state. The status of the state is less clear in Teitel's humanity law, which is closer to a vision of global law than international law. That said, there is no indication that she would want to get rid of states, although she does argue strongly that state sovereignty should be relativised, thus losing its absolute value when the protection of humanity is at stake – this protection not being limited to violent conflicts, but including also issues such as poverty, disease and environmental threats. Domingo's vision of international organisations-led global law is the most critical towards states. Yet, for him, too, the real problem is the central place given to the state, as well as its personification, rather than the simple existence of states per se, since this personification has dehumanised the human person and deprived her of human dignity.[185] The state would likely still exist in Domingo's global law, but it would be simply one institution among others, comparable to the family and the municipalities, which are often – in Domingo's mind – preferable administrators of life due to their spontaneous and natural character.

States therefore have a role in all accounts of law of humanity, but that role is strictly constrained as states are conceived as 'fiduciaries of humanity' or 'officials of law of humanity'. Whilst states would likely still remain subjects of the new law of humanity, they would have that subjectivity only insofar as it is necessary for them to play their fiduciary/official role. Moreover, state sovereignty would be relativised and made conditional on the effective fulfilment of this role.

C. Change through Concepts

The third key characteristic of the law of humanity theories is that they perceive concepts as the key tool in transforming international law in the law of humanity direction. Even though the accounts of law of humanity are more or less *lex ferenda*, they are characteristically legal accounts. Teitel, for example, emphasises that her humanity's law entails a move away from interstate politics and towards 'an increasingly law-based order' where courts play a key role.[186] At the heart of the theories, however, is not really the creation of new rules, but rather interpretation. This is perhaps most obvious in the work of Peters and Waldron, neither of whom is very interested in changing the core structures and concepts of international law but would rather focus on changing the way we understand

[185] Domingo (n 1) xvi.
[186] Teitel (n 10) 63.

those structures and concepts so that considerations of humanity are always primary. Further, interpretation is quite obviously the key also for Teitel, for whom

> [h]umanity law's ascendancy and diffusion has not occurred through a counter-hegemonic challenge to sovereignty from above, from a pretended higher or supreme normative order that seeks to impose itself over and above the state, but rather in large measure through interpretation or reinterpretation of legal norms by a large range of actors including domestic actors, political and judicial.[187]

Furthermore, Delmas-Marty's cultural exchange is almost entirely about interpretation of rules and making them compatible with local contexts. The importance of interpretation might seem more surprising in the case of Domingo, however, considering his top-down approach. Nonetheless, the focus on interpretation is actually integral to his project. As his global law is guided primarily by core principles aiming for the protection of the human person and governed through several overlapping institutions, it is quite natural that interpretation –always tilted in favour of humanity – gains a key role in the system. For Domingo, this new global law must 'integrate the highest values of different legal traditions while acknowledging the living synthesis of diverse and often disparate cultures'.[188] As he writes, the

> new legal order must above all be a jurisdictional law and not an interstate jurisdictional model: consensual, not bureaucratic, positive, or official. It should be proposed and not imposed – based more on laws and codes and led by civil society protected by global institutions and not by hierarchical and technocratic state entities.[189]

As such, his system is also fluid and based on interpretation. It is most of all about a new mentality, not about an exact set of rules.[190]

Because of this focus on interpretation, the primary tools of the law of humanity project are concepts. As the argument goes, the increased importance of certain concepts has an impact on values and interpretation, inevitably changing the way we perceive and practise international law and eventually changing it into law of humanity. So what are the concepts that guide this system? The four approaches studied above have somewhat different focuses, and it is therefore obvious that different concepts have different emphases within them. However, there are three concepts that play a key role in all of them and are the most fundamental in some of them. These three are also the concepts around which the approaches are built, so that other humanity-focused legal concepts are seen to derive from or support them.

The first concept is *human rights*, which is probably the concept most frequently mentioned, if all the texts discussed above are studied together. All

[187] ibid 165–66.
[188] Domingo (n 1) xv.
[189] ibid xviii.
[190] ibid 100–02.

of the authors would likely agree with Domingo when he writes that human beings are 'bearers of rights, always and everywhere', not by attribution, 'but by virtue of their nature, essence, substance, or however one calls this intrinsic condition innate to persons'.[191] The authors nevertheless each give a somewhat different role to human rights. For some of the authors, such as Waldron and Peters, human rights are the fundamental norms of international law, although Peters has sought in her most recent work to go beyond human rights in deriving individual rights from all areas of international law.[192] Others give human rights a more modest role. As we learned above, for Domingo, human rights form 'an integral part of global law', yet they constitute only 'a point of departure' or a new beginning for the global law of humanity.[193] Indeed, in Domingo's mind, human rights law grants an overly large role to the state and can even be harmful in its linkage to the notion of nationality.[194] Similarly, Teitel writes that her humanity law 'depends on a discourse and structure of claims-making that has become the *lingua franca*, surpassing while also encompassing human rights law and norms'.[195] For her, too, human rights are only a stepping stone to the more global humanity law, which is not tied to the idea of the subject within a state. Moreover, being keenly aware of the problems related to the balancing of rights, Teitel does not believe that human rights can be hierarchically equal, and thus gives preference to those rights that are related to survival.

The second concept is *human security*, which is given more concrete form in the legal world in the responsibility to protect concept. Human security and the responsibility to protect play a key role especially in Teitel's and Peters's texts. Teitel's humanity law is focused primarily on ensuring the survival of human individuals and groups. Consequently, human security takes precedence in her theory, while human rights and human dignity come second – even though Teitel does certainly emphasise that survival alone is not enough. Perhaps even more importantly here, however, Teitel sees the increased importance of human security as radically transforming how we perceive international law and international relations, as international security becomes only a 'part and parcel' of broader human security or 'the security of persons and peoples'.[196] This shift of emphasis from state to human security thus alters the very 'normative foundations of the international legal order'.[197] For Peters, the humanisation of international law increased dramatically beginning from the year 1999. The most important factor in this development was the endorsement of human security through the responsibility to protect concept, mainstreamed by the 2001 Report

[191] ibid 125.
[192] Peters, *Beyond Human Rights* (n 9).
[193] Domingo (n 1) 142–44.
[194] ibid 59–60.
[195] Teitel (n 10) 204–06.
[196] ibid 109.
[197] ibid 4.

of the International Commission on Intervention and State Responsibility. The emergence of the responsibility to protect removed sovereignty from its privileged position in international law in that sovereignty was now derived from humanity, which is 'the *telos* of the international legal system'.[198] Hence, for Peters too, human security and the responsibility to protect are not only important concepts, but are also catalysts for change in international law.

The third key concept is *human dignity*. This concept has a particularly prominent role in Domingo's work, as for him personhood and human dignity are inseparable. Human dignity is therefore the basis of any proper law.[199] Domingo devotes an entire section to the history of the concept of dignity and its role for his global law of humanity. Furthermore, both Delmas-Marty and Cançado Trindade emphasise the role of human dignity as the most fundamental concept of law.[200] Peters and Teitel, too, mention the concept of dignity frequently and seem to consider it a foundational concept of their vision, although the concept is not discussed as thoroughly as in Domingo's work, but, rather, is treated as the self-evident core of the law of humanity. For Teitel, human dignity is strongly linked to human security and therefore forms a basis for humanity rights. While she argues that humanity rights must start from self-preservation, she nevertheless goes on to add that human security and humanity rights still have to be about more than preventing bodily harm, as humanity law 'also encompasses a certain conception of humanity as related to dignity'.[201] Human dignity therefore seems to be a foundational concept of the law of humanity, one that guides its interpretation but also changes its direction.

In what follows in this book, I treat the aforementioned three concepts – human rights, human security and human dignity – as the foundational concepts of the law of humanity project. This does not, however, mean that the humanity discourse in international law would not use other concepts, such as crimes against humanity or a common heritage of (hu)mankind, for example. These and other concepts do play an important role as well. Nevertheless, I distinguish them from human rights, human security and human dignity as they play a very specific and limited legal role in international law and the law of humanity, whereas the three key concepts of the project are claimed to guide all legal thinking and interpretation (at least) in the law of humanity.

[198] Peters, 'Humanity as the A and Ω of Sovereignty' (n 9) 514.
[199] Domingo (n 1) 134–35.
[200] Cançado Trindade (n 12) 638; Delmas-Marty, *Aux quatre vents du monde* (n 133) 85–86.
[201] Teitel (n 10) 155–58.

3

Concepts of Law of Humanity

AT THE HEART of the law of humanity discourse lays an assumption that the increased circulation of the key law of humanity concepts – namely, human rights, human security and human dignity – will transform international law into law of humanity and improve the lives of individuals everywhere. In this chapter, I will engage with this assumption by analysing each of the aforementioned concepts in turn. My argument is that, due to their indeterminacy, the concepts can be used to achieve multiple purposes; not only those sought by the law of humanity theorists. Hence, there are no guarantees that the increased reference to the concepts will necessarily bring about the outcomes desired by the law of humanity theorists.

I. THE PROMISES AND THE CHALLENGES

The concepts of human rights, human security and human dignity all hold great promise for the law of humanity project. At the heart of the project lies the notion that persons are bearers of inalienable human rights, always and everywhere.[1] Although Anne Peters has recently emphasised that individual rights in the international legal system cannot be reduced to human rights[2] and Rafael Domingo has treated human rights most of all as a tool for protecting human dignity,[3] human rights are nevertheless a fundamental building block of the project. This is so for at least four reasons. First, international human rights law – along with international criminal law and international investment law – has played a crucial part in putting the individual on the map of international law. Second, as the importance of international human rights law grew, it started to affect more traditional areas of international law through interpretation. As both Cançado Trindade and Merón have argued, human rights have produced a ripple effect with the consequence that human rights considerations

[1] R Domingo, *The New Global Law*, reprint edn (Cambridge, Cambridge University Press, 2011) 125.

[2] A Peters, *Beyond Human Rights: The Legal Status of the Individual in International Law* (J Huston trans, Cambridge, Cambridge University Press, 2016).

[3] Domingo, *The New Global Law*, 142–44.

now permeate almost the entire plane of international law.[4] Third, human rights are seen to help in the law of humanity project's attempt to reduce the role of states in international law and/or to relativise state sovereignty.[5] Finally, human rights are supposed to alter the structure of international law, providing it with a new foundation by changing the way we perceive law at the global level. Indeed, international human rights law tends to emphasise its special character and thus construct itself 'in direct opposition to the tried and tested methods of international law'.[6] Whereas international law is often seen to be trapped in the 'agnosticism of classical liberalism', human rights law is seen to resurrect the idea that there is some eternal core which law must serve and thus 'put the international legal system on an entirely new footing, one that is much more geared towards the pursuit of a broad vision of justice'.[7]

The attractiveness of human security for the law of humanity project lies especially in the notion that human security is seen to position the human being at the centre of international security.[8] As the argument goes, persons are no longer subordinated to states; rather, states and other institutions are subordinated to persons,[9] in a new deterritorialised 'society of humankind'.[10] Although these ideas have not been successfully institutionalised in global governance and international law, commentators such as Barbara von Tigerstrom argue that human security has already acted as a framework through which debates and developments in international law and politics are rethought, critically scrutinised and interpreted.[11] Indeed, according to Ruti Teitel, human security alters the 'normative foundations of the international legal order',[12] whereas Anne Peters argues that the emergence of the responsibility to protect concept has ousted sovereignty from its position as the foundation of international law and replaced it with humanity.[13] Furthermore, some argue that the mainstreaming of

[4] AA Cançado Trindade, *International Law for Humankind* (Leiden, Brill Academic Publishers, 2010); T Meron, *The Humanization of International Law* (Leiden, Brill Academic Publishers, 2006). See also VP Tzevelekos, 'Revisiting the Humanisation of International Law: Limits and Potential. Obligations Erga Omnes, Hierarchy of Rules and the Principle of Due Diligence as the Basis for Further Humanisation' (2013) 6 *Erasmus Law Review* 62.

[5] F Mégret, 'Apology of Utopia: Some Thoughts on Koskenniemian Themes, with Particular Emphasis on Massively Institutionalized International Human Rights Law' (2013) 27 *Temple International & Comparative Law Journal* 455, 463.

[6] ibid.

[7] ibid 463–64.

[8] Commission on Human Security, *Human Security Now* (2003) 4.

[9] S Tadjbakhsh and A Chenoy, *Human Security: Concepts and Implications* (Abingdon, Routledge, 2007) 13.

[10] ibid 20–21.

[11] B von Tigerstrom, *Human Security and International Law: Prospects and Problems* (Oxford, Hart Publishing, 2007) 90, 211–13. See also G Oberlietner, 'Human Security: A Challenge to International Law' (2005) 11 *Global Governance* 185, 198; Y Roznai, 'The Insecurity of Human Security' (2014) 32 *Wisconsin International Law Journal* 95, 113–14.

[12] R Teitel, *Humanity's Law* (Oxford, Oxford University Press, 2011) 4.

[13] A Peters, 'Humanity as the A and Ω of Sovereignty' (2009) 20 *European Journal of International Law* 513, 514.

human security means the universalisation of a certain set of values which initiate a move from a 'society of states' to a deterritorialised 'society of humankind'.[14]

Most recently, there has been a significant rise in publications and judicial decisions that employ the concept of human dignity. The concept, it is hoped, will provide much needed guidance to the interpretation of human rights. According to Mark Lagon and Anthony Clark Arend, for example, the emergence of the human dignity discourse is a welcomed addition to or replacement for the human rights discourse, which 'does not seem to fully address the challenges to the human person in the contemporary international system'.[15] As they write:

> [I]f human rights are to have meaning beyond norm elaboration in resolutions, treaties, and law and are to be enjoyed in practice, the test of impact is whether they actually yield the agency and social recognition that constitute human dignity.[16]

Catherine Dupré makes the argument even more strongly, stating that if 'the twentieth century marked for some the end of history and of human rights, the twenty-first century definitely seems to be the century of human dignity'.[17] And Thomas Banchoff declares that human dignity has more political force than human rights, since rights must be balanced against each other whereas 'human dignity is, by definition, inviolable'.[18] Similarly, there has been a turn in the human security discourse towards 'freedom to live in dignity', which is supposed to either supplement or replace the freedom from want and freedom from fear approaches.

It is therefore no wonder that some theorists of law of humanity have put a lot of hope on the concept of human dignity. Increased use of the concept is supposed to help shift international law in the law of humanity direction while also guiding decision-making; but, at the same time, human dignity is also commonly viewed as some kind of end result or goal of the law of humanity. According to Domingo, for example, his global law is based on the human person, who is the centre of that order because of her unique human dignity.[19] In contrasting international law with the new global law of humanity, Domingo draws parallels with the role of sovereignty in international law and human dignity in law of humanity. As he writes, sovereignty 'is to international law

[14] Tadjbakhsh and Chenoy, *Human Security*, 20–21.

[15] MP Lagon and AC Arend, 'Introduction: Human Dignity in a Neomedieval World' in MP Lagon and AC Arend (eds), *Human Dignity and the Future of Global Institutions* (Washington DC, Georgetown University Press, 2014) 7.

[16] MP Lagon and AC Arend, 'Constructing a Dialogue on Dignity: The Path Ahead' in Lagon and Arend, *Human Dignity*, 322.

[17] C Dupré, *The Age of Dignity: Human Rights and Constitutionalism in Europe* (Oxford, Hart Publishing, 2015) 1.

[18] T Banchoff, 'Religion and the Global Politics of Human Dignity: The Catholic Church and Beyond' in Lagon and Arend, *Human Dignity* (n 15) 257.

[19] Domingo (n 1) xxi.

what dignity is to global law: its foundation'.[20] Indeed, some authors have claimed that human dignity has already 'inverted the relationship between the state and individuals' by putting the human person 'at the normative center of constitutionalism', thus turning it into an instrument for 'protecting humanity in all its integrated and evolving dimensions'.[21]

Commentators also argue that human dignity can guide decision-making in the new global legal order. According to Lagon and Arend, for example, human dignity can act as a guiding principle in the contemporary world where states have lost their dominant role and hence offer 'both the inspiration and an implementation yardstick for global institutions'.[22] Similarly, Dupré emphasises the concept's potential for interpretation in a globalised world,[23] whereas Judge Christian Byk argues that human dignity 'helps define what humanity is and it gives us the opportunity of a discussion on the limits of human power'.[24] Furthermore, Habermas argues that human dignity can play an 'inventive function', leading both to 'more complete exhaustion of existing civil rights and to the discovery and construction of new ones'.[25]

However, in order to provide a solid foundation for something like a new global law of humanity, human rights, human security and human dignity would have to manage to 'strike consistently utopian postures without falling prey to the gravitational pull of apology, essentially founding international law anew on the basis of commonly shared values'.[26] In other words, the concepts would have to be able to solve cases dealing with conflicting rights or conflicts between rights and other essential community interests.

For this to be possible, however, we would need a theory of the concepts that explains their authority while clarifying their content in practical situations.[27] This seems like quite a task. If the authority of the concepts are to be commonly accepted, they necessarily have to remain neutral and abstract in character, for only then can they be accepted globally in different cultures and different contexts.[28] Yet, this would mean that they cannot remain concrete enough to help

[20] ibid 99.

[21] Dupré, *The Age of Dignity*, 171–72. For an earlier view on somewhat similar lines, see O Schachter, 'Human Dignity as a Normative Concept' (1983) 77 *American Journal of International Law* 848, 853–54.

[22] Lagon and Arend, 'Constructing a Dialogue on Dignity', 332.

[23] Dupré (n 17) 166–68.

[24] C Byk, 'Is Human Dignity a Useless Concept? Legal Perspectives' in M Düwell et al, *The Cambridge Handbook of Human Dignity: Interdisciplinary Perspectives* (Cambridge, Cambridge University Press, 2014) 364.

[25] J Habermas, 'The Concept of Human Dignity and the Realistic Utopia of Human Rights' (2010) 41 *Metaphilosophy* 464, 467–68.

[26] Mégret, 'Apology of Utopia', 463.

[27] EJ Criddle and E Fox-Decent, *Fiduciaries of Humanity: How International Law Constitutes Authority* (Oxford, Oxford University Press, 2016) 94.

[28] G Frankenberg, 'Human Rights and the Belief in a Just World' (2014) 12 *International Journal of Constitutional Law* 35, 57.

solve concrete cases. Similarly, a functional legal system would seem to require some sort of rule hierarchy; but hierarchy between rights does not match well with their universal and inalienable character, for a superior right would render all other rights anything but inalienable and universal in cases of conflict.[29]

II. HUMAN RIGHTS

The ways in which the aforementioned conflicts, or paradoxes,[30] lead to the indeterminacy of human rights is demonstrated well in critical legal scholarship.[31] This indeterminacy is visible on multiple levels in the practice of human rights law. At the most general level, it is reflected in what Koskenniemi calls the 'field constitution' of human rights, namely 'the process whereby an aspect of reality comes to be characterised in terms of rights'.[32] Some issues are translated into human rights language and recognised as human rights issues, whereas other are not. This is by no means a merely technical issue. Rather it is politics *par excellence*.[33] This is even clearer in the application of already accepted rights. Even such a fundamental right as the right to life is far from clear-cut when applied in practice – particularly issues concerning the beginning and end of life. For example, in *Vo v France* the European Court of Human Rights stated that it was not within its competence to assert when human life begins, the issue falling under the margin of appreciation of national authorities. It continued that it is 'convinced that it is neither desirable, nor even possible as matters stand, to answer in the abstract the question whether the unborn child is a person for the purposes of Article 2 of the Convention', especially since in that particular case it considered it 'unnecessary to examine whether the abrupt end to the applicant's pregnancy falls within the scope of Article 2'.[34] And even assuming that we would agree that the foetus is protected by the right to life, abortion cases still require a delicate balancing of rights.[35] Similarly, we tend to disagree on whether we have the right to euthanasia. Consequently, when it had to decide on the right to peaceful suicide in *Haas v Switzerland*, the Court stated that the member states of the Council of Europe are 'far from having reached a consensus with regard to an individual's right to decide how and when his or her life should end', and consequently held that 'States enjoy a considerable margin of appreciation in this area'.[36]

[29] C Douzinas, 'The End(s) of Human Rights' (2002) 26 *Melbourne University Law Review* 445, 463.
[30] C Douzinas, 'The Paradoxes of Human Rights' (2013) 20 *Constellations* 51.
[31] M Koskenniemi, 'Human Rights, Politics, and Love' (2001) *Mennesker & Rettigheter* 33.
[32] ibid 35.
[33] ibid 35–36.
[34] *Vo v France* no 53924/00 (2004) 40 EHRR 12, para 85.
[35] See, eg *Tysiac v Poland* no 5410/03 (2007) 45 EHRR 42.
[36] *Haas v Switzerland* no 31322/07 (2011) 53 EHRR 33, para 55.

At the level of rules, the indeterminacy is demonstrated by the fact that human rights tend to come with exceptions, the scope and conditions for application of which are never clearly defined. This is the case, for example, with the rights (such as Articles 8–11 of the European Convention on Human Rights and several rights in the International Covenant on Civil and Political Rights) that can be infringed upon without a violation if the infringement is prescribed by law, meets one of the legitimate interests set out in the relevant articles and is 'necessary in a democratic society'. The last condition, in particular, requires complex political balancing, including references to 'reasonability' and 'proportionality', and the application of the margin of appreciation doctrine. Any such balancing will ultimately hinge upon 'cultural and political assumptions' on whether a good society should prioritise this or that value or vision of the good life.[37] Balancing tends, therefore, to be 'an issue of political value; of struggle and compromise between alternative views'.[38] There is no clear rule on how to find the correct balance between privacy and security, for example – or between several freedoms and public health in the contemporary case of the COVID-19 pandemic.

Moreover, as more and more interests have been turned into the human rights language,[39] most contemporary human rights conflicts involve the weighing of competing rights claims, as one person's right to act or speak in a certain way, or to possess something, constrains another person's similar rights or her right to be protected from certain type of behaviour. Again, there is no simple rule on how to solve these conflicts. Instead, human rights actors increasingly have to resort to the kind of utilitarian calculations that the human rights movement has for so long protested against.

These controversies are further highlighted when we move from the domestic and regional to the global level. Mégret writes:

> Limitations on rights now have to be evaluated in relation to a world that is considerably more diverse, and in which we have even less reason to think that we can agree on what might constitute 'morality,' 'public order,' and 'the rights of others,' or 'proportionality,' 'necessity,' and a 'democratic society'.[40]

Accordingly, it has been argued by critics that human rights are in practice little more than a 'presumptive claim whose scope has to be addressed against a range of other competing social priorities or public goods, such as law and public order, morality, or the protection of the rights of others'.[41]

[37] Koskenniemi, 'Human Rights, Politics, and Love', 36–38.

[38] M Koskenniemi, 'The Effect of Rights on Political Culture' in P Alston, MR Bustelo and J Heenan (eds), *The EU and Human Rights* (Oxford, Oxford University Press, 1999) 105.

[39] C Douzinas, 'Identity, Recognition, Rights or What Can Hegel Teach Us about Human Rights?' (2002) 29 *Journal of Law and Society* 379.

[40] Mégret (n 5) 468.

[41] ibid 466.

Although the political and indeterminate nature of human rights is not a problem per se,[42] it does become one if human rights are assumed to be able to form some (utopian) foundation of the law of humanity, or if it is assumed that more focus on human rights automatically delivers desired results. In fact, the more successful human rights become, and the more they are relied upon, the more problematic their indeterminacy becomes – at least for something like the law of humanity project. As Allen Buchanan writes, 'The more seriously the international legal system takes the protection of human rights and the more teeth this commitment has, the more problematic the lack of a credible public justification for human-rights norms becomes'.[43] The more important human rights become in public policy and court practice, the more pertinent it is that human rights can provide coherent solutions in actual cases.

It is, then, becoming increasingly clear for the human rights community that human rights cannot act as guides of global law and policy 'without re-engaging the fundamental philosophical questions of human rights theory'.[44] Indeed, there has recently been renewed interest in finding a philosophical foundation of human rights – many commentators believing that this could help us solve the 'problem' of their indeterminacy.

These attempts can be divided into several approaches. The first is a naturalistic one. Usually drawing from moral theories or even natural law theory, the proponents of this approach hold that human rights derive their authority from some deeper order of values, not from law or practice, and that they are rights that we have simply by virtue of our humanity and which can be identified by ordinary moral reasoning.[45]

The naturalistic conception faces several problems, however. Perhaps the most obvious one is the question of why all humans should have some rights irrespective of law. The answer of most of the naturalistic accounts is that human rights protect or derive from those characteristics without which we would not be fully human. This, however, requires determination of what those features are. This is often presented in more legalistic terms as an issue of personhood.[46]

[42] In many ways, it is worth celebrating. See, eg J Rancière, 'Who Is the Subject of the Rights of Man?' (2004) 103 *South Atlantic Quarterly* 297.

[43] A Buchanan, 'Human Rights and the Legitimacy of the International Order' (2008) 14 *Legal Theory* 39, 40–41.

[44] E Fox-Decent and EJ Criddle, 'The Fiduciary Constitution of Human Rights' (2009) 15 *Legal Theory* 301, 305.

[45] CR Beitz, *The Idea of Human Rights* (Oxford, Oxford University Press, 2011) 48–50; R Cruft, SM Liao and M Renzo, 'The Philosophical Foundations of Human Rights: An Overview' in R Cruft, SM Liao and M Renzo (eds), *Philosophical Foundations of Human Rights* (Oxford, Oxford University Press, 2015) 4. See, eg A Gewirth, *The Community of Rights* (Chicago, University of Chicago Press, 1998); J Griffin, *On Human Rights* (Oxford, Oxford University Press, 2009); J Tasioulas, 'Towards a Philosophy of Human Rights' (2012) 65 *Current Legal Problems* 1.

[46] JR Slaughter, 'However Incompletely, Human' in C Douzinas and C Gearty (eds), *The Meanings of Rights: The Philosophy and Social Theory of Human Rights* (Cambridge, Cambridge University Press, 2014) 275–76.

Referring to personhood does not solve the issue, however, but only raises the further question of who counts as a person and why.[47] Agency and capacity of moral consideration are typical threshold criteria, but all such candidates can push – and have, indeed, pushed throughout history – a substantial number of human beings out of the sphere of human rights.[48] Furthermore, the naturalistic conception also struggles to explain why some moral rights should be turned into legal rights,[49] and seems to suggest that legally accepted rights – such as second and third generation rights, or group rights – should not be accepted as human rights.[50] And most fundamentally, the naturalistic conception seems to be quite incapable of dealing with the fact that, in practice, the protection of the rights of some might well require interference with the rights of others. Whilst the naturalistic approach greatly narrows the list of fundamental rights, it does not seem to have a mechanism for deciding cases where some of the remaining rights collide.

Some thinkers have tried to circumvent the aforementioned problems by shifting focus from personhood and moral capacity to human needs. Human rights are, according to this view, derived from those basic needs that are required to sustain physical existence and have a healthy psychological and social life,[51] or to ensure the opportunities and choices that are necessary for a 'life worthy of human dignity'.[52] However, although this need-based version does manage to escape some of the difficulties of the agency/personhood version, such as the problem of second and third generation rights, it still suffers from the oscillation between under- and overinclusiveness: either it cannot differentiate in a convincing manner between human rights and the rights of non-human species, or it must propose 'characteristics we will endlessly squabble about'.[53]

Others thinkers go to the other extreme. Noting the problem of basing human rights on any substantive quality, they 'strip the human of all particularities, including bodily ones, until it becomes as abstract and generic as possible – a contentless, all-purpose, "human"'.[54] Thus, what is left is only some sort of almost mystical human essence which cannot be defined, but which nevertheless unites us all after we have been stripped of all our 'contingent

[47] See, eg Griffin, *On Human Rights*, 95; C Wellman, *Real Rights* (Oxford, Oxford University Press, 1997) 107, 113; A Buchanan, 'Moral Status and Human Enhancement' (2009) 37 *Philosophy & Public Affairs* 346; P Singer, *Animal Liberation*, 2nd edn (Bournemouth, Pimlico, 1995); J McMahan, '"Our Fellow Creatures"' (2005) 9 *The Journal of Ethics* 353.

[48] A Phillips, *The Politics of the Human* (Cambridge, Cambridge University Press, 2015) 28.

[49] Criddle and Fox-Decent, *Fiduciaries of Humanity*, 93.

[50] P Macklem, *The Sovereignty of Human Rights* (Oxford, Oxford University Press, 2015) 8.

[51] Cruft et al, 'The Philosophical Foundations', 14. For a defence of this view, see M Renzo, 'Human Needs, Human Rights' in Cruft et al, *Philosophical Foundations of Human Rights*.

[52] MC Nussbaum, *Creating Capabilities: The Human Development Approach* (Cambridge, MA, Harvard University Press, 2011) 33–34.

[53] Phillips, *The Politics of the Human*, 29. See also Cruft et al, 'The Philosophical Foundations' (n 45) 14–15.

[54] Phillips (n 48) 33.

and accidental characteristics'.[55] This kind of approach would seem to solve the problem of exclusion in the personhood approach. Yet, as Costas Douzinas notes, abstracting some essence of humanity from everything that makes us human is 'bizarre'.[56] As Anne Phillips explains, women or those with darker skins, or other people deviating from the norm, 'should *not* have to present themselves as disembodied abstractions … in order to claim their equal status in the world'.[57] The more contentless the subject of human rights is made, the more difficult it becomes to address those inequalities that have ignited the most important human rights struggles – and the less contentless human rights become, the less possible it is to use them as a guide for decision-making or as solutions to concrete cases.

If none of the naturalistic conceptions of human rights are able to meet the requirements for functioning as a foundation for a new system of global law, the main competitor, namely an agreement approach, does not fare much better. Instead of claiming that human rights derive from some common human nature which would give rise to moral obligations, this approach argues that there are some values which all cultures can agree to respect and which can therefore guide legal and political decision-making.[58] This approach can take at least two forms. According to the 'common core' version, we can, by comparing social–moral codes, discover a certain moral minimum that all cultures share, whereas, according to the 'overlapping consensus' version, we can agree on some commonly accepted human rights, which different societies can interpret from the perspective of their own norms, thus embedding them in their own culture.[59]

The agreement theory solves the issue of exclusion inherent in (at least some versions of) the naturalistic approach, thus appearing more capable of receiving universal support. However, the approach seems even less capable of guiding decision-making than the naturalistic one, as it leaves human rights helplessly abstract. As Criddle and Fox-Decent point out, it is not enough to identify some right as a human right, for 'the mere fact that virtually all states have recognised a particular human right often tells us little about the scope or legal consequences of the right'.[60] Moreover, the agreement theory seems to deprive human rights of their critical edge.[61] Cultures are not uniform, and making human rights defer to the prevailing cultural norms may deprive them of their utopian pull, turning them into mere apology.

[55] F Fukuyama, *Our Posthuman Future: Consequences of the Biotechnology Revolution*, reprint edn (New York, Picador, 2003) 149–50.

[56] C Douzinas, *Human Rights and Empire: The Political Philosophy of Cosmopolitanism*, new edn (London, Routledge-Cavendish, 2007) 53.

[57] Phillips (n 48) 36–37 (original emphasis).

[58] Beitz, *The Idea of Human Rights*, 73–74.

[59] See JR Bauer and DA Bell (eds), *The East Asian Challenge for Human Rights* (Cambridge, Cambridge University Press, 1999); J Donnelly, *Universal Human Rights in Theory and Practice*, 2nd edn (Ithaca, NY, Cornell University Press, 2002) ch 5.

[60] Criddle and Fox-Decent (n 27) 94.

[61] Beitz (n 45) 78 and 86.

Whereas the naturalistic and agreement approaches seek to base human rights on something outside the practice of human rights – that is to say on universal, innate qualities of humanity or on common values of all cultures – the third approach to human rights starts from opposite position. Taking as its basis 'the doctrine and practice of human rights as we find them in international political life',[62] the so-called practical approach holds that even though peoples may not be able to agree on the exact content of human rights, they can at least agree that human rights do and should play an important role in international practice.[63] Human rights, according to this conception, are therefore those rights that the international community sees as so important that they limit the internal autonomy of states and may even justify interference with the internal matters of those states that do not protect them.[64]

The practical conception escapes the problem that the human rights recognised in treaties and courts do not conform to those identified by philosophers. However, it faces two different problems. The first is that, in interpreting the practice of human rights, the practical approach needs to constantly interpret what the intentions of the actors participating in the practice are – which, as any lawyer dealing with treaties knows, is painfully difficult, if not impossible. Second, and more fundamentally, the political conception cannot easily explain why the discursive role that human rights play in political practice would give it normative value.[65] Hence, it risks falling into mere apology by becoming a tool for the global powers to protect their particular interests. Some authors, such as Beitz, have tried to shield their theory against these problems by introducing certain minimum standards, seeking to place human rights on a 'middle ground' between universal rights and domestic social justice. Yet, as sophisticated as Beitz's approach is, it seems to be vulnerable either to the critique of naturalistic conceptions or to the critique presented here, depending on where the balance between the approaches is struck. Hence, while the practical approach seems to be very well suited to describing and explaining the practice of human rights in international relations, it cannot provide a solid foundation for human rights as the basis for a new global law.

Closely related to the practice approach is a legal one. As Patrick Macklem writes, the legal approach is 'less concerned with the normative dimensions of human rights as a discursive political practice' and more concerned with the role they play 'in the constellation of international legal norms in which they find themselves'.[66] According to the legal approach, the existence of rights is

[62] ibid 102–03.

[63] Cruft et al, 'The Philosophical Foundations' (n 45) 19; J Rawls, *The Law of Peoples*, new edn (Cambridge, MA, Harvard University Press, 2001) 3–4.

[64] Cruft et al, 'The Philosophical Foundations' (n 45) 6. See, eg Rawls, *The Law of Peoples*, 79–81; Beitz (n 45); J Raz, 'Human Rights in the Emerging World Order' (2010) 1 *Transnational Legal Theory* 31.

[65] Macklem, *The Sovereignty of Human Rights*, 14–15.

[66] ibid 33–34.

determined not by philosophical considerations, moral theory or political practice, but by international law.[67] Even if many proponents of this approach hold that human rights are both moral and legal rights, the legal element is emphasised in the sense that human rights are fundamental moral interests which have been deemed to be important enough to create moral duties recognised by law.[68]

The legal approach is able to grasp something that the other approaches seem to ignore or brush aside, namely that human rights become meaningful only as legal rights, and in particular when they are put into practice.[69] As Macklem correctly observes, 'The debate between universalism and relativism occurs *in* international law, in contexts where legal entitlements protecting cultural differences clash with legal entitlements protecting competing interests'.[70] Yet, I do not think that the legal approach, either, can turn human rights into the normative foundation of a new global law of humanity. One possible problem would be that human rights are useful most of all as a counterbalance to the negative effects of the already existing legal system.[71] In particular, the main role of human rights law is to monitor and control the exercise of state sovereignty.[72] It is therefore not at all clear what role, if any, human rights would play in the new, less state-centric, global law of humanity.

This first obstacle does not have to be an insurmountable one, of course.[73] Indeed, it is commonly argued that human rights are entitlements against any public institution.[74] More problematic for the legal approach is that it risks losing the utopian promise of human rights: the more human rights are constitutionalised and legalised, the more they lose their potential to act as a tool of protest and critique of power. When actors in power have to take human rights seriously, the rights language is fused into mainstream politics and administration – in other words, bureaucratised. To ensure that the indeterminate rules are interpreted and applied in an efficient, reasonable way, authorities are forced to create 'complex balancing practices and rights-exceptions schemes that defer to general considerations of administrative policy, public interest, economic efficiency, and so on – precisely the kind of criteria that rights were once introduced to limit'.[75] To apply these schemes, experts are needed, leading to indeterminate rules meant to constrain the power of experts, but only interpretable by experts,

[67] ibid 18; A Buchanan, *The Heart of Human Rights* (Oxford, Oxford University Press, 2014).

[68] S Besson, 'Human Rights and Constitutional Law' in Cruft et al, *Philosophical Foundations of Human Rights* (n 45) 281.

[69] Koskenniemi (n 31) 35.

[70] Macklem (n 50) 23 (original emphasis).

[71] ibid 22.

[72] ibid 2. See also A Buchanan, 'Why International Legal Human Rights?' in Cruft et al, *Philosophical Foundations of Human Rights* (n 45) 256–61.

[73] Peters, *Beyond Human Rights*, 477.

[74] Besson, 'Human Rights and Constitutional Law', 283; Peters (n 2) 477.

[75] M Koskenniemi, 'Human Rights Mainstreaming as a Strategy for Institutional Power' (2010) 1 *Humanity: An International Journal of Human Rights, Humanitarianism, and Development* 47, 49.

and so on.[76] For those thinkers for whom human rights are first and foremost a way of protest, this means that human rights become 'hijacked' by experts and bureaucrats.[77] But whether one sides with these critics or not, the process means at least that the legal approach does not seem to be able to answer at all the issue of indeterminacy that this section began from. In this sense, the legal approach closes the circle and returns us back to the starting point.

Finding a philosophical foundation for human rights, then, has proven extremely difficult. Yet, there is one more perspective worth considering, for could it be enough that human rights have become universal in the sense that they have been generally accepted to be of fundamental value (whatever they are exactly) and in that sense have started to guide legal discussion? Do we really need a single foundation of human rights if they still gain specific meanings step-by-step in legal practice? These are the questions asked by those who represent what is sometimes called an 'anti-foundationalist' or 'foundationless' approach to human rights.[78] In its strongest form, the anti-foundationalist account rejects the idea that human rights could be grounded on any substantive foundation. Going further than the proponents of the practice- and law-based approaches, anti-foundationalists argue that discussing the foundations of human rights is 'not only inefficient, but also harmful to the practice of human rights'.[79]

Within philosophy, this view is represented most famously by Michael Ignatieff and Richard Rorty. According to Ignatieff, we need to stop thinking of human rights as 'the universal credo of a global society' or 'a secular nature',[80] because not only are such notions likely to be at least partly false, but they are also bound to be inherently contestable or even abusable.[81] Ignatieff therefore asks us to stop discussing these foundational questions and advocates for building 'support for human rights on the basis of what such rights actually do for human beings'.[82] Similarly, Rorty argues that human rights cannot be founded on human nature.[83] A key mistake of foundationalists, writes Rorty, is that they imagine that human rights violations are committed by people 'deprived of truth, of moral knowledge', and whose behaviour can therefore be altered

[76] J Petman, 'Deformalization of International Organizations Law' in J Klabbers and A Wallendahl (eds), *Research Handbook on the Law of International Organizations* (Cheltenham, Edward Elgar Publishing, 2012) 399. See also Koskenniemi, 'Human Rights Mainstreaming as a Strategy for Institutional Power', 54.

[77] C Douzinas, *The End of Human Rights* (Oxford, Hart Publishing, 2000) 241–45; Douzinas, *Human Rights and Empire*, 24.

[78] B Schaefer, 'Human Rights: Problems with the Foundationless Approach' (2005) 31 *Social Theory & Practice* 27; M Granik, 'The Human Rights Dialogue: Foundationalism Reconsidered' (2013) 60 *Theoria: A Journal of Social & Political Theory* 1.

[79] Granik, 'The Human Rights Dialogue', 5.

[80] M Ignatieff, *Human Rights as Politics and Idolatry* (A Gutmann ed, Princeton, Princeton University Press, 2003) 95.

[81] Schaefer, 'Human Rights: Problems', 29–30.

[82] Ignatieff, *Human Rights as Politics and Idolatry*, 54.

[83] Schaefer (n 78) 30–31.

by discovering truths about what it means to be a human, formulating moral rules. According to Rorty, human rights violators are better seen as individuals deprived of security and sympathy.[84] Human rights are thus best protected by cultivating sentiments and teaching sympathy – or, as legal scholars have argued,[85] by turning them into legal rules for behaviour – rather than by relying on the power of human reason.

Perhaps something like this might also be in the minds of law of humanity theorists? Perhaps there is no need for foundations of human rights as long as human considerations take an even more central role in global law and hence help to posit the individual at the centre of the legal order? As Anne Peters writes, human rights have expanded recently in at least two ways. First, human rights have expanded in substance. Some new rights are codified into treaties, such as the right against forced disappearance, whereas others are acknowledged without codification, such as the right to be free from discrimination on the basis of sexual orientation or the right to water. There are also rights which were already enshrined in the Universal Declaration of Human Rights but which have been concretised or specified only more recently. Furthermore, economic, social and ecological rights have become more widely accepted. Second, 'the circle of addressees of human rights has also widened' as international lawyers are now increasingly willing to accept that international organisations and even multinational corporations may have human rights obligations.[86]

There are, however, at least two problems with the anti-foundationalist approach. The first relates to the arguments provided by Ignatieff and Rorty. Commentators have noted that their visions of human rights are not as foundationless as they would like to believe. Amy Gutmann, for example, argues that Ignatieff's reason for defending human rights, namely human agency, is in fact an attempt to found human rights and not merely a pragmatic idea, as Ignatieff claims,[87] for 'to say that human rights are needed for human agency is to say something nontrivial about "why we have rights"'.[88] Similarly, Brian Schaefer argues that the hidden foundationalist basis of Rorty's argument can be detected in his argument that human rights are important because they help to fulfil an 'Enlightenment utopia', consisting of 'a widespread sympathy for others, and a respect for one another's security'. But it is not quite this point which Schaefer attacks as foundationalist. As he anticipates, Rorty would probably counter that argument 'by saying that he has adequately accounted for the value of the

[84] R Rorty, 'Human Rights, Rationality and Sentimentality' in O Savić and B Krug (ed), *The Politics of Human Rights* (London, Verso, 1999) 77.

[85] W Osiatynski, *Human Rights and Their Limits* (Cambridge, Cambridge University Press, 2009) 175.

[86] J Klabbers, A Peters and G Ulfstein, *The Constitutionalization of International Law* (Oxford, Oxford University Press, 2011) 167–68.

[87] A Gutmann, 'Introduction' in Ignatieff (n 80) xviii, xxiv–xxv.

[88] ibid xviii.

Enlightenment utopia by endorsing a progress of sentiments and implying that it is only in such a utopia that valuable sentiments are realised to the greatest extent'.[89] This does not solve the problem according to Scahefer, however, 'for we would now wonder how a progress of sentiments could be justified without reference to foundations'. As he writes, 'Rorty appears to believe he can avoid talk of foundations by appealing to sentiments', but it is difficult to understand how 'we could justify a progress of moral sentiments without making an appeal to facts about human beings, facts that would appeal to the very sort of human nature whose existence Rorty denies'.[90]

If even the anti-foundationalist approach cannot escape foundationalism, we are back at square one. But even if it could – for Ignatieff's and Rorty's accounts probably do not exhaust all possible anti-foundationalist arguments – a second problem remains, for if any discussion of foundations is discarded, human rights claims are bound to multiply almost endlessly. This is not necessarily a bad thing; it might well open avenues for creative political projects. But it does raise the problem of effectiveness. As human rights language becomes increasingly hegemonic and covers an ever-wider array of topics, without a foundation it becomes less and less capable of solving disputes between conflicting claims, for it has already absorbed all of the competing views within itself without solving them in any way.[91]

While there is thus much to compliment in the human rights revolution of the past few decades, there is a danger in making too much of the increased circulation of the human rights language. That language can be used to further all kinds of projects and interests, many of which are no doubt desired, but some of which might be very problematic. Human rights can therefore doubtlessly be used to bring about welcome change, but they certainly do not do so by necessity. Human rights are not outside politics but are very much a political project in themselves, and deployable by other such projects.[92] Moreover, if we get too tangled up with the discourse, there is a danger that it might blind our eyes to the root causes of the conflicts that human rights are used to solve. As Susan Marks writes, 'human rights institutions and officials have grappled only partially and rather problematically with the question of why abuses occur, how vulnerabilities arise, and what it will take to bring about change'.[93] Consequently, human rights violations are often made to seem arbitrary and random, and their systemic context is consequently removed from view.[94] As Marks emphasises,

[89] Schaefer (n 78) 37.
[90] ibid 37–38.
[91] I owe this point to Martti Koskenniemi.
[92] W Brown, '"The Most We Can Hope For …": Human Rights and the Politics of Fatalism' (2004) 103 *South Atlantic Quarterly* 451; D Kennedy, 'International Human Rights Movement: Part of the Problem? Boundaries in the Field of Human Rights' (2002) 15 *Harvard Human Rights Journal* 101.
[93] S Marks, 'Human Rights and Root Causes' (2011) 74 *MLR* 57, 70.
[94] ibid 75.

this is not because of failings of particular institutions or officials, but rather because of how the entire system of human rights law is configured.[95]

III. HUMAN SECURITY

If it is impossible to base a new law of humanity on human rights, the same seems to be true of human security – for mostly similar reasons. Human security is a people-centred approach to security and international law and politics, based on the idea that the human individual, rather than the state, should be the referent object of security.[96] Building on concepts such as 'positive peace', 'stable peace' and 'basic human needs' 'that were coined from the late 1960s onwards to conceptualise and highlight the need to combine the human rights paradigm with a more grass-roots promotion of fundamental human needs', proponents of human security aim to alter the old paradigm of security which 'privileged national security concerns over the elementary demands of millions of people'.[97] In contrast to the state-centred model, then, the aim of human security is 'to safeguard the vital core of all human lives from critical pervasive threats, in a way that is consistent with long-term human fulfillment'.[98]

The indeterminacy of the concept of human security is perhaps best demonstrated through a struggles perspective. At the same time as the human security movement as a whole has struggled over the ownership of 'security' against realist and other competing accounts, other struggles have been fought within the movement over the definition of 'human security'. What these struggles demonstrate is the conceptual theory point that the meaning of human security – like that of any concept – has less to do with its representation than with its use,[99] concepts existing only 'in movement', that is, when they are 'used as moves, as political instruments of action'.[100]

The ambiguity of human security was built into it from the very beginning. In order to safeguard the vital core of human life, human security brings together knowledge from several previously separate paradigms. Two such paradigms

[95] ibid 70–71.

[96] S Alkire, 'A Conceptual Framework for Human Security', Working Paper 2 (Oxford, CRISE, 2003) 3; L Axworthy, 'Human Security and Global Governance: Putting People First' (2001) 7 *Global Governance* 19; Oberlietner, 'Human Security: A Challenge'; Tigerstrom, *Human Security and International Law*, 16–17.

[97] P Niemelä, *The Politics of Responsibility to Protect: Problems and Prospects* (Helsinki, The Erik Castrén Institute of International Law and Human Rights, 2008) 29.

[98] Alkire, 'A Conceptual Framework for Human Security', 2.

[99] On this point regarding a different concept, see F Kratochwil, 'Has the "Rule of Law" Become a "Rule of Lawyers"? An Inquiry into the Use and Abuse of an Ancient Topos in Contemporary Debates' in G Palombella and N Walker (eds), *Relocating the Rule of Law* (Oxford, Hart Publishing, 2009) 195.

[100] K Palonen, 'Rhetorical and Temporal Perspectives on Conceptual Change: Theses on Quentin Skinner and Reinhart Koselleck' (1999) 3 *Finnish Yearbook of Political Thought* 41, 46.

stand above all others. The first is, of course, that of security. Key to the emergence of the concept of human security was the end of the Cold War and the growing awareness of the effects of increasing globalisation.[101] In the post-Cold War environment, large interstate wars seemed less likely than before, but intrastate conflicts became bloodier than ever.[102] At the same time, concerns about the underside of globalisation increased.[103] Not only was it understood that the traditional security approach was ill-equipped to deal with such transnational threats as terrorism, organised crime, the trafficking of persons, weapons and drugs, and environmental degradation, but it also became increasingly clear that crisis states, torn by violence and extreme poverty, provided a dangerous breeding ground for these phenomena.

The second key paradigm behind human security is that of human development. Drawing from the work of Amartya Sen and Mahbub ul Haq, human security was from the beginning 'concerned with how people live and breathe in a society, how freely they exercise their many choices, how much access they have to market and social opportunities, and whether they live in conflict or in peace'.[104] The concept is meant to draw the attention of decision-makers to the fact that traditional security approaches can tackle only a limited number of the dangers threatening the lives of human beings around the world.[105] As the drafters of the 1994 Human Development Report emphasised,

> the concept of security has for too long been interpreted narrowly: as security of territory from external aggression, or as protection of national interests in foreign policy or as global security from the threat of nuclear holocaust ... Forgotten were the legitimate concerns of ordinary people who sought security in their daily lives.[106]

Hence, the novelty of the concept of human security was not only the notion that security threats are now transnational, but also, and equally importantly, the idea that there was a need to shift the focus onto the actual needs of actual human beings by distinguishing human development from mechanical, purely economic growth.[107] Building a bridge to Franklin Roosevelt's 1941 State of the Union Address, the Report emphasises that human security requires

[101] SN MacFarlane and YF Khong, *Human Security and the UN: A Critical History* (Bloomington, Indiana University Press, 2006) 8–9.

[102] International Commission on Intervention and State Sovereignty, *The Responsibility to Protect: The Report of the International Commission on Intervention and State Sovereignty*, pap/cdr edn (Ottawa, IDRC Books, 2002) para 1.16.

[103] Tigerstrom (n 11) 18–19; Axworthy, 'Human Security and Global Governance', 19–21.

[104] United Nations Development Programme, *Human Development Report 1994*, 5th edn (Oxford, Oxford University Press, 1994) 23.

[105] D Amnéus, *Responsibility Protect by Military Means – Emerging Norms on Humanitarian Intervention?* (Stockholm, Department of Law, Stockholm University, 2008) 143.

[106] United Nations Development Programme, *Human Development Report 1994*, 22.

[107] M Duffield, 'Human Security: Linking Security and Development in an Age of Terror' in S Klingebiel (ed), *New Interfaces between Security and Development: Changing Concepts and Approaches* (Bonn, German Development Institute (DIE), 2006) 18–19. See also Axworthy (n 96).

both 'freedom from want' and 'freedom from fear', the former referring to an economic understanding of what is required for a free, healthy life and the latter referring mainly to safety from physical aggression.[108]

In seeking to shift attention from states to human beings, the 1994 Human Development Report, which mainstreamed the concept of human security, drew from both the security and development paradigms, and combined them with other related approaches. The outcome was highly complex and ambitious, and was soon criticised for vagueness and indeterminacy. According to the Report, threats to human security can be divided into seven main categories: economic security, food security, health security, environmental security, personal security, community security and political security.[109] And as commentators soon asked, 'if human security is all these things, what is it not?'[110]

The ambiguity of the concept of human security is clearly demonstrated in academic debates about its precise definition. Many commentators would surely agree on the point that 'if the term "human security" were defined more narrowly, it would accrue greater analytical and policy value'.[111] Yet, they cannot agree on how to limit the definition. Some suggest a definition that focuses primarily on 'transnational threats to international norms arising from inadequacies in internal state systems', requiring some form of international intervention.[112] Others try to sharpen the focus of human security by concentrating solely on violent threats, no matter whether they occur inside national borders or transnationally.[113] Still others find the focus on violent threats problematic. As Bellamy and McDonald write, to suggest that 'terrorism which kills fewer than 5,000 people per year – even in a year as unusually bloody as 2001 – should be given political priority (and hence more resources) over the "general" threat of malnutrition, which kills over 40,000 people every day', is absurd.[114] The more the concept is narrowed, then, the more it starts to resemble other approaches, such as the traditional security approach or the development discourse, with the consequence that the concept loses its holistic, 'revolutionary' meaning.[115]

[108] M Wählisch, 'Human Security: Concept and Evolution in the United Nations' (2014) 18 *Max Planck Yearbook of United Nations Law Online* 1, 6.

[109] United Nations Development Programme (n 104) 24–25.

[110] R Paris, 'Human Security: Paradigm Shift or Hot Air?' (2001) 26 *International Security* 87, 92.

[111] N Thomas and WT Tow, 'The Utility of Human Security: Sovereignty and Humanitarian Intervention' (2002) 33 *Security Dialogue* 177, 179.

[112] ibid.

[113] K Krause, 'The Key to a Powerful Agenda, If Properly Delimited' (2004) 35 *Security Dialogue* 367; A Mack, 'A Signifier of Shared Values' (2004) 35 *Security Dialogue* 366; SN Macfarlane, 'A Useful Concept That Risks Losing Its Political Salience' (2004) 35 *Security Dialogue* 368.

[114] AJ Bellamy and M McDonald, '"The Utility of Human Security": Which Humans? What Security? A Reply to Thomas & Tow' (2002) 33 *Security Dialogue* 373, 374.

[115] S Alkire, 'A Vital Core That Must Be Treated with the Same Gravitas as Traditional Security Threats' (2004) 35 *Security Dialogue* 359; L Axworthy, 'A New Scientific Field and Policy Lens' (2004) 35 *Security Dialogue* 348; FO Hampson, 'A Concept in Need of a Global Policy Response' (2004) 35 *Security Dialogue* 349; J Leaning, 'Psychosocial Well-Being over Time' (2004) 35 *Security Dialogue* 354; D Winslow and T Hylland Eriksen, 'A Broad Concept That Encourages Interdisciplinary Thinking' (2004) 35 *Security Dialogue* 361.

The academic debate over the definition of human security is therefore pestered by a paradox. As Taylor Owen explains, 'the closer the concept gets to its original conceptualization, focusing on all threats to the individual, the more difficult both human security policy and theory become'.[116] Every step towards sharper focus and increased utility comes at the price of ignoring non-violent threats, whereas every step in the opposite direction, towards inclusiveness, sacrifices analytic rigour and policy effectiveness. It is therefore not possible to determine the meaning of human security through academic definitions, as that meaning does not lie in the concept's representation but in its use.

The use of concepts is usually guided by particular interests and their meaning is therefore in constant movement. Indeed, when states have decided to support human security in their foreign policy, they have usually tried to shape its definition so that it fits their particular interests. To give some examples, the survival and rights-based 'freedom from fear' approach to human security has been a useful tool for Canada, a country which had already gained recognition as a peacekeeper in post-conflict situations,[117] whereas the broader, economics-based 'freedom from want' approach allowed Japan to circumvent many of the military limitations set by its post-World War II constitution, as well as to strengthen its economic status in the aftermath of the Asian 1997 crisis.[118] Similarly, the food security aspect of human security became very influential in Brazil because food security issues had in any case become 'a firm part of "normal" political discourses and debates' in the country. And, unsurprisingly, economic security has become important in places where extreme poverty is most widespread, such as sub-Saharan Africa.[119]

Hence, states have preferred different conceptions of human security as a result of their different political and security interests.[120] As human security is a useful way to legitimate policies,[121] it is no wonder that fierce battles are fought over who gets to determine its content at any given time, keeping the concept in constant motion.[122] These battles are not fought only by states, but also by several international organisations, non-governmental organisations, experts and academics.[123]

However, it is not only the intentions of different actors that matter in the struggles which keep those concepts in motion. These interests are shaped by

[116] T Owen, 'Human Security – Conflict, Critique and Consensus: Colloquium Remarks and a Proposal for a Threshold-Based Definition' (2004) 35 *Security Dialogue* 373, 381. See also Paris, 'Human Security: Paradigm Shift', 94–96.

[117] Tadjbakhsh and Chenoy (n 9) 28–29.

[118] ibid 29–30.

[119] S Breslin and G Christou, 'Has the Human Security Agenda Come of Age? Definitions, Discourses and Debates' (2015) 21 *Contemporary Politics* 1, 4–5.

[120] ibid 5.

[121] D Chandler, 'Review Essay: Human Security: The Dog That Didn't Bark' (2008) 39 *Security Dialogue* 427.

[122] Breslin and Christou, 'Has the Human Security Agenda Come of Age?', 5.

[123] See generally M Duffield, *Development, Security and Unending War* (Cambridge, Polity, 2007) chs 2 and 4.

existing circumstances: they are dependent on time and context, as the rhetorical value and strategic possibilities opened by concepts and their various definitions change from one situation to another, and context also determines to some extent which arguments are acceptable and which are not. The concept of human security rose to international prominence at a very specific moment in history, when the threat of global conflict seemed to have been resolved and the economic crises of Asia and Latin America or the post-9/11 war on terror were not yet on the horizon. At this moment of history, it was possible to start rethinking security from a clean slate. The financial crises and the 9/11 terrorist attacks, as well as the attacks on the Madrid underground and London buses, allowed new interests to be furthered through the concept. The 1997 Asian financial crisis gave states such as Japan a strong incentive to support the development-focused approach to human security, whereas the war on terror and the growing concern about the bloody non-international armed conflicts that had been occurring throughout the 1990s tilted the scale heavily in favour of the 'freedom from fear' approach, especially within Western states. Following terrorist attacks, several Western states started to see human security as an opportunity to take a leading position in global security while still protecting their new security interests. The most important example of this is Canada, which established the International Commission on Intervention and State Sovereignty, and made freedom from fear the driving force of its own foreign policy, as well as the policy of the Human Security Network. But the EU also played a significant role in establishing the supremacy of the freedom from fear approach with its 'Human Security Doctrine for Europe', developed by the Barcelona Study Group (a collection of influential experts and academics) in 2004. With this somewhat contradictory document, the Union surely wanted to reinforce its image 'as a successful example of peaceful development based on cooperation, and on core values of respect for diversity, rule of law, human rights, democracy, and citizen participation'. But the EU also wanted to respond to 'the strategic environment after Iraq and September 11' – an environment in which it wanted to play a more active role in issues of global security.[124] Moreover, health security gained increasing prominence as a human security issue as soon as diseases such as HIV, SARS and others (many of which had been issues in the Global South for a long time) 'crossed borders from the developing to the developed world' and in the process 'made the transition from being "their" diseases to "ours"'.[125] Food security also became mainstreamed, but only after the link between food and war was sufficiently established, thus linking food security with scarcity, sufficiency and survival in the developed world, in contrast to the malnutrition, chronic illness and death present elsewhere.[126]

[124] Tadjbakhsh and Chenoy (n 9) 205.

[125] Breslin and Christou (n 119) 3. See further F Lisk, A Bindenagel Šehović and S Sekalala, 'Health and Human Security: A Wrinkle in Time or a New Paradigm?' (2015) 21 *Contemporary Politics* 25.

[126] Breslin and Christou (n 119) 8–9; see also B Richardson and J Nunes, 'What Can Security Do for Food? Lessons from Brazil' (2015) 21 *Contemporary Politics* 70.

The meaning of human security is thus really a matter not of finding the optimal definition of the concept, but rather of a contingent struggle determined by the concrete intentions of particular actors with their own interests, bound always to changing contexts. These struggles have very concrete consequences. The hegemonic definition of important concepts determines which issues get attention, how resources are allocated and which issues are ignored. For example, after Western powers, led by Canada and the EU, managed to establish 'freedom from fear' as the prevalent conception of human security in the aftermath of 9/11, resources were shifted from economic and development issues to those dealing with 'civil wars, physical safety and humanitarian violations of human dignity'.[127] Furthermore, as this 'political security' aspect of human security was increasingly translated into the language of responsibility to protect, focus shifted further away from the original idea of empowering individuals and onto the intervening and intervened states.[128]

Finally, the meaning of human security has changed as a consequence of competing expert rationales, vocabularies and ways of viewing the world – in other words, of competing regimes,[129] each seeking to reverse established hierarchies 'in favour of the structural bias in the relevant functional expertise'.[130] A powerful floating signifier such as human security necessarily attracts these regimes, which try to shape the concept so that it furthers the regime's rationale and agenda. Although there are constant attempts to hide the hegemonic nature of these struggles behind the language of technical cooperation,[131] they operate, for example, behind the opposition between 'freedom from want' and 'freedom from fear' approaches to human security.

At the background of the freedom from want approach is the development regime. From the viewpoint of this regime, human security is threatened most of all by poverty and can be improved by following the teachings of, and by granting more resources to, development agencies and experts, particularly those influenced by the capabilities approach developed by Amartya Sen, Martha Nussbaum and others. Human security, from this viewpoint, is mostly about increasing the 'capabilities' of individuals. That is to say, human security is about securing necessary conditions for human development and flourishing.[132]

[127] A Francechet, 'Global Legalism and Human Security' in SJ MacLean, DR Black and TM Shaw (eds), *A Decade of Human Security: Global Governance and New Multilateralisms* (Farnham, Ashgate Publishing, 2006) 33.

[128] O Hassan, 'Political Security: From the 1990s to the Arab Spring' (2015) 21 *Contemporary Politics* 86.

[129] M Koskenniemi, 'Hegemonic Regimes' in MA Young (ed), *Regime Interaction in International Law: Facing Fragmentation* (Cambridge, Cambridge University Press, 2011); A Fischer-Lescano and G Teubner, 'Regime-Collisions: The Vain Search for Legal Unity in the Fragmentation of Global Law' (2003) 25 *Michigan Journal of International Law* 999.

[130] M Koskenniemi, 'The Fate of Public International Law: Between Technique and Politics' (2007) 70 *MLR* 1, 4.

[131] Koskenniemi, 'Hegemonic Regimes', 319–20.

[132] Tadjbakhsh and Chenoy (n 9) 105–06.

Consequently, in aiming to ensure human security, the regime also constructs a certain 'truth' about the human. The idea of the capability approach is that human life in its bare form must be guaranteed certain minimum conditions through which human beings can nourish capabilities which make life 'truly human'.[133] Mere survival does not therefore yet amount to 'truly human life', at least in the sense given to the term by Nussbaum.[134] Instead, only once the capabilities of humans are 'nurtured and developed through the exercise of practical reason and moral choice' does life become 'truly human'.[135] At the heart of the capabilities approach-influenced notion of human security, then, is the 'truth' of the human individual as an active, creative creature, but also as an autonomous chooser who is able to make free rational decisions in a rather standard liberal sense and thus take control of her life. Hence the focus on elevating lives to 'fully human life' through outside interventions.[136]

Behind the 'freedom from fear' approach, by contrast, is the security regime. From the perspective of the security regime, human security is not threatened so much by poverty as by various threats to physical integrity. As such, the approach is focused primarily on present emergencies rather than on sustainable development.[137] Therefore, at the heart of human security is primarily physical survival, which lies in the security experts' domain. The human constructed by the security regime is primarily a biological being, defined by her 'vital core', reducible more or less to those elements which ensure existence.[138] The problem of poverty and development is replaced by transnational circulation of threats to survival and the focus is constantly on terrorism, organised crime, trafficking of all sorts of goods and persons, and so on.[139] More or less in line with the way of thinking that Michel Foucault traces to the eighteenth century, the aim of this form of security is to eliminate the dangerous element of circulation by 'making a division between good and bad circulation and maximizing the good circulation by diminishing the bad'.[140] While it is not profitable to suppress circulation, the aim is to predict and manage a future which remains 'not exactly controllable, not precisely measured or measurable'.[141] Main threats to human security

[133] MC Nussbaum, *Sex and Social Justice* (Oxford, Oxford University Press, 2000) 39.

[134] MC Nussbaum, *Women and Human Development: The Capabilities Approach* (Cambridge, Cambridge University Press, 2001) 1–4.

[135] N Marhia, 'Some Humans Are More Human than Others: Troubling the "Human" in Human Security from a Critical Feminist Perspective' (2013) 44 *Security Dialogue* 19, 22–23.

[136] ibid 21–22.

[137] Tadjbakhsh and Chenoy (n 9) 205.

[138] M Pandolfi, 'From Paradox to Paradigm: The Permanent State of Emergency in the Balkans' in D Fassin and M Pandolfi (eds), *Contemporary States of Emergency: The Politics of Military and Humanitarian Interventions* (New York, Zone Books, 2010) 160.

[139] See further M de Larrinaga and MG Doucet, 'Sovereign Power and the Biopolitics of Human Security' (2008) 39 *Security Dialogue* 517, 524–25. See also Roznai, 'The Insecurity of Human Security', 107–08.

[140] M Foucault, *Security, Territory, Population: Lectures at the Collège de France, 1977–78* (M Senellart, F Ewald and A Fontana trans, New York, Picador, 2007) 18.

[141] ibid 20.

are therefore presented as flows of all kind – of small arms, drugs, victims of trafficking, sexually transmitted diseases and so on – because their global and circulatory nature renders them unmanageable and beyond remedy.[142]

What I hope to show with these two examples is how differently regimes can perceive a concept like human security. What is at stake is not only small disagreements on how to define human security, but also entirely different ways of perceiving the 'human' of human security. In aiming to fulfil their mission in accordance with their worldview, all regimes must construct some kind of vision of what this 'human' consists of, or at least what its most fundamental features are. This notion of the human determines, again, what forms of security can be imagined.[143] Thus, the security regime is premised on bodily safety, the food regime highlights the human as a biological being by beginning from bodily functions, the development regime emphasises the capacities and freedoms of individuals to develop themselves freely, the environment regime underlines the dependency of the human on the environment and forces of nature, and so on.

Although I have focused only on two regimes here, the field is determined through countless such struggles over the 'truth' of human security. In these struggles, the victories of one regime are also losses for competing ones, with very concrete results regarding the allocation of resources. One commentator complains, for example, that economic security risks becoming a redundant concept because it has largely become associated with raising people out of less than US$1.25 per day poverty, with the consequence that those complex interlinkages that human security was supposed to unearth have again become buried out of sight.[144] In a similar vein, another commentator shows that climate change has 'hijacked' the environmental security discourse, marginalising 'localised environmental sources of human security', such as dirty water, and moving the discourse away from human security.[145] Consequently, very real human insecurities and vulnerabilities experienced by people as a consequence of environmental issues (including the climate change) 'have been marginalised in the climate security debates'.[146]

Much like human rights, then, the concept of human security, too, can be, and has been, used to support myriad different aims. As such, it is far from inevitable that the increased circulation of the concept will lead to the outcomes promised in the law of humanity discourse. In fact, some of its outcomes are likely to be very troubling from the perspective of the law of humanity theorists. Critics have, for example, pointed out that human security and the responsibility to

[142] Larrinaga and Doucet, 'Sovereign Power and the Biopolitics', 524–25. See also Roznai (n 11) 107–08.
[143] Marhia, 'Some Humans Are More Human than Others', 21.
[144] SM Tang, 'Rethinking Economic Security in a Globalized World' (2015) 21 *Contemporary Politics* 40.
[145] Breslin and Christou (n 119) 8.
[146] L Elliott, 'Human Security/Environmental Security' (2015) 21 *Contemporary Politics* 11, 17.

protect can be used to support military interests and securitization,[147] and even to justify neo-imperialist projects.[148] Consequently, it has also often been the case that populations in strategic regions are prioritised over other populations, including those whose human security is most at risk.[149] Indeed, it has been argued that many human security measures have focused mostly on the question of what to do with the global 'surplus population' which our capitalist system necessarily produces as it renews and stabilises itself.[150] By focusing on 'improving the collective resilience of a given population against the contingent and uncertain nature of its existence',[151] human security measures in the developing world have maintained a homeostatic condition where basic needs are secured but possibilities for improving material standards of living are non-existent.[152]

IV. HUMAN DIGNITY

The problems regarding human rights and human security, discussed in the previous two sections, have not gone unnoticed among academics and practitioners. Perhaps for this reason, there has recently been a significant rise in publications and judicial decisions that employ the concept of human dignity. But does human dignity really fare that much better than human rights and human security as a candidate for a sound basis for a new law of humanity?

There are many critics who would answer that question in the negative, perhaps even concluding that human dignity is a 'shibboleth of all the perplexed and empty-headed moralists', as the nineteenth-century philosopher Arthur Schopenhauer once did.[153] According to one commentator, for example, 'appeals to dignity are either vague restatements of other, more precise notions or mere slogans that add nothing to the understanding of the topic'.[154] Others state that the concept of human dignity is incapable of explaining or justifying interests, and is therefore merely 'a notion that is used by academics, judges, and legislators when rational justifications have been exhausted'.[155] And according

[147] S Klingebiel, 'New Interfaces between Security and Development: Introduction' in Klingebiel, *New Interfaces between Security and Development*, 5.

[148] M Mamdani, 'Responsibility to Protect or Right to Punish?' (2010) 4 *Journal of Intervention and Statebuilding* 53.

[149] C Thomas, 'Global Governance, Development and Human Security: Exploring the Links' (2001) 22 *Third World Quarterly* 159, 173–74; M Duffield and N Waddell, 'Securing Humans in a Dangerous World' (2006) 43 *International Politics* 1, 13–14.

[150] D Harvey, *The New Imperialism* (Oxford, Oxford University Press, 2005) 140.

[151] Duffield, *Development, Security and Unending War*, 16–17.

[152] ibid 115.

[153] Arthur Schopenhauer, cited in M Rosen, *Dignity: Its History and Meaning* (Cambridge, MA, Harvard University Press, 2012) 1.

[154] R Macklin, 'Dignity Is a Useless Concept' (2003) 327 *British Medical Journal* 1419.

[155] M Bagaric and J Allan, 'The Vacuous Concept of Dignity' (2006) 5 *Journal of Human Rights* 257, 260.

to one critic, human dignity is an empty vessel – 'a mirror onto which each person projects his or her own values'.[156]

One should, however, resist the temptation of jumping to conclusions too quickly here – especially if one is about to focus on human dignity predominantly as a legal concept, as I am here. For there is a great difference in stating that human dignity is indeterminate in the abstract – in the analytical or philosophical sense – and arguing that it is so in legal practice. The former president of the Supreme Court of Israel, Aharon Barak, for example, defends the concept of human dignity in legal practice by arguing that what might be unclear and vague for philosophers and other scholars might not be so for practising jurists and particularly for judges. As he reminds his readers, judges do not enjoy the same kind of discretion as philosophers, but 'live in a legal framework, which determines rules on whose opinion is decisive and whose is not'.[157]

Whilst there is no doubt much truth in Barak's argument, I am nevertheless not quite as willing as he is to accept that human dignity's problems of indeterminacy are purely philosophical and theoretical – at least at the global level, where different traditions collide. The very practical problems in the application of the concept are illustrated vividly in the commonly cited case of *Manuel Wackenheim*, sometimes referred to as the 'French dwarf-throwing case'.[158] As its moniker suggests, the case dealt with an activity where a person with dwarfism is clothed in padded attire and a helmet and thrown around. The applicant of the case, Mr Wackenheim, had appeared since July 1991 in such dwarf-throwing events, organised by a company called Société Fun-Productions, entertaining the clients of discotheques by allowing them to throw him onto an airbed. At the end of October 1991, the mayor of Morsang-sur-Orge ordered a ban on the dwarf-tossing events scheduled to take place at a local discotheque on the basis of public order and safety. The order was challenged and eventually annulled by the Administrative Court of Versailles. However, the persistent mayor appealed the decisions to the Conseil d'État, invoking the concept of human dignity, which the Court indeed sympathised with. According to the Conseil d'État, protection of dignity was an example of the acceptable inclusion of morality within the definition of 'public order'. Since 'an attraction of this sort' infringed, in the Court's opinion, 'the dignity of the human person in its very objective',

[156] LR Barroso, 'Here, There, and Everywhere: Human Dignity in Contemporary Law and in the Transnational Discourse' (2012) 35 *Boston College International & Comparative Law Review* 331, 332.

[157] A Barak, *Human Dignity: The Constitutional Value and the Constitutional Right* (Cambridge, Cambridge University Press, 2015) 10.

[158] UN Human Rights Committee, *Manuel Wackenheim v France*, Communication No 854/1999, UN Doc CCPR/C/75/D/854/1999 (2002). Christoph Möllers also aptly demonstrates the indeterminacy of human dignity and its practical consequences in his analysis of the ECtHR case *KU v Finland*. See C Möllers, 'The Triple Dilemma of Human Dignity: A Case Study' in C McCrudden (ed), *Understanding Human Dignity*, Proceedings of the British Academy Vol 192 (Oxford, Oxford University Press/British Academy, 2013).

the mayor was acting within his powers in banning the activity. The story was the same regarding a similar ban issued by the mayor of Aix-en-Provence on 20 March 1992.[159] The decisions of the Conseil d'État, in which it emphasised that its decisions were not tied to particular local circumstances, meant that other mayors were also allowed to ban dwarf-throwing activities, and this quickly led to the end of the practice. Finding himself left unemployed, Mr Wackenheim applied to the Human Right Committee, arguing that France had discriminated against him and violated his rights to freedom, employment, respect for private life and an adequate standard of living. According to Mr Wackenheim, it was actually the ban on dwarf-throwing that violated his human dignity rather than the activity itself, as human dignity hinges on the right to make autonomous decisions in one's life and the right to work in the profession that one has chosen for himself.[160] The Committee did not, however, hold France to have violated Mr Wackenheim's rights, finding that the bans had been 'necessary in order to protect public order, which brings into play considerations of human dignity that are compatible with the objectives of the Covenant'.[161]

At the heart of the case was the question of what Wackenheim's dignity actually entailed. In Wackenheim's view, protection of his dignity meant that he should be given autonomy to make free decisions about his life, as well as the right to work, whereas the French authorities felt that it meant protecting him, and the whole of humanity, from exploitation and humiliation – or what is deemed as such by an 'objective' third party. Both the French courts and the UN Human Rights Committee ended up opting for the latter option, privileging the objective notion of dignity for the benefit of humankind, even at the expense of the livelihood and autonomy of the applicant. Yet the decision could just as well have gone the other way. The notion of human dignity, entailing that human beings have intrinsic worth, leads to two consequences at the same time: it grants individuals 'absolute, inalienable' rights and freedoms, while it simultaneously requires that those individuals are protected from threats to their dignity even against their express will.[162] Or, as Martti Koskenniemi might say, it gives at once birth to both ascending arguments, deriving from the sovereignty of the individual, and descending arguments, deriving from some kind of objective notion of humanity or dignity that is out of the reach of an individual, having more to do with our collective existence.[163] Hence, it is almost always possible to use human dignity on both sides of a debate, as is evidenced, for example, by

[159] Conseil d'État, *Commune de Morsang-Sur-Orge* (27 October 1995) Dalloz Jur 1995, 257; Conseil d'État, *Ville d'Aix-en-Provence* (27 October 1995) Dalloz Jur 1996, 177.

[160] *Wackenheim* (n 158) paras 2.1–3.

[161] ibid para 7.4.

[162] R Andorno, 'Human Dignity and Human Rights as a Common Ground for a Global Bioethics' (2009) 34 *Journal of Medicine & Philosophy* 223, 232–33.

[163] On ascending and descending arguments, see M Koskenniemi, *From Apology to Utopia the Structure of International Legal Argument* (Cambridge, Cambridge University Press, 2005).

the debate on euthanasia.[164] As Mohammed Bedajoui, the former president of the International Court of Justice, once admitted, the concept of human dignity is fragile, 'for in the name of the same argument of "human dignity" some refute the legitimacy of euthanasia, whilst others claim it as the ultimate right of those who wish to "die in dignity"!'[165]

The *Wackenheim* case suggests, then, that using human dignity in legal decision-making might not be quite as smooth as some commentators suggest – at least at the international or global level. Judge Barak might have a point that previous legal practice and hierarchy of authority might constrain the judge's discretion considerably at the domestic level, provided that there are clear precedents and uniform legal culture. However, these are unlikely to be found at the global level. Instead, international judges and other international decision-makers are bound to operate within a cacophony of different legal cultures which are bound to be in contradiction over many important issues.

This much becomes clear, for instance, from the commonly cited distinction between autonomy-based and obligation-creating uses of human dignity. The autonomy-based usage is expressed, for example, in two excerpts from the Israeli Supreme Court. In *Veckselbum v The Defence Minister*, the Court stated that 'At the base of this concept [of human dignity] stands the recognition that man is a free creature who develops his body and mind as he sees fit',[166] and in *The Movement for Quality Government in Israel v The Knesset*, it held that: '[at] the centre of human dignity are the sanctity and liberty of life. At its foundation are the autonomy of the individual will, the freedom of choice, and the freedom of man to act as a free creature.'[167] The usage is also visible in US Supreme Court cases, such as *Rice v Cayetano*, where Kennedy J stated that an affirmative action measure was unconstitutional because it demeaned 'the dignity and worth of a person to be judged by ancestry instead of by his or her own merit and essential qualities',[168] and *Planned Parenthood v Casey*, where Kennedy, O'Connor and Souter JJ framed the abortion decision as one where human dignity requires freedom of the individual and the family from governmental intrusion. Another illustrative example is the Canadian Supreme Court's decision in *Sauvé v Canada*, in which Justice Gonthier employed the link between human dignity and autonomy as the basis for the entire criminal law system, writing that 'it could be said that the notion of punishment is predicated on the dignity of the individual: it recognizes serious criminals as

[164] Bagaric and Allan, 'The Vacuous Concept of Dignity', 266.

[165] UNESCO, 'Speech by Mr Mohammed Bedjaoui', Proceedings of the Third Session of the International Bioethics Committee of UNESCO, vol i, 144. See also R Dworkin, *Life's Dominion: An Argument about Abortion, Euthanasia, and Individual Freedom* (New York, Vintage Books, 1993) 238–39.

[166] *Veckselbum v The Defence Minister* (1993) HCJ 5688/92, IsrSC 47(2) 812, 830.

[167] *The Movement for Quality Government in Israel v The Knesset* (2006) HCJ 6427/02, IsrSC 61(1) 619, 685.

[168] Cited in C McCrudden, 'Human Dignity and Judicial Interpretation of Human Rights' (2008) 19 *European Journal of International Law* 655, 700.

rational, autonomous individuals, who have made choices'.[169] And there is also a Slovenian case in which the court held that forced medication constitutes 'a most humiliating act and a degradation of the human being as a person, as it constitutes a deprivation of liberty or a deprivation of the right to decide about oneself'.[170]

The autonomy-based usage of human dignity is therefore founded on the notion of the human as a rational, autonomous being in full possession of her body. It aims to help the 'individual to take control over his life without any interference, or indeed any help, from others or from the state', and therefore 'surrounds the individual in a sort of protective sphere, and thus isolates individuals from each other'.[171]

By contrast, the obligation-creating usage conceives human dignity as something objective and independent from the desires of individuals. This is illustrated, for example, in the *Life Imprisonment* case, in which the German Constitutional Court stated that the freedoms guaranteed in the constitution are not those 'of an isolated and self-regarding individual but rather of a person related to and bound by the community', and the individual must therefore 'allow those limits on his freedom of action that the legislature deems necessary in the interest of the community's social life'.[172] Another well-known case that illustrates the non-subjective, obligations-founding character of the German approach to human dignity is the *Peep Show* decision.[173] In this case, the Federal Administrative Court denied a licence for a peep show on the basis that the show would violate human dignity, irrespective of the fact that the women who acted in the shows did so with their own consent. In explaining its decision, the Court held that because the significance of human dignity is out of the range of an individual, it must be protected even against the contrary wishes of the women performing in the shows, as the will of those women differs from the objective value of human dignity. As Susanne Baer comments, the Court

> never asked the women why they were there; what they did, wanted, or had to do; or how they felt about it. The Court never inquired into the existence or nature of the activity, instead attributing what it perceived as harm. This harm was, then, a violation of specific morals rather than economic deprivation or sexual violence, both well-documented as aspects of prostitution. Thus, the Court used the notion of dignity to regulate rather than to liberate the women involved.[174]

[169] *Sauvé v Canada (Chief Electoral Officer)* (2002) 3 SCR 519; 2002 SCC 68 (Gonthier J, dissenting at para 73), cited in E Daly, *Dignity Rights: Courts, Constitutions, and the Worth of the Human Person* (Philadelphia, University of Pennsylvania Press, 2013), 108.

[170] U-I-60/03-4-12-2003, Official Gazette RS, No 131/2003 and OdlUS XII, 93, para 1, cited in Daly, *Dignity Rights*, 105.

[171] Dupré (n 17) 125.

[172] 45 BVerfGE 187 (1977). Cited in McCrudden, 'Human Dignity and Judicial Interpretation of Human Rights', 700.

[173] BVerfGE 64, 274 (1981); BVerfGE 84, 314 (1990).

[174] S Baer, 'Dignity, Liberty, Equality: A Fundamental Rights Triangle of Constitutionalism' (2009) 59 *University of Toronto Law Journal* 417, 458–59.

A similar approach to sexual self-determination has been taken by the Israeli Supreme Court regarding pornography,[175] and by the Constitutional Court of South Africa regarding prostitution. In deciding in the *Jordan* case that the prohibition of prostitution was not unconstitutional, Judges O'Reagan and Sachs JJ of the latter Court explained that 'Even though we accept that prostitutes may have few alternatives to prostitution, the dignity of prostitutes is diminished … by their engaging in commercial sex work'.[176] Finally, a French court held in the *Senanayake* case, dealing with blood transfusion, that:

> The French understanding of autonomy is much narrower than the Anglo-Saxon one … it is the capacity to define and respect universal duties, laws, towards others as well as towards oneself as member of Humanity. … It encompasses an objective dimension, founded in the belonging of the individual to humanity, and leads to giving a greater importance, whenever a human value is at stake, to the universal standard over singular preferences.[177]

A comparison between the autonomy-based and obligation-founding uses of human dignity suggests that the concept is indeed indeterminate and empty enough that it can be filled with very different contents. It is not even unheard of for both parties in the same case to refer to opposing notions of human dignity.[178] This does not make the concept useless, but it does render it primarily an apparatus for decision-makers to legitimate their decisions – decisions which have very concrete outcomes.[179]

Human dignity is an efficient decision-making apparatus for at least three reasons.[180] First, human dignity collects together different forces and somehow networks them together. This is to a large extent thanks to its analytical emptiness. As many commentators suggest, the reason why human dignity is found in the preamble of so many international documents is probably because it is vague enough that the drafters could agree on it when there was no other common ground.[181] Whilst there are many approaches to human dignity, as well as different theoretical attempts to link human dignity and human rights, what is most important here is that human dignity is still relied on by countless human rights scholars and legal theorists, from human rights believers to pragmatists. Thus, irrespective of whether human dignity is invoked because the author sincerely

[175] *Shin v Council for Cable TV and Satellite Broadcasting* (2004) HCJ 5432/03, IsrSC 58(3) 65.

[176] *Jordan v The State* (2002) (6) SA 642 (CC), cited in McCrudden (n 168) 706.

[177] M Heers, conclusions in CAA Paris (9 June 1998) 6 Revue francaise de droit administratif, 1231–42, cited in S Hennette-Vauchez, 'When Ambivalent Principles Prevail: Leads for Explaining Western Legal Orders' Infatuation with the Human Dignity Principle' (2007) 10 *Legal Ethics* 193, 202–03.

[178] Möllers, 'The Triple Dilemma of Human Dignity: A Case Study'.

[179] See further U Soirila, 'Othering through Human Dignity' (2018) 15 *No Foundations: An Interdisciplinary Journal of Law and Justice* 127.

[180] For a more general, philosophical discussion of the concept of apparatus, see G Agamben, *What Is an Apparatus? And Other Essays* (Stanford, Stanford University Press, 2009).

[181] R Urueña, 'Deciding What Is Humane: Towards a Critical Reading of Humanity as a Normative Standard in International Law' in B van Beers, L Corrias and WG Werner (eds), *Humanity across International Law and Biolaw* (Cambridge, Cambridge University Press, 2014) 187.

believes that there is some verifiable thing called 'human dignity', or whether the author simply wants to take advantage of the energy invested in the concept, there seems to be wide consensus on, or at least promotion of, the idea that human dignity is some kind of transcendental raison d'être of human rights. What seems to be at stake, then, is the ability of human dignity to tie together different views and hence save the credibility, and perhaps even existence, of the human rights system as a theoretical construction.

Second, in addition to collecting together, or capturing, a wide array of forces drawn from different discourses and practices and attaching them together, the apparatus of human dignity allows decision-makers to direct these forces to accomplish concrete results in concrete cases. In other words, human dignity has the powers to make diffused, manifold, often contradictory forces and sentiments become operative and to use them to accomplish strategic functions. Many of these functions are witnessed above. Human dignity has been used to protect the autonomy or freedom of the individual against interventions from the state or from other individuals, who are each shielded in their own protective bubble, and it has been used to obligate individuals to follow certain norms against their wishes. Individuals have been allowed or forbidden to engage in controversial activities, such as sex work, abortion, euthanasia, unconventional sexual practices and blood transfusion, and this has produced concrete results, such as a woman becoming a mother, an affirmative action being struck down, or an individual losing her or his job. But sometimes human dignity has been used even more clearly as part of a project. For example, Hennette-Vauchez has described how an influential group of French scholars seized the success of the human dignity concept 'as a favourable occasion for promoting a particular meaning of the principle whose strategic asset was to convey or enable an otherwise quite despised "*jusnaturalist*" representation of legal orders'.[182] In practice, this has been accomplished by taking a strong normative approach to human dignity and by classifying judicial and legislative uses of the concept on the basis of their compliance or non-compliance with the 'real' meaning of human dignity, which has been, according to Hennette-Vauchez, almost exclusively that of human dignity being used to defend 'society' against the deviating individual.[183] The concrete results of this strategic move have been impressive. Not only has French legal scholarship become, in Hennette-Vauchez's words, 'quite significantly characterised by its acceptance of objective values' that can be used as a potential limitation on rights, but 'the idea according to which Law has an anthropological function of defining and preserving the human dimension of mankind [is also] much more commonly accepted today than it was [some] decades ago'.[184]

[182] Hennette-Vauchez, 'When Ambivalent Principles Prevail', 204. See also S Hennette-Vauchez, 'Human Dignity in French Law' in Düwell et al, *The Cambridge Handbook of Human Dignity*.
[183] Hennette-Vauchez, 'When Ambivalent Principles Prevail' (n 177) 206–07.
[184] ibid 207–08.

Finally, in employing the concept of human dignity, decision-makers and experts not only get to impose on the individual and society a particular vision, or knowledge, of what good life looks like,[185] but also get to define what the 'human' of human dignity is like.[186] Is a dignified human individualistic, rational and always in control of herself, or is she first and foremost a member of her society and her species, even to the extent that she becomes completely enmeshed with and inseparable from the norms of the majority? Or is she a combination of these, or something else entirely? Indeed, as Rene Urueña has argued, the subject created in human dignity cases is 'whoever human rights institutions say she is'.[187] It is, of course, important to resist the temptation of making this seem too much like a one-way street, for it is also possible for the applicants or respondents of a particular case or other actors to make use of the indeterminacy of concepts such as human dignity to subjectivise themselves and to use human rights actively and creatively to create political conflicts and shape their own worlds.[188] This does not, however, counter Urueña's argument; it just adds a new level to it. Sometimes the individual may be able to win the decision-makers over through creative micropolitics,[189] but ultimately that depends on the decision-maker, the apparatus of human dignity always eventually returning to them the power to shape the ideal subject of law – a power that they have eagerly, although often heterogeneously, used, as evidenced by the cases studied above.

To conclude, although human dignity might be incapable of providing much analytical help when conflicting rights or visions of dignity collide, it is nevertheless indisputably 'useful' in de facto justifying decisions in these cases by hiding the political nature of the decision. The concept allows decision-makers to achieve concrete, political results in concrete cases (whatever one might think of these results). This, however, is not enough to provide a solid normative foundation for a global law of humanity, or to guide its decision-making. Although human dignity is a useful concept for the decision-maker, it is incapable of providing an objective yardstick for measuring and balancing competing arguments.

Furthermore, even if the meaning of human dignity could be crystallised through legal practice at the global level – which sounds like a very difficult task – it is far from clear that that would be a desirable outcome. Indeed, some critics, myself included, have argued that both the autonomy-based and obligation-creating uses of human dignity are still based on a similar hierarchical structure as their predecessor, the Roman law concept of *dignitas*, which was a status-based concept, attached to human life only through the office that an

[185] See Baer, 'Dignity, Liberty, Equality', 458–59.
[186] Urueña, 'Deciding What Is Humane', 188.
[187] R Urueña, *No Citizens Here: Global Subjects and Participation in International Law* (Helsinki, Helsinki University Printing House, 2010) 106.
[188] Rancière, 'Who Is the Subject of the Rights of Man?' See also generally J Butler, *The Psychic Life of Power: Theories in Subjection* (Stanford, Stanford University Press, 1997).
[189] WE Connolly, *Why I Am Not a Secularist* (Minneapolis, University of Minnesota Press, 1999).

individual held, and which could therefore be gained or lost.[190] Indeed, in both contemporary uses, too, the apparatus of human dignity is mediated through another apparatus – personhood in the autonomy-based usage and (personhood or) humanity in the obligation-creating one. Although in most cases this peculiar construction hardly matters, and, indeed, remains securely hidden, it may start to reveal its problematic face when its limits are tested and the question becomes who counts as a 'person', 'human' or whatever the mediating apparatus might be. Hence, I would side with Anne Phillips, who argues that the use of the concept of human dignity should be replaced with that of equality. As she explains, human dignity 'is often just another way of describing what it is to treat others as our equals', but 'when it isn't – when it edges into problematically substantive notions of what it is to be a human – it edges into something we would do better to avoid'.[191] Perhaps even more importantly, however, whereas human dignity tends to be a matter of complex philosophical, theological or legal discussions, equality is usually something claimed by those who are de facto unequal. We are not born equal, but become so precisely by claiming our equality. Equality is therefore not something we need to prove through arguments of shared humanity or personhood, but a process which is brought into existence 'at the moment we claim it'.[192]

***

This chapter has argued that human rights, human security and human dignity are all indeterminate concepts that are used for multiple different purposes as experts, practitioners and academics struggle over their ownership and seek to harness them to fulfil their vision of good life or even to further their particular interests. Hence, the law of humanity discourse risks becoming ideological if it loses sight of the difference between what is said about the concepts and what the consequences of their increased circulation are or might be. The law of humanity theorists therefore should not expect the increased circulation of these concepts to lead automatically to the outcomes they desire. Instead, there is a need to pay more attention to how the concepts are actually used in practice.

[190] Phillips (n 48); S Hennette-Vauchez, 'A Human Dignitas – Remnants of the Ancient Legal Concept in Contemporary Dignity Jurisprudence' (2011) 9 *International Journal of Constitutional Law* 32; D Herzog, 'Aristocratic Dignity?' in M Dan-Cohen (ed), J Waldron, *Dignity, Rank, and Rights* (Oxford, Oxford University Press, 2012); Soirila, 'Othering through Human Dignity'; U Soirila, 'Human Dignity Mediated: Personhood, Humanity, and the Logic of Property in Law and Bioethics' in A Griffiths, S Mustasaari and A Mäki-Petajä-Leinonen (eds), *Subjectivity, Citizenship and Belonging in Law: Identities and Intersections* (Abingdon, Routledge, 2016). For an attempt to turn the hierarchical structure into a positive force, see J Waldron, *Dignity, Rank, and Rights* (Oxford, Oxford University Press, 2012).

[191] Phillips (n 48) 103.

[192] ibid 69. See also J Rancière, *Disagreement: Politics and Philosophy* (Minneapolis, University of Minnesota Press, 1999); Rancière, 'Who Is the Subject of the Rights of Man?' (n 42).

4

Humanity Language in Action

IF THERE IS no certainty that the increased circulation of the key concepts of the law of humanity project necessarily leads to the outcomes assumed and desired by its theorists, it becomes pertinent to analyse how these concepts, and humanity language at large, have actually been used in global governance, and with what outcomes. That is the task of this chapter. In so doing, the chapter adopts a descriptive approach. Relying mostly on the extensive work done by others, the aim of the chapter is to bring together information from seemingly distinct fields and hence paint as broad a picture as possible of the use of the humanity language in action.

Hence, if the previous chapter argued that the law of humanity risks falling into the trap of 'false necessity', this chapter seeks to cover some of the blind spots left in my own analysis by addressing its 'false contingency'. As Susan Marks teaches, at the heart of the idea of false contingency is the notion that there are always structural limits, pressures and forces that shape and constrain the uses of analytically indeterminate concepts, thus rendering them less indeterminate in practice than an abstract analysis would lead one to believe.[1]

Like any project or idea, the law of humanity project, too, has coexisted with different mindsets and forms of power, some of which it shares some affinity with and many of which are entirely alien to it. In doing so, it has necessarily become embedded in complex networks of power relations and discourses. This chapter asks how these circumstances have affected the use of humanity language in the practice of global governance. In particular, the chapter seeks to find out how the outcomes of these uses match the representation of the law of humanity project. Hence, it focuses especially on those aspects of the uses of humanity language that can be mirrored and compared to the stated aims of the law of humanity project, namely the protection and empowerment of human persons and the diminishing or altering of the role of the state.

[1] S Marks, 'False Contingency' (2009) 62 *Current Legal Problems* 1.

I. RIGHTS AND OBLIGATIONS OF INDIVIDUALS: INTERNATIONAL HUMAN RIGHTS, INVESTMENT AND CRIMINAL LAW

The 1990s witnessed the final breakthrough of three international legal regimes focused on the individual, namely international human rights law, international investment law and international criminal law. Although all of the regimes had already existed for some time, it was not until after the end of the Cold War that they truly blossomed. Human rights law was quickly mainstreamed to most areas of the UN and regional activities, the amount of bilateral investment treaties multiplied and new *ad hoc* international criminal tribunals were eventually followed by the establishment of the International Criminal Court (ICC).

With the final breakthrough of these regimes came a dramatic rise in humanity rhetoric. As human rights came to guide most of the decision-making in global governance – at the very least, rhetorically – international criminal law was also framed as a matter of human rights promotion, 'particularly the protection of life, dignity and freedom from discrimination',[2] and presented as a 'conscience of humankind'. Consequently, the notion of humanity is not only presented as the source of the ICC's normative authority, but is also continuously invoked in the practice of international criminal law, international crimes being commonly presented as attacks on 'humanity' or 'humankind.[3] Perhaps most famously, this focus on humanity and the human person was captured in a passage of the *Tadić* decision, in which the International Criminal Tribunal for the Former Yugoslavia (ICTY) declared that a 'State-sovereignty-oriented approach has been gradually supplanted by a human-being-oriented approach'.[4]

The connection between investment law and humanity rhetoric may seem less obvious. Yet, Mont Pèlerin Society members had already used human rights language in the 1950s to defend unrestricted international investment,[5] in particular the 'right to sell and leave',[6] and to 'justify supervision of post-colonial states to ensure they protected the rights of traders'.[7] Following this tradition, the champion of international trade and investment, Ernst-Ulrich Petersmann, replied to the mounting questioning on the legitimacy of the World Trade Organization (WTO) at the turn of the millennium by adopting the very

[2] F Mégret, 'What Sort of Global Justice Is "International Criminal Justice"?' (2015) 13 *Journal of International Criminal Justice* 77, 86.

[3] LDA Corrias and GM Gordon, 'Judging in the Name of Humanity International Criminal Tribunals and the Representation of a Global Public' (2015) 13 *Journal of International Criminal Justice* 97, 99–101.

[4] *Prosecutor v Dusko Tadic* (Appeals Chamber Decision on the Defence Motion for Interlocutory Appeal on Jurisdiction) IT-94-1-AR72 (2 Oct 1995) para 97.

[5] J Whyte, *The Morals of the Market: Human Rights and the Rise of Neoliberalism* (London, Verso, 2019) 146–50.

[6] Q Slobodian, *Globalists: The End of Empire and the Birth of Neoliberalism* (Cambridge, MA, Harvard University Press, 2018) 145.

[7] Whyte, *The Morals of the Market*, 155.

human rights language of the protesters, reinterpreting it so as to demand more effective protection of economic freedoms and property rights.[8] Indeed, according to Petersmann, the global protection of human dignity requires 'mutually beneficial trade and investment',[9] and increased investment protection reflects the process of 'increasing recognition of citizens as legal subjects and "democratic owners" of international law'.[10] Similarly, it is commonly argued that international investment law operates in the interests of the whole of humanity, the protection of investment ensuring the welfare benefits which derive from increased capital flows.[11] As the standard liberal assumption goes, the protection of private interests and private property will produce trickle-down effects, reduce poverty and increase human well-being in general.[12]

In addition to having acted as forerunners of the rise of the humanity rhetoric, the regimes of international human rights law, international investment law and international criminal law also reflect and exemplify the trends analysed in this chapter. To start with, the concrete outcomes of the regimes and the use of humanity language within them are subject to much academic debate. There is, for example, no doubt that human rights law has provided a remedy for countless individuals who have had their rights violated. In particular, human rights law has been very efficient in combating status-based discrimination. Yet, human rights law has been either unable or unwilling to do the same when it comes to material inequality, and human rights actors have increasingly – although perhaps unfairly – become seen by the public as some kind of elitist experts.

Similarly, although the expansion of the global investment regime has certainly empowered some individuals – the investors – and there are many success stories of foreign investment having enriched host countries, there are an equal number of cases where the economic benefits have remained low, despite states relinquishing their sovereignty, or where the privatisation often linked to foreign investment has caused catastrophic outcomes from the perspective of the local population.[13] Even more importantly, the regime seems inimical to mass

[8] E-U Petersmann, 'The WTO Constitution and Human Rights' (2000) 3 *Journal of International Economic Law* 19; E-U Petersmann, 'From "Negative" to "Positive" Integration in the WTO: Time for "Mainstreaming Human Rights" into WTO Law?' (2000) 37 *CML Rev* 1363.

[9] E-U Petersmann, 'Introduction and Summary: "Administration of Justice" in International Investment Law and Adjudication?' in P-M Dupuy, E-U Petersmann and F Francioni (eds), *Human Rights in International Investment Law and Arbitration* (Oxford, Oxford University Press, 2009) 9. Generally, see E-U Petersmann, 'Time for a United Nations "Global Compact" for Integrating Human Rights into the Law of Worldwide Organizations: Lessons from European Integration' (2002) 13 *European Journal of International Law* 621.

[10] Petersmann, 'Introduction and Summary', 35.

[11] A Peters, *Beyond Human Rights: The Legal Status of the Individual in International Law* (J Huston trans, Cambridge, Cambridge University Press, 2016).

[12] E-U Petersmann, 'Constitutional Theories of International Economic Adjudication and Investor-State Arbitration' in Dupuy et al, *Human Rights in International Investment Law and Arbitration*, 186–87.

[13] See, eg N Tzouvala, 'Food for the Global Market: The Neoliberal Reconstruction of Agriculture in Occupied Iraq (2003–2004) and the Role of International Law' (2017) 17 *Global Jurist* 1.

politics and democracy, and can in this way 'be understood as a means for safeguarding hierarchy and power within each and every state'.[14]

Finally, international criminal law, too, has been the target of heated critique focused on the discrepancy between the discourse and the practice. As Mégret writes, for example, the idea that international criminal law is exercised for the benefit of 'Humanity' can be questioned on the basis that 'if Humanity is indeed the prime beneficiary of international criminal justice, it shows little sign of being aware of this'. As Mégret explains, the 'global public' of international criminal justice is limited to a few specialised non-governmental organisations (NGOs), and the oft-invoked NGO efforts in the creation of the ICC were in reality far from social movements or mass mobilisation.[15] Moreover, although the victim rhetoric is overwhelming in international criminal law, the 'victims' referred to in the discourse are typically not any concrete persons, with their particular harms and suffering, but rather 'The Victims' in abstract, the rhetoric, employed, for example, by NGOs and prosecutors, transcending legally recognised victims.[16] According to Kendall and Nouwen, 'The Victims' act as the 'sovereign' of international criminal law, in the sense that they are those on whose behalf international criminal justice is rhetorically exercised, just like national prosecutions are carried out on behalf of the Crown or the state.[17] Yet, not unlike Giorgio Agamben's genealogy of economics and government in *The Kingdom and the Glory*, that reference point – the throne – is empty, producing a bipolar machine where practice is legitimated by a reference to some transcendent source of power whose power lies only in that practice that glorifies it.[18] 'The Victims' are therefore fundamentally important for legitimating the action of international criminal tribunals, but since the abstractions 'cannot speak back' and challenge the representation itself,[19] the consequence is that there is an increasing gap between those who represent and those who are represented.[20] As Kendall and Nouwen write, the abstraction of 'The Victims' 'does not actually exercise power itself' but rather 'works as a placeholder for the agency of others', the active subjects representing the 'international community'.[21]

The human rights, investment and international criminal law regimes similarly set the tone for another key issue of the law of humanity project – namely,

[14] N Tzouvala, 'The Ordo-Liberal Origins of Modern International Investment Law: Constructing Competition on a Global Scale' in JD Haskell and A Rasulov (eds), *New Voices and New Perspectives in International Economic Law: New Voices, New Perspectives* (Springer, 2020) 37.

[15] Mégret, 'What Sort of Global Justice', 86.

[16] S Kendall and S Nouwen, 'Representational Practices at the International Criminal Court: The Gap between Juridified and Abstract Victimhood' (2013) 76 *Law & Contemporary Problems* 235, 253–54.

[17] ibid 254.

[18] G Agamben, *The Kingdom and the Glory: For a Theological Genealogy of Economy and Government* (L Chiesa and M Mandarini trans, Stanford, Stanford University Press, 2011).

[19] Kendall and Nouwen, 'Representational Practices at the International Criminal Court', 255.

[20] ibid 261.

[21] ibid 253–56.

the complex relation between the humanity discourse and the state. In this regard, too, the outcomes are complex. The evidence does not seem to support the claim of the withering of the state, but it does seem to point to its disciplining. For example, it would be difficult to see human rights diminishing the role of the state – although it may shape it. In fact, human rights have at least so far been so intimately linked to the state that some commentators, such as Patrick Macklem, are ready to go so far as to argue that human rights – in their current stance – make sense only in an international legal system built around states. According to Macklem, international law validates some claims of sovereign power and refuses to validate others, and in so doing produces 'an ongoing distribution of sovereign power among geographically concentrated collectivities that international law recognises as States'.[22] The role of human rights, then, is to mitigate the negative effects of this distribution of power.[23] The protection provided by human rights compensates for the losses that some collectivities and individuals suffer in the great game of international law. And in so doing, human rights secure the legitimacy of states and of the international legal order as a whole.[24]

Regardless of whether one agrees with Macklem's theoretical views or not, some of the foundations of his argument are supported by the practice of human rights law. Human rights are rights that individuals hold against their states or, conversely, obligations that states have towards their citizens and other people under their jurisdiction. Hence, human rights claims are brought to courts or monitoring bodies by an individual against a state, or by one state against another. The horizontal dimension of human rights,[25] which would arguably be necessary for global law, has so far remained mostly a matter of academic debate, as have the precise human rights obligations of international institutions.[26]

Human rights law, then, is built around the state, and hence seems to solidify the key role of the state in international law. Nevertheless, it is important to add that this role is a very specific and limited one. At the same time as human rights law empowers the state and commands it to take an active role in securing

[22] P Macklem, *The Sovereignty of Human Rights* (Oxford, Oxford University Press, 2015) 29–30.

[23] ibid 22.

[24] ibid passim.

[25] JH Knox, 'Horizontal Human Rights Law' (2008) 102 *American Journal of International Law* 1; S Baughen, 'Customary International Law and Its Horizontal Effect: Human Rights Litigation between Non-State Actors' (2015) 67 *Rutgers Law Review* 89.

[26] A Clapham, *Human Rights Obligations of Non-State Actors* (Oxford, Oxford University Press, 2006); O De Schutter, 'Human Rights and the Rise of International Organizations: The Logic of Sliding Scales in the Law of International Responsibility', CRIDHO Working Paper 2010/4 (Univeristé catholique de Louvain, 2010); G Acquaviva, 'Human Rights Violations before International Tribunals: Reflections on Responsibility of International Organizations' (2007) 20 *Leiden Journal of International Law* 613; P Alston (ed), *Non-State Actors and Human Rights* (Oxford, Oxford University Press, 2005); G Verdirame, *The UN and Human Rights: Who Guards the Guardians?* (Cambridge, Cambridge University Press, 2011).

the human dignity of its citizens, it monitors the exercise of its sovereignty and limits the ways in which the state can use its discretion.[27] The limits are constantly redrawn in the practice of human rights law, not only in the decisions of human rights courts, but also, for example, in the lending requirements of the World Bank, which often demands loan-seeking states to take certain measures which are seen to improve their human rights standards.

The subtlest, but perhaps most comprehensive, way of disciplining state power through human rights standards comes in the form of indicators and periodic reviews.[28] An excellent example is the Universal Periodic Review (UPR). Established in 2006, the UPR is supposed to provide a universal, holistic, objective and transparent review of a state's human rights situation. Based on peer review, states are supposed to learn about best practices from each other during the UPR process. As Cowan and Billaud write, 'UPR feeds into the already existing – and politically controversial – institutional processes of expertise, "knowledge transfer" and "capacity building"', but is also often perceived 'as an individually endured public "exam"'.[29] The UPR treats states as isolated entities, removed from any historical, political or economic context, or of its relations with other states and non-state actors, measuring their performance according to certain 'universal' standards.[30] In so doing, the UPR process solidifies 'the international human rights system's focus on the state as the primary duty bearer',[31] but also 'pushes at the boundary of non-interference' in its recommendations by fellow states and in its pressure to adopt certain practices, institutional structures and standards.[32]

Thus, although international human rights law has solidified the position of the state as a key actor in international law, it has been very effective in producing a certain type of state, with rather limited discretion. This disciplining of the state is even clearer in the case of international investment law. As Kate Miles writes, investment protection is usually presented as a project which divorces disputes from the 'politicized environment of the host state' and moves them to the realm of the universal and neutral rule of law, guided by the teachings of global administrative law.[33] This is reflected, for example, in the view that investment arbitrators and judges should not see themselves only as agents of the

[27] Macklem, *The Sovereignty of Human Rights*, 2; W Osiatynski, *Human Rights and Their Limits* (Cambridge, Cambridge University Press, 2009) 26–27.

[28] SE Merry, *The Seductions of Quantification: Measuring Human Rights, Gender Violence, and Sex Trafficking* (Chicago, University of Chicago Press, 2016); JK Cowan and J Billaud, 'Between Learning and Schooling: The Politics of Human Rights Monitoring at the Universal Periodic Review' (2015) 36 *Third World Quarterly* 1175.

[29] Cowan and Billaud, 'Between Learning and Schooling', 1175–76.

[30] ibid 1179.

[31] ibid.

[32] ibid 1181.

[33] K Miles, 'International Investment Law and Universality: Histories of Shape-Shifting Part I: General Part' (2014) 3 *Cambridge Journal of International and Comparative Law* 986, 987.

parties, but also as 'independent guardians of constitutional justice'.[34] In achieving this shift from domestic actors to global ones,[35] international investment law is very efficient in 'constraining the power and authority of the legislature, executive and judiciary', and thus restricting the state's ability to protect its sovereign concerns.[36] In other words, global investment law participates in the process of reshaping the state. The state structure remains important in facilitating investment and maintaining free markets, but the state's role is minimised in almost all other ways, as typically public functions – such as guaranteeing access to food and water, the exploitation of natural resources, healthcare and transportation – are privatised and taken over by foreign investors.

Even if states remain key facilitators of investment, it is not easy for them to resist its disciplining function. The global economic order is built so that states must ensure sufficient capital flow into their country. In order to do this, they have to guarantee desirable conditions for investments, for example by ratifying investment protection agreements, which 'often demand compliance by host states even if these norms intrude upon areas of sovereign control, such as monetary policies or the exploitation of resources'.[37] Together with arbitral decisions, which tend to favour strong protection of private property and investment, these agreements and their subsequent compliance 'have stabilized expectations of appropriate state behavior'.[38] In a way, then, the power of the investment regime lies in the very existence of the investment dispute settlement system. As Martti Koskenniemi argues:

> While the number of actual cases will always be limited, the fact of the existence of a disciplinary system will by itself create an immediate effect in the relations between public power and international investors. When one of the parties and only *one of them*, may say to the other 'if you do not agree with my conditions, then see you in court', then the balance of power has shifted decisively in favour of that party … This effect will be automatically visible in the thousands upon thousands of situations where negotiations are being held between an investor and a public body about the conditions under which the investment is to be managed. But its effect is likely to be even greater in the innumerable situations where a public authority contemplates some policy measure and will take account of the possibility of a reaction on the part of a foreign investor.[39]

The outcome of this disciplinary process is that investor interests and the notion of the value of privatisation are internalised by domestic actors, if not already,

[34] Petersmann, 'Constitutional Theories of International Economic Adjudication' 190. See also A Stone Sweet and F Grisel, 'Transnational Investment Arbitration: From Delegation to Constitutionalization?' in Dupuy et al (n 9).

[35] T-H Cheng, 'Power, Authority and International Investment Law' (2004) 20 *American University International Law Review* 465, 469.

[36] ibid 493–94.

[37] ibid 467.

[38] ibid 470–71.

[39] M Koskenniemi, 'It's Not the Cases, It's the System' (2017) 18 *Journal of Investment & Trade* 343, 351–52 (original emphasis).

as a consequence of the current hegemony of neoliberalism[40] and the benefits it may produce for local elites. The process therefore ensures 'that trade liberalization remains a largely uncontested recipe for welfare as governments are busily privatizing essential services and attracting investors by binding their hands in innumerable ways'.[41] Conversely, collective domestic planning becomes almost impossible.[42]

Finally, the international criminal law project, too, has a complicated relationship with the state. On the one hand, the regime shares cosmopolitans' typical scepticism towards the state. As Pádraig McAuliffe notes, theorists of international criminal justice – like cosmopolitan theorists generally – attempt to 'disrupt the relationship between the individual and the State and relegate the latter from its status as the primary actor in the international system'.[43] For example, writing in the context of international criminal law, Geoffrey Robertson argues that state sovereignty is the 'traditional enemy' of human rights,[44] while Steven C Roach sees it is an 'enduring obstacle' to the development of international criminal law.[45] Others may not share this hostile attitude towards the state but, rather, argue that international criminal tribunals are likely to start living a life of their own, becoming cosmopolitan institutions with their own rationality[46] and operating as an 'engine of an expanding global rule of law'.[47] A consequence of this development is that state action starts to seem 'more like a dilution of an international tribunal than a necessary and beneficial complement to it'.[48] Thus, 'even in a context where the importance of the local is periodically recognized, it is always by reference to the overarching commitment of international criminal tribunals to cosmopolitan values'.[49]

On the other hand, international criminal law relies on the state to capture accused individuals, help with investigations and so on, while bolstering states in several small ways. In fact, some commentators have gone so far as to claim that international criminal law 'purifies' states (and the international community)

[40] S Singh, 'The Fundamental Rights of States in Neoliberal Times' (2015) 4 *Cambridge Journal of International and Comparative Law* 461.

[41] Koskenniemi, 'It's Not the Cases', 352–53.

[42] ibid 345.

[43] P McAuliffe, 'From Watchdog to Workhorse: Explaining the Emergence of the ICC's Burden-Sharing Policy as an Example of Creeping Cosmopolitanism' (2014) 13 *Chinese Journal of International Law* 259, 268.

[44] G Robertson, *Crimes against Humanity: The Struggle for Global Justice* (London, Penguin, 2012) 624.

[45] SC Roach, *Politicizing the International Criminal Court: The Convergence of Politics, Ethics, and Law* (Lanham, MD, Rowman & Littlefield Publishers, 2006) 19.

[46] Mégret (n 2) 85.

[47] T Krever, 'International Criminal Law: An Ideology Critique' (2013) 26 *Leiden Journal of International Law* 701, 702.

[48] McAuliffe, 'From Watchdog to Workhorse', 269.

[49] Mégret (n 2) 85–86.

by punishing some individuals. According to Edwin Bikundo,[50] the prosecuted individuals serve as scapegoats – or *pharmakos*, in the Derridean sense – both belonging to and being excluded from the community: belonging enough that their sacrifice serves to purify the community, but excluded enough to be easily sacrificed without jeopardising the community in its entirety.[51] As put by Mégret, the prosecuted individuals are made to 'appear as more or less interchangeable free agents ultimately responsible to mankind, rather than figureheads for a range of particularly problematic national situations' with deep structural roots deserving separate attention.[52]

Nevertheless, and as was the case with human rights and investment law, international criminal law's vision of a 'good' state is very specific. Hence, international criminal law also contributes to disciplining the state, in particular by allowing international interventions. According to Tor Krever, for example, the international criminal law's 'selective and highly politicized interventions have operated to reproduce one-sided narratives of complex conflicts, demonizing some perpetrators as *hostis humani generis*, while legitimating military interventions in the name of humanity', sometimes with significant transformations of the societies in question.[53] Similarly, Immi Tallgren has argued that the international criminal regime constrains the policy options of states, 'up to a point of erasing the sovereignty of states not complying',[54] whilst at the same time obscuring many of the choices that go into the everyday practices of international criminal law.[55] In this way, international criminal law hides political battles and naturalises 'phenomena which are in fact the pre-conditions for the maintenance of the existing governance'.[56]

To conclude, then, the breakthrough of international human rights law, international investment law and international criminal law during the last decade of the past millennium played a key role in distributing humanity discourse to different areas of international law, global governance and world politics. With this rise of the humanity discourse came increased focus on the individual and concerns of 'humanity', but also many questionable outcomes. Moreover, although the rise of the humanity discourse has not heralded the withering of the state, the discourse has brought about disciplining of the state, all of the regimes implying certain requirements that a human rights- and international

[50] E Bikundo, 'Humanity's Exemplary Justice: From Hostis to Hostia Humani Generis' in B van Beers, L Corrias and WG Werner (eds), *Humanity across International Law and Biolaw* (Cambridge, Cambridge University Press, 2014) 64–66.

[51] J Derrida, *Dissemination* (B Johnson trans, Chicago, University of Chicago Press, 1983) 130–34.

[52] Mégret (n 2) 87–88.

[53] T Krever, 'Dispensing Global Justice' [2014] *New Left Review* 67, 97.

[54] I Tallgren, 'The Voice of the International: Who Is Speaking?' (2015) 13 *Journal of International Criminal Justice* 135, 147.

[55] Mégret (n 2) 81.

[56] I Tallgren, 'The Sensibility and Sense of International Criminal Law' (2002) 13 *European Journal of International Law* 561, 595.

criminal law-abiding or investment-friendly state should meet. As we will see, these trends have subsequently surfaced in one form or another, in most instances where the humanity rhetoric has been employed in global governance.

II. HUMANITARIAN OCCUPATIONS

Perhaps the most paradigmatic example is the case of the UN's international territorial administration (ITA) missions in the 1990s and afterwards in Bosnia and Herzegovina, East Slavonia, Kosovo and East Timor. Although ITA is an established practice, some commentators argue that these specific missions contain new elements that make them a deviation from rather than a continuation of previous practice.[57] According to Gregory H Fox, for example, the missions constitute a completely new mode of ITA – 'humanitarian occupation' – which was made possible by the post-Cold War environment in which the 'question of how nations are governed had moved beyond the social contract between state and citizen and become a question for the broader international community'.[58]

According to Fox, the term 'humanitarian occupation' is fitting for two reasons. First, the missions are humanitarian because their purpose is to end human rights abuses and to protect human life. This humanitarian rationale has been so strong, argues Fox, that the missions are best seen as social engineering projects aimed at reforming governmental institutions for the benefit of the life of the administered population. Second, the governing authority assumed by the administration in all these projects matched that of occupiers – hence the latter part, 'occupation'. Humanitarian occupation means, for Fox, 'the assumption of governing authority over a state or a portion thereof, by an international actor for the express purpose of creating a liberal, democratic order'.[59] However, unlike in previous cases, such as the trusteeship system, the welfare of the population is, according to Fox, 'genuinely' the primary concern of humanitarian occupiers.[60]

Whether these 'humanitarian occupations' truly represent a radical break from the past or are a culmination of a historical continuum is outside the scope of this chapter.[61] What is relevant, however, is that the missions were

[57] GH Fox, *Humanitarian Occupation* (Cambridge, Cambridge University Press, 2008) chs 1–3.
[58] ibid 72.
[59] ibid 3–4.
[60] See also M Ruffert, 'Administration of Kosovo and East-Timor by the International Community Shorter Articles, Comments and Notes' (2001) 50 *International and Comparative Law Quarterly* 613, 629.
[61] For the latter view, see R Wilde, *International Territorial Administration: How Trusteeship and the Civilizing Mission Never Went Away* (Oxford, Oxford University Press, 2010); C Stahn, *The Law and Practice of International Territorial Administration: Versailles to Iraq and Beyond*, reissue edn (Cambridge, Cambridge University Press, 2010).

conducted in the name of humanity and intervened in core areas of the administered states' sovereignty.[62] They are thus part of a more general shift towards human rights and responsibility to protect in humanitarian law and the law of occupation. Initially, the law of occupation was interested mostly in relations between states and their elites. Of the 15 articles on 'belligerent occupation' in the Hague Conventions of 1899 and 1907, only three were related to physical integrity of civilians, whereas the rest concerned property, and the primary aim was to maintain the ousted government's title to sovereignty.[63] The 1949 Geneva Convention IV had already sought to find a new balance between the rights of the population and the occupants, and the 1977 Additional Protocol I to the Geneva Conventions took a further step towards an individualised human rights approach. Yet the scope of who was protected remained a problem, until it was eventually tackled by the ICTY in 1999 in the *Tadic* decision,[64] which adopted a very flexible approach to the category of protected people. The 'humanised' approach is also reflected in Additional Geneva Protocol II, which extends protection to civilians in non-international armed conflicts. As a consequence of all these transformations, it is now commonly argued that the emphasis is on the duty of occupiers to actively protect human rights: the occupier is seen as a trustee who must actively increase the welfare and human rights of the occupied population, guided by the principle of humanity.[65] Fulfilling this task, however, requires that occupiers have more extensive powers. Indeed, these powers have expanded to cover almost all areas over which contemporary governments exercise power, in stark contrast to the previous conception of minimal governmental intervention. Further, focus has shifted – at least in rhetoric – from the rights of the occupied sovereign to the needs of the population.[66] The occupier's powers are therefore seen to have expanded 'into a broad grant of authority to transform the occupied economy, the landscape, even local institutions'. In the words of Eyal Benvenisti, almost as soon as the welfare of the population was deemed the most important aim of the occupant to pursue, it was 'transformed into a legal tool extensively invoked by occupants in those areas in which they wished to intervene'.[67]

While it is fiercely debated whether the law of occupation applies to the Security Council or to other UN organs, the logic of extending administrative powers for the protection of human rights and human life is clearly visible in all

[62] Fox, *Humanitarian Occupation*, 2.

[63] See further E Benvenisti, *The International Law of Occupation*, 2nd edn (Oxford, Oxford University Press, 2012) 7–15.

[64] *Prosecutor v Dusko Tadic* (Appeals Chamber Judgment) IT-94-1-A (15 July 1999) ch IV of the judgment.

[65] JL Cohen, *Globalization and Sovereignty: Rethinking Legality, Legitimacy, and Constitutionalism* (Cambridge, Cambridge University Press, 2012) 235.

[66] Benvenisti, *The International Law of Occupation*, 6–7.

[67] ibid 10–11.

four 'humanitarian occupation' missions, as well as in the occupation of Iraq by the USA and its allies.

The first humanitarian occupation was the Bosnia mission in 1995. After four years of fruitless diplomacy and peacekeeping, the international community decided to put an end to the bloody conflict between Serbs, Croats and Muslims. The end result was the Dayton Agreement, the content of which was more or less dictated by intervening states.[68] The agreement subjected Bosnia-Hertzegovina's (BiH) institutions 'to a remarkable series of checks by international norms and institutions' and created a constitution which stated that the European Convention on Human Rights would apply directly in BiH and 'have priority over all other law'.[69] Furthermore, BiH was to remain or become party to 15 human rights treaties and cooperate fully with their supervisory bodies.[70] Wide implementation responsibilities were assigned to the UN, the Refugee Agency (UN High Commission for Refugees, UNHCR), the International Committee of the Red Cross, the North Atlantic Treaty Organization (NATO), Organization for Security and Co-operation in Europe (OSCE) and the World Bank. Civilian authority was put in the hands of the 'international community', represented through the Office of the High Representative, which was granted jurisdiction 'over virtually every aspect of economic reconstruction, human rights and institutional rehabilitation', as well as the authority to interpret the Dayton documents.[71] As Fox writes, 'Dayton thus tied the Bosnia constitutional order directly to international norms and institutions, which were erected as a fail-safe to ensure minimum standards of human rights'. The post-Dayton politics in BiH were therefore 'wholly the creation of outsiders, who ran roughshod over any local attempts to chart a different direction'.[72] Perhaps the most important of these actors was the Peace Implementation Council (PIC), a group of 55 states and organisations, established ad hoc to sponsor and direct the peace implementation process. The Council effectively guided the High Representative and decided the policy for BiH. Amongst the PIC's main aims were the economic transformation of BiH into a state which could guarantee market-driven economic growth, a swift return of refugees and displaced persons, and the creation of democratically accountable institutions.[73] Drastic changes in legislation were perceived as necessary for attracting foreign investors – presented as a top priority – and forced through with coercive measures.[74]

[68] Fox (n 57) 76–78.

[69] General Framework Agreement for Peace in Bosnia and Herzegovina with Annexes (signed 14 December 1995) 35 ILM 75, 89 (1996) Art II(2).

[70] ibid Arts II(7)–(8).

[71] Fox (n 57) 81.

[72] ibid 83–84.

[73] A Orford, *Reading Humanitarian Intervention: Human Rights and the Use of Force in International Law*, reissue edn (Cambridge, Cambridge University Press, 2007) 130. See further Declaration of the Peace Implementation Council, www.ohr.int/?p=54080.

[74] ibid 131–32.

The second humanitarian occupation mission was the most limited of the four. The United Nations Transitional Administration in East Slavonia, Baranja and Western Sirmium (UNTAES) was a response to ethnic cleansings in Croatia. Security Council Resolution 1037 (1996) granted UNTAES a rather narrow mandate compared to other UN-led missions. Its task was to govern the region during a transitional period during which the Erdut Agreement between the Croatian government and local Serb groups – including, among other things, demilitarisation and the return of displaced people to their homes – would be put in force. In particular, the UN administration were to guarantee the protection of international human rights.[75] The mandate also covered civil administration, the holding of elections, the return of refugees and economic reconstruction. Not long before the mission ended in 1998, the Secretary-General assessed that UNTAES had managed to reintegrate the area institutionally to Croatia, but 'the reintegration of the people had hardly begun'.[76]

The third humanitarian occupation mission is the still ongoing territorial administration of Kosovo. In 1999, the international community sought to repeat the 'success' of Dayton, in an attempt to end bloody hostilities between the Kosovo Liberation Army and the Federal Republic of Yugoslavia (FRY). However, the negotiations in Rambouillet in February 1999 did not succeed, and it was not until June 3 that the FRY reached – after months of intense NATO bombing – an agreement with EU envoy Martti Ahtisaari and Russia's envoy Victor Chernomyrdin. The agreement was approved and elaborated upon on June 10 by the UN Security Council, acting under Chapter VII of the UN Charter. The Security Council decided that international civil and security presence would be established in Kosovo, civil authority would be controlled by a Special Representative of the UN Security General (SRSG) and peace would be guaranteed by NATO. The legal details of the administration of Kosovo were distributed across several documents. Together, however, the documents delegated 'virtually all the classical powers of a state' to international actors.[77] All legislative and executive powers were vested in the UN Mission in Kosovo (UNMIK), civilian administration was to be controlled by the UN, humanitarian affairs by the UNHCR, institution building by the OSCE and reconstruction by the EU. The SRSG oversees these four components of the UNMIK. The Security Council ordered the UNMIK to establish institutions for multi-ethnic government, the application of international human rights instruments, democratic governance and a market-based economy,[78] and the interim administration has indeed made full use these powers.[79]

[75] Basic Agreement on the Region of Eastern Slavonia, Baranja and Western Sirmium (1995) UN Doc A/50/757, S/1995/951, Art 6.

[76] UNSC, 'Report of the Secretary-General on the Situation in Croatia' (1997) UN Doc S/1997/487, 12.

[77] Fox (n 57) 93.

[78] UNSC Res 1244 (10 June 1999) UN Doc S/RES/1244.

[79] Fox (n 57) 95.

The fourth UN-led humanitarian occupation also occurred in 1999, as a response to the massacre of the East Timorese by pro-Indonesian militias, following a vote on the political status of East Timor. In its Resolution 1272, the UN Security Council, acting again under Chapter VII, established the UN Transitional Administration in East Timor (UNTAET) to take overall responsibility for the administration of East Timor and to exercise all legislative and executive authority. The administration was constrained by seven international human rights instruments. Indonesian laws continued to apply only to the extent that they were compatible with these instruments, and the UNTAET very quickly rescinded a series of Indonesian security regulations which were seen to be inconsistent with international human rights law. Although the 'UNTAET's organizational structure came to resemble that of a government, divided into eight ministerial like portfolios',[80] a minimalist human rights agenda soon took over from community building efforts,[81] and the administration's relations with the East Timorese themselves remained very controversial until the end of the mission in 2002. The East Timorese found the UNTAET to be very unreceptive to any of their wishes and complained repeatedly of autocratic rule. Perhaps most controversial was that the UNTAET concluded a treaty with the World Bank on a local governance project. The World Bank took control of the economic governance of the country, aiming to transform the society's 'culture of subsistence and informal economy' into 'one that develops capitalism, creates opportunity and ultimately formalizes the economy'.[82] Whilst the Bank provided funding for health and education, it also decided early on that East Timor should have a small state, with as many areas as possible open for the private sector and especially foreign investors. As a consequence, the country was soon 'overrun by foreign, mainly Australian, companies making large profits out of contracts negotiated with INTERFET [International Force East Timor] or UNTAET'.[83] Furthermore, the World Bank reformed East Timor's agriculture radically, guided by the Bank's long-established vision that agriculture should be a commercial activity included in global value chains, even if it jeopardises local food security and food sovereignty – a policy which led to disastrous effects following the global food crisis of 2008.[84]

Of relevance here is also the occupation of Iraq by the USA and its allies. While the Iraq mission differed from the 'humanitarian occupations' in the sense that it was conducted by individual states rather than the UN, it nevertheless repeated the pattern of huge transformations conducted in the name of human

[80] ibid 103.

[81] J Klabbers, 'Redemption Song? Human Rights versus Community-Building in East Timor' (2003) 16 *Leiden Journal of International Law* 367.

[82] OP Richmond and J Franks, 'Liberal Peacebuilding in Timor Leste: The Emperor's New Clothes?' (2008) 15 *International Peacekeeping* 185, 197.

[83] Orford, *Reading Humanitarian Intervention*, 135–36.

[84] Tzouvala, 'Food for the Global Market', 23–25.

rights. Again, such transformations were eventually supported by the Security Council in its Resolutions 1483 and 1500. Other Security Council members had initially objected to the US and UK's plans to invade Iraq. Nevertheless, there was not much that the Council could do once the two states decided to take matters into their own hands. Resolutions 1483 and 1500 thus express a kind of *modus vivendi*: it is ambiguous enough to legitimate the occupation and significant transformation of the society in the name of its people's human rights – considered especially in light of the preceding practice of humanitarian occupations – without mandating the occupiers to do so.[85] As Benvenisti writes, the Resolutions refuted the claim that occupation is illegal, reaffirmed the territory and sovereignty of Iraq, recognised the continued applicability of international humanitarian law in occupied territories and confirmed the role of the modern occupier as a heavily informed regulator. Indeed, the Resolutions invoked the law of occupation while at the same time calling the occupiers to assist the Iraqi people in reforming their institutions and promoting economic reconstruction, sustainable development and the protection of human rights.[86]

Like in the UN's humanitarian occupation missions, the reforms conducted by the occupiers of Iraq were massive. The Coalition Provisional Authority (CPA), established to administer Iraq for the duration of the occupation, asserted at the outset that the goals of the interim administration were to introduce wide-ranging reforms in Iraq. All CPA Regulations and Orders spelled out the legal basis for the legislation and routinely invoked the well-being of the Iraqi people.[87] CPA Orders numbers 1 and 2 and the first CPA Regulation on 16 May 2003 sought the de-Ba'athification of Iraqi society. The removal of Ba'ath party members from administration led to a serious power vacuum and instability, as over two million people lost their posts (membership of the party had been a prerequisite for government positions).[88] Iraq's Penal Code was amended several times in the name of international human rights law.[89] A Central Criminal Court was established in the name of the Iraqi population, along with a Special Tribunal in the name of public order and the international rule of law.[90] A Human Rights Ministry was set up and the minimum age of work was changed in the Labour Code in order to protect the health, safety and morals of children.[91]

The most extensive transformations concerned the economy. As Chief Administrator Paul Berner declared at the beginning of the occupation, the CPA sought to transform Iraq from a state-owned to a 'dynamic' private sector

[85] N Bhuta, 'The Antinomies of Transformative Occupation' (2005) 16 *European Journal of International Law* 721, 735–36.

[86] Cohen, *Globalization and Sovereignty*, 224.

[87] Benvenisti (n 63) 257–59.

[88] ibid 259.

[89] ibid 260.

[90] ibid 261.

[91] ibid 260–61.

economy, supported by corresponding legislation.[92] Iraqi private banking was radically changed through a new Bank Law, the transformation of the Central Bank of Iraq and the opening of the banking sector to foreign ownership. Flat tax rates were introduced. 'All tariffs, custom duties, import taxes and licensing fees for goods entering or leaving Iraq were suspended until the end of the occupation.'[93] The new investment law was described as one of the most open in the world. Company formation, ownership and shareholding were opened to foreigners. Bankruptcy laws were changed to encourage risk-taking. Intellectual property laws were aligned with WTO standards. A new stock exchange was established, and media and traffic regulation enacted. When the plan for privatising state-owned enterprises was met with fierce resistance, control over them was switched to ministers, with the plan of gradually fading their separate legal entity and eventually getting rid of them altogether.[94] As Ntina Tzouvala describes, Iraq's farming was reconfigured along neoliberal, corporate lines and absorbed into global value chains, with massive impacts on the local population.[95] The CPA justified these changes by stating that it worked closely with the Governing Council and in cooperation with international financial institutions in order to fulfil its responsibilities towards the Iraqi people, aiming to improve conditions of life.[96] All in all, the CPA transformed Iraq 'from a centralized dictatorship into a market-based democracy' by completely reprogramming the Iraqi legal, political and economic systems.[97]

As was the case with humanitarian occupations, the changes were done in the name of human rights. The link between human rights and transformation is demonstrated clearly in the former US Deputy Assistant Attorney General in the Office of Legal Counsel John Yoo's testimony in a Senate hearing regarding human rights, constitutionalism and rule of law in Iraq – subsequently republished as a journal article.[98] In the testimony, Yoo fiercely defended an expansive reading of the law of occupation, arguing that a broad discretion to reform the occupied state was necessary to ensure the protection of human rights and democracy, as well as the occupier's own security. As Yoo stated:

> Given the barbaric nature of the Hussein regime, the United States must eliminate the institutions of the Hussein government to carry out all of the duties placed upon it by Geneva IV and to protect the basic human rights given to the Iraqi people.[99]

[92] Cited in GH Fox, 'The Occupation of Iraq' (Social Science Research Network, 2004) SSRN Scholarly Paper ID 595163, www.papers.ssrn.com/abstract=595163.
[93] ibid 27.
[94] For more information on all these changes, see ibid 24–32.
[95] Tzouvala (n 13).
[96] Benvenisti (n 63) 262–63.
[97] ibid 268.
[98] J Yoo, 'Iraqi Reconstruction and the Law of Occupation' (2004) 11 *UC Davis Journal of International Law & Policy* 7.
[99] ibid 21.

Hence, 'it almost certainly will be necessary for the United States to change Iraqi law to dismantle current Iraqi government institutions and create new ones to take their place'.[100]

Indeed, many of the actions of the USA in Iraq could quite convincingly be supported by human rights law, although the changes to the economic system and the transition of Iraq to a democracy are rather difficult to justify, considering that they were conducted without consulting the Iraqi people adequately.[101] The legal interpretation of the situation therefore depends mostly on whether one adopts a conservationist or transformative approach to the law of occupation, although the transformative stance entails more or less replacing the law of occupation and humanitarian law with human rights law.[102] As Nehal Bhuta characterises the situation, the occupiers take a gamble in the name of a 'new and better order'. They derive their authority from a promise of a beautiful future and hence seek to relativise the rules which bind them and legitimate their actions ex post facto.[103]

What, then, have been the outcomes of the humanitarian missions and what kind of vision of statehood and international order do they reflect? Humanitarian occupations are commonly presented as simple temporary humanitarian missions, aimed at the protection of human life. Yet, even the brief analysis above shows that they are much more than that. As Anne Orford comments:

> Perhaps the function of administration is simply to protect the life of the inhabitants of the territory through establishing order. And yet we can see from the description of the legal questions that arise in practice that international administrators do far more than this. They detain people, establish systems of judicial administration, redistribute property, set and collect taxes, nationalize industry, run schools, adjudicate disputes, allocate resource contracts, create central banks, provide services and so on. International officials undertake all these tasks while benefiting from an extremely broad regime of immunities and privileges developed to enable the conduct of international public service or diplomatic relations.[104]

As intrusive as these measures are, for many international scholars they are completely justified due to the assumption that they are executed not in the interest of the occupiers but for the enforcement of the values shared by the international community. Indeed, many commentators see international administration as part of the same 'community-based' development of international law and international relations as *erga omnes* obligations, universal

[100] ibid 22.
[101] Benvenisti (n 63) 269–71.
[102] Cohen (n 65) 238; Fox (n 57) 241.
[103] Bhuta, 'The Antinomies of Transformative Occupation', 738.
[104] A Orford, 'Book Review Article: International Territorial Administration and the Management of Decolonization' (2010) 59 *International & Comparative Law Quarterly* 227, 243.

jurisdiction and international crimes.[105] As Carsten Stahn writes, international administration

> is rooted in a cosmopolitan tradition of thought to the extent that it seeks to create conditions for a stable and humane universal order, in which state interests are balanced against certain communitarian interests and fundamental human rights and freedoms.[106]

In fact, for Stahn, international territorial administration is 'a genuine form of international executive authority ... in which international authorities have replaced the state as the main executive agent on the international plane'. Hence, international territorial administration gives, according to Stahn, 'a certain meaning to the concept of a 'shared' conception of responsibility'.[107]

Yet, were we to agree with Stahn and others that international territorial administration enforces community values, the question would arise what exactly these values would be. According to a thorough study conducted by Korhonen, Gras and Creutz, they are liberal ones:

> One of the inherent characteristics in post-conflict governance from the 1990s onwards has been the normative agenda of liberalism pursued by international administrations ... It includes eg the holding of multi-party elections, constitutionalism, the rule of law, the human and minority rights, good governance, and economic liberalization.

What is remarkable about these projects is that 'the question whether this "liberal peacebuilding package" fits the post-conflict target country' is never addressed but the liberal agenda is pursued as if it were neutral and universally accepted. Consequently,

> the success of the international mission is measured in terms of the imported liberal agenda; the holding of the elections, the drafting of a liberal constitution, the establishing of the human rights commissions or the criminal courts to deal with past atrocities etc. No other measure is considered.[108]

What, then, comes across strongest from the humanitarian occupation missions – and international territorial administration in general – is that they have shaped the administered state into the aforementioned liberal model. As Wilde argues, the missions have actually quite rarely simply responded to the consequences of a conflict, as is commonly assumed. In fact, often the governmental vacuum that the territorial administration seeks to patch is created by the territorial administration itself. Thus, the UN does not necessarily seek to

[105] Wilde, *International Territorial Administration*, 262–63.

[106] Stahn, *The Law and Practice of International Territorial Administration*, 751.

[107] ibid 758–59.

[108] O Korhonen, J Gras and K Creutz, *International Post-Conflict Situations: New Challenges for Co-operative Governance* (Helsinki, The Erik Castrén Institute of International Law and Human Rights, 2006) 37–38. See also Stahn (n 61) 752–54; Klabbers, 'Redemption Song?'.

simply remedy a governmental breakdown but has often aimed to 'engineer a fundamental change in government policy'.[109] Instead of acting reactively to bridge existing gaps, international territorial administration operates actively, displacing local actors in order to create different policy changes.[110] In light of the analysis above, the most important such changes include privatisation, the establishment of strong property rights and investment-friendly legislation, the shrinking of the public sector and the inclusion of all local production into global value chains – even at the expense of local interests, such as food security.

The humanitarian occupation missions should not, then, be associated with arguments about the erosion of the state per se, as many cosmopolitans would like to do. By contrast, Fox emphasises that in all cases borders were preserved and populations kept intact – in many cases against the wishes of all parties. Consent from targeted states was achieved through coercion where necessary.[111] Hence, the aim of humanitarian occupation is actually the 'rehabilitation of a state', affirming 'the state's centrality to the international legal order'.[112] Wilde agrees with this conclusion, writing that international territorial administration bolsters 'the norm that the global political space should be divided into Westphalian states'.[113]

What were eroded, however, were state sovereignty and self-determination in the sense of collective planning. The state to be maintained, and created from scratch, if need be, is a very particular one: liberal, (low-intensity) democratic and market based. Moreover, humanitarian occupations were clearly guided by the idea that sovereignty is to be earned by protecting the population. Thus, 'the legal right to self-determination [became] one of the factors to be weighed in deciding how administration might serve international policies in the future, rather than a constraint that binds those who make such decisions in the present'.[114] This may, indeed, have been the largest difference between the humanitarian occupations and previous missions of international territorial administration. Whereas international law has previously respected the state's capacity for self-government, in humanitarian occupations 'international actors have effectively *become* national governments'.[115] Indeed, in all the cases discussed above, international actors 'took on a dizzying array of tasks in governing day to day, from profound matters of policy to mundane custodial functions'.[116]

[109] Wilde (n 61) 12–18.
[110] ibid 233.
[111] Fox (n 57) 73.
[112] ibid 7.
[113] R Paris, *At War's End: Building Peace after Civil Conflict* (Cambridge, Cambridge University Press, 2004) 655; Wilde (n 61) 256.
[114] Orford, 'Book Review Article', 234.
[115] Fox (n 57) 2 (original emphasis).
[116] ibid 72–73.

All in all, then, humanitarian occupations redistributed authority on a global scale, withdrawing it from states deemed unworthy and assigning it to 'the international community' – meaning different UN organs, global governance institutions and some powerful states acting for the 'common good'. Indeed, the 'exercise of legislative, executive and judicial functions by international administrators within the framework of governance missions comes very close to replicating the traditional power structures between a state and its people in practice',[117] with international governing institutions having assumed direct responsibility for law and order. However, as Orford writes, these institutions have exercised these powers 'without a developed account of their political (as opposed to technical or humanitarian) practice, and without any international legal categories adequate to the tasks upon which they are engaged', with the consequence that the 'international order becomes comprehensible as a system in which "functions" are vested in this or that social group or actor, in the way that a manager might vest a task in this or that organizational department'. In this order, status and the rights of sovereigns have been replaced with 'the welfare of populations'.[118]

III. WAR ON TERRORISM

Although the occupation of Iraq did not quite meet the definition of a humanitarian occupation, it could perhaps be seen as a kind of swansong of the practice. Indeed, by the early 2000s, the prevailing political climate had already made such large-scale UN operations practically impossible. Rather, following 9/11, the focus of international cooperation shifted to the war on terrorism that each state could fight against its internal enemies.

It might be tempting to characterise the war on terrorism as a kind of backlash against the ideas of the law of humanity project. After all, the immediate notion that comes to mind when hearing the phrase 'war on terrorism' is how little international law and human rights meant for the USA and its allies as soon as they got in their way.[119] From covert operations and extraordinary renditions to the abuse of captives in Guantanamo and elsewhere, there is no doubt that the war on terrorism undid many victories won within international law and human rights law during the past decades. Indeed, according to many commentators, human rights had become one of the first casualties of the war on terrorism,[120] as states quickly moved to 'take back' some of the human rights commitments

[117] Stahn (n 61) 518.

[118] Orford (n 104) 243.

[119] KL Scheppele, 'Empire of Security and the Security of Empire' (2013) 27 *Temple International & Comparative Law Journal* 241, 245.

[120] R Foot, 'The United Nations, Counter Terrorism, and Human Rights: Institutional Adaptation and Embedded Ideas' (2007) 29 *Human Rights Quarterly* 489, 490.

they had made before the attacks and strike a new balance between human rights and security.[121]

Yet, humanity language actually played an important strategic role in both resisting and enabling measures against terrorism. On the side of resistance, the concepts of human rights, human security and human dignity were used to raise moral and legal outrage against the measures of the USA and its allies. The High Commissioner, Special Rapporteurs, treaty bodies, NGOs and academics all criticised the counter-terrorist measures not only for being blatantly in violation of human rights norms, but also for eroding trust in the human rights system in general.[122] Most of these human rights concerns were compiled together by Martin Scheinin, the UN Special Rapporteur on the Promotion and Protection of Human Rights and Fundamental Freedoms while Countering Terrorism.[123] The Special Rapporteur raised concern about the fact that Security Council Resolution 1373 (2001) 'made only one passing reference to human rights, in a very specific context', and did not grant the newly established Counter-Terrorism Committee (CTC) a proper mandate to monitor how states abided by human rights norms in implementing their anti-terror obligations.[124] Although this problem was corrected at least to some extent later on, the actions of the CTC left many states with the impression that it advocated for 'promoting measures of counter-terrorism irrespective of their adverse consequences for human rights'.[125]

The relentless work of the human rights actors and activists eventually paid off, however – to a degree. Although human rights violations continued and the CTC remained 'insensitive to a number of potentially affected rights and risks',[126] powerful states, acting through UN organs, were forced to give at least a surface-level impression that they wished to respect human rights norms. In the interpretation of the Special Rapporteur, Security Council Resolution 1624 (2005) finally conferred 'a human rights mandate upon the Counter-Terrorism Committee in the implementation of the resolution', following a more human rights-friendly approach to counter-terrorism activities, already reflected in Resolutions 1456 (2003) and 1535 (2004), which prescribed 'that States must ensure that any measure taken to combat terrorism comply with all their

[121] M Scheinin, 'Law and Security: Facing the Dilemmas', EUI Working Paper 58 (2009), http://cadmus.eui.eu//handle/1814/12233.

[122] J Fitzpatrick, 'Speaking Law to Power: The War against Terrorism and Human Rights' (2003) 14 *European Journal of International Law* 241, 245–46.

[123] See also ibid.

[124] ECOSOC, 'Report of the Special Rapporteur on the Promotion and Protection of Human Rights and Fundamental Freedoms While Countering Terrorism, Martin Scheinin' (2005) 62nd session, UN Doc E/CN.4/2006/98, para 53.

[125] ibid para 63.

[126] UNGA, 'Report of the Special Rapporteur on the Promotion and Protection of Human Rights and Fundamental Freedoms While Countering Terrorism, Martin Scheinin' (2010) 65th session, UN Doc A/65/258, para 44.

obligations under international law, and should adopt such measures in accordance with international law, in particular international human rights, refugee and humanitarian law'.[127] Moreover, this trend continued, according to the Special Rapporteur, in Security Council Resolution 1822 (2008) and General Assembly Resolution 62/272, which seemed to indirectly recognise that all UN action against terrorism 'must fully comply with international law, including human rights law, refugee law and international humanitarian law'.[128]

The humanity language was not used only to resist the war on terrorism, however; it was used to support it as well. This occurred in at least two ways. First, states supported their counter-terrorism measures on the basis of their own citizens' rights to life and security, arguing – quite plausibly, from a human rights law perspective – that effective counter-terrorist measures are necessary for the protection of these rights and are hence demanded by the states' most central human rights obligations.[129] Hence, although the human rights language indeed made a quick comeback after its initial rejection in the war on terrorism, this was not just because of the fierce resistance by the human rights movement. It was also useful for international actors to at least give the impression that they care about human rights,[130] in order to convince troubled states to sustain their counter-terrorism efforts and make cooperation easier at both the international and domestic levels.[131]

Second, the war on terrorism connected to an already ongoing trend of humanity language being used to make the Security Council a more efficient tool for the USA and its allies. Although it is true that whatever actual power the Security Council has, that power derives almost exclusively from that of its five permanent members, the Council nevertheless plays a role in legitimising and providing authority for the measures of those same powers.[132] Indeed, in acting partly through the Security Council in its counter-terrorism activities, the USA 'was able to issue directives to all Member States of the United Nations with binding legal force'.[133] This was enabled by an already-existing trend to use humanity language to create

> a subtle shift in the understanding of the position of the Security Council – from a political executive body established by a treaty to enforce peace and provide collective security in a crisis, to the executive organ of the international community, enforcing its global constitutional law.[134]

[127] ibid para 40.
[128] ibid para 41.
[129] P Hoffman, 'Human Rights and Terrorism' (2004) 26 *Human Rights Quarterly* 932, 949.
[130] Foot, 'The United Nations, Counter Terrorism, and Human Rights', 511–12.
[131] Hoffman, 'Human Rights and Terrorism', 935–36.
[132] M Koskenniemi, 'The Police in the Temple Order, Justice and the UN: A Dialectical View' (1995) 6 *European Journal of International Law* 325, 327–28.
[133] Scheppele, 'Empire of Security and the Security of Empire', 246.
[134] Cohen (n 65) 270.

According to Jean Cohen, this shift was justified through a dynamic constitutional method of interpretation based on three key interpretative moves: the emphasis on human over state security; the reconceptualisation of human rights in terms of security; and the redefinition of sovereignty as a function – the responsibility to protect – so as to 'disaggregate' it. The consequence of these moves was that the distinction between the protection of human rights as the main rule and security as an exception could be blurred, giving birth to an enforcement model with a new focus on global law and community values, rather than international peace strictly understood.[135]

The novel possibilities created by this reshaping of the function of the Security Council were put to use by the USA and its allies during the war on terrorism. When the Security Council adopted Resolution 1373 in the wake of 9/11, it departed radically from its previous practice and language. The Resolution included 'far-reaching, general obligations for states to prevent and combat terrorism', including orders to take actions to prevent support and financing of terrorism, for example by freezing funds of any possible suspects, to strengthen border security and surveillance of migrants and refugees, and even to become parties to UN anti-terrorism conventions and criminalise terrorism in domestic laws.[136] Instead of *forbidding* a state from doing something, as it normally tends to do, the Security Council now directed all states *to act* and do something very specific and far-reaching (change their domestic laws) in order to 'create a world-spanning net of legal interdiction'.[137] In so doing, the Security Council created a body of legal norms that a state was automatically bound by: it started to legislate.[138] Hence, at the same time as the USA was sidestepping international law left and right, it also promoted new legislation to support its project, creating what some have called 'global security law'.[139]

It therefore would not be quite correct to view the war on terrorism as a backlash against the law of humanity language. Rather, it is better seen as its obscene underside. Humanity language has played an important role in the campaign, but many of its results are likely to give the theoretical proponents of the law of humanity project a pause. For one, terrorists came to be treated as 'enemies of mankind' and excluded from the sphere of law, not unlike Agamben's *homo sacer*.[140] Whilst it is true that law was present in places like Guantanamo in the sense that they were extremely regulated areas,[141] it is equally the case that the

[135] ibid 270–72.
[136] ibid 272–74.
[137] Scheppele (n 119) 252–54.
[138] PC Szasz, 'The Security Council Starts Legislating' (2002) 96 *American Journal of International Law* 901. See also JE Alvarez, 'Hegemonic International Law Revisited' (2003) 97 *American Journal of International Law* 873; Scheppele (n 119) 259.
[139] Scheppele (n 119) 246.
[140] G Agamben, *Homo Sacer: Sovereign Power and Bare Life* (Stanford, Stanford University Press, 1998).
[141] F Johns, 'Guantánamo Bay and the Annihilation of the Exception' (2005) 16 *European Journal of International Law* 613.

USA and its allies sought to exclude captured terrorists from the protection of law by playing with the meaning of legal concepts such as 'prisoner of war' and 'extraterritorial jurisdiction'.[142] Furthermore, like the *homo sacer*, the terrorists, too, helped in the creation of a community and in its boundary-making. In truly Schmittian spirit, the creation of an enemy, an 'other', helped to create an 'us' – in this case, the 'international community'.

Second, the war on terrorism helped develop an efficient international legal technique for disciplining individuals, namely the terrorist sanction regime. The foundation for this regime had been created back in 1999 by Security Council Resolution 1267, which addressed Taliban support for terrorists. Building on this basis, a set of Resolutions created a complex, smart sanction regime which poses a grave danger to basic due process and property rights of individuals. Those placed on the UN's terrorist list are to have their assets frozen and their movement restricted. Persons can be put on the list and targeted with sanctions without being told the reasons and evidence for the listing, or being able to show that it is unjustified.[143] All in all, the terrorist sanction regime constitutes an odd modification of the individualisation and humanisation of international law. It certainly draws attention from states to individuals, but it does so by disciplining rather than empowering individuals, by threatening their human rights.

Finally, when discussing the outcomes of the war on terrorism from a law of humanity perspective, it is also worth mentioning the way in which it diverted attention and resources from other human rights considerations. As the Chair of the International Executive Committee of Amnesty International, Paul Hoffman, commented during the early years of the war on terrorism:

> Without denying the legitimacy of responding to threats of terrorist attacks, a central problem with the 'war on terrorism' is that it ignores other equally or more pressing challenges to human security. For hundreds of millions of people in the world today, the most important source of insecurity is not a terrorist threat but grinding, extreme poverty.[144]

True security depends on all of the world's peoples having a stake in the international system and receiving the basic rights promised by the Universal Declaration of Human Rights, regardless of race, gender, religion or any other status. The 'war on terrorism' undermines that prospect by ignoring all other causes of human insecurity, while undermining human rights norms that offer a promise of human security for all human beings. The challenge of terrorism is

[142] For a legal analysis, see M Mofidi and AE Eckert, 'Unlawful Combatants or Prisoners of War: The Law and Politics of Labels' (2003) 36 *Cornell International Law Journal* 59; M Milanovic, *Extraterritorial Application of Human Rights Treaties: Law, Principles, and Policy* (Oxford, Oxford University Press, 2011).

[143] Cohen (n 65) 272–74; EJ Criddle and E Fox-Decent, *Fiduciaries of Humanity: How International Law Constitutes Authority* (Oxford, Oxford University Press, 2016) 314–15.

[144] Hoffman (n 129) 953.

real and cannot be ignored; however, it must not blind states to the other challenges that are just as pressing as the fight against terrorism.[145]

To move to the second key theme of this chapter, namely, international authority and the state, the use of humanity language in the war on terrorism enabled a significant shift of authority to the 'international community', represented in this case by certain UN organs, and a shift of power to the USA, which was de facto acting through those organs. Kim Lane Scheppele has convincingly described the war on terrorism as a disciplinary operation in which national governments around the world were convinced to shape their domestic legislation more in line with the model given by the USA. Some states were convinced to do so by disguising the war on terrorism as a UN mission operated by the international community in the name of humanity, whereas others were convinced by the fiction that all states retained their sovereign law-making powers as they would still set their own domestic counter-terrorism laws and define terrorism themselves.[146] Moreover, many national governments were given the possibility to 'rearrange their own domestic political architecture in ways that benefited national executives by strengthening their powers relative to others in their domestic sphere'.[147]

The outcome, however, was always the same: the strategies 'produced a concerted, coordinated anti-terrorism campaign that has united most countries in the world in a common template of action'.[148] Although they were granted a certain margin of discretion, states were swiftly convinced to develop domestic policies which were remarkably similar, allowing 'the core' – most importantly, the USA – to control what went on in 'the periphery', thus disciplining 'populations both in the center and [at] the periphery while appearing to shape only the latter'.[149] As Scheppele writes, 'the new global security law operates primarily by permitting strong states to shape the content of the internal legal systems of weak states, which facilitates the peripheral regimes doing the jobs they have been delegated'.[150]

IV. RESPONSIBILITY TO PROTECT

Although world politics changed drastically in the era of the war on terrorism and it is unlikely that we will witness more humanitarian occupation missions, at least in the near future, many of the key ideas of the missions nevertheless did not die, but live on in different guises. The most notable of these is

[145] ibid 954.

[146] Scheppele (n 119) 248–49. See also M Koskenniemi, 'International Law and Hegemony: A Reconfiguration' (2004) 17 *Cambridge Review of International Affairs* 197, 200.

[147] Scheppele (n 119) 247.

[148] ibid 249.

[149] ibid 251.

[150] ibid 277.

the responsibility to protect (R2P) concept, which incorporates the idea that if states cannot protect their populations, the international community must intervene and rebuild and reform if necessary.[151]

The R2P concept was introduced to the world in the Report of the International Commission on Intervention and State Sovereignty (ICISS).[152] The Report was based on a radical rethinking of state sovereignty, but drew from already ongoing trends reflected, for example, in the humanitarian occupation missions. Although duly recognising the importance of state sovereignty as 'a cornerstone of the UN Charter' and the 'best line of defence' against inequalities of power and resources, the ICISS emphasised that international law and politics had changed in important respects as a consequence of the breakthrough of human rights and human security.[153] Most importantly, the notions of people's and individual sovereignty had risen to both contest and complement state sovereignty. And although the ICISS seemed very hesitant to rank these notions of sovereignty in any way, arguing that the 'more traditional notion of state sovereignty should be able comfortably to embrace the goal of greater self-empowerment and freedom for people',[154] the ICISS Report as a whole gives a clear message that in a situation of conflict, individual sovereignty prevails. In the words of Alex Bellamy, whereas the traditional conception of sovereignty was based on self-determination – that is, the idea 'that people might choose to live and be governed in many different ways and outsiders have no right to impose their particular way of life on others'[155] – the R2P concept 'rests on the proposition that individuals have *inalienable* human rights that may never be rescinded'.[156]

This shift of attention from state sovereignty to the sovereignty of individuals was connected to another reconceptualisation – equally relevant from the law of humanity perspective – namely, the conception of state sovereignty not as control, but as responsibility to respect and protect human dignity and human rights.[157] The idea of sovereignty as responsibility is not entirely novel, of course. According to Luke Glanville, 'sovereign authority has been understood to involve varied and evolving responsibilities since it was first articulated in the sixteenth and seventeenth centuries'.[158] Hobbes emphasised that the legitimate sovereign is she who brings the safety of people and that no one can be forced

[151] Wilde (n 61) 264. See also JE Nijman, *The Concept of International Legal Personality: An Inquiry into the History and Theory of International Law* (The Hague, Asser Press, 2004) 471–72.

[152] ICISS, *The Responsibility to Protect: The Report of the International Commission on Intervention and State Sovereignty*, pap/cdr edn (Ottawa, IDRC Books, 2002) para 1.32.

[153] ibid paras 125–28.

[154] ibid para 2.31.

[155] AJ Bellamy, *Responsibility to Protect* (Cambridge, Polity, 2009) 15.

[156] ibid 19–20 (original emphasis).

[157] ICISS, *The Responsibility to Protect*, para 2.14.

[158] L Glanville, *Sovereignty and the Responsibility to Protect: A New History* (Chicago, University of Chicago Press, 2013) 5.

to obey a sovereign that does not protect her life; de Vattel held that only those nations that fulfilled their responsibilities deserved the respect of other nations; and later Schmitt argued that the obedience of the citizens 'is only the correlate of the true protection that [the state] guarantees'[159] – although for Schmitt the state emerged out of a legal vacuum and most of all united the people to fight external enemies.[160] Closest to its ICISS form, the notion of sovereignty as responsibility was used by Francis Deng and his colleagues in their work on international displaced people as well as conflict management in Africa.[161] Yet, as Jennifer Welsh notes, R2P does seem to take things one step further than these previous conceptions of sovereignty by holding that 'the process by which individuals consent to the power of the state, in order to secure their rights, also makes the state's external rights (such as non-intervention) contingent upon its internal justice and constitution'.[162] This is reflected in the central notion of R2P that, when the state manifestly fails to protect its population, it is the responsibility of the international community to step in.

This conception of sovereignty as responsibility further means that state sovereignty is no longer a de jure matter but a de facto one. Although legal rights do still matter, sovereignty is most fundamentally premised on the capacity to protect life effectively – an instrumental rather than intrinsic value.[163] And this effective protection, or failure of it, is 'a factual matter that can be determined by the international community'.[164] Hence, state sovereignty is no longer a binary matter that either exists or does not exist, but a matter of spectrum: a state can be sovereign to a greater or lesser extent, depending on how effective it is in protecting life. In other words, R2P enabled the 'unbundling' of sovereignty that authors such as Robert Keohane had campaigned for. As Keohane argues, this 'unbundling' means that sovereignty should be given a different meaning and weight depending on the state and the context, in particular taking into account that the 'unitary conception of sovereignty is inimical both to human rights and to political stability'.[165] The result is that sovereignty is not something absolute

[159] C Schmitt, *Leviathan in the State Theory of Thomas Hobbes: Meaning and Failure of a Political Symbol* (Westport, CT, Greenwood Press, 1996) 96.

[160] A Orford, *International Authority and the Responsibility to Protect* (Cambridge, Cambridge University Press, 2011) 127.

[161] FM Deng (ed) et al, *Sovereignty as Responsibility: Conflict Management in Africa* (Washington, Brookings Institution Press, 1996).

[162] JM Welsh, 'Norm Contestation and the Responsibility to Protect' (2013) 5 *Global Responsibility to Protect* 365, 391.

[163] N Shawki, 'Responsibility to Protect: The Evolution of an International Norm' (2011) 3 *Global Responsibility to Protect* 172, 173.

[164] Orford, *International Authority and the Responsibility to Protect*, 16.

[165] RO Keohane, 'Political Authority after Intervention: Gradations in Sovereignty' in JL Holzgrefe and RO Keohane (eds), *Humanitarian Intervention: Ethical, Legal and Political Dilemmas* (Cambridge, Cambridge University Press, 2003) 278. See also SD Krasner, *Sovereignty: Organized Hypocrisy* (Princeton, Princeton University Press, 1999); S Tutuianu, *Towards Global Justice: Sovereignty in an Interdependent World* (The Hague, Asser Press, 2012).

and negative, arising out of nothingness, but a bundle of prerogatives, contingent on the state's fulfilment of its functions – functions that can, crucially, be performed by others as well, if need be.[166]

The R2P concept has been subject to radical transformations since the publishing of the ICISS Report, but many of its key innovations with regard to state sovereignty have remained and become mainstreamed. The concept had a very slow start, partly due to rather mundane reasons of world politics, but most importantly because the 9/11 terrorist attacks occurred almost at the same time as the ICISS Report was published. Yet, it was the war on terrorism that helped the human security language make its final breakthrough in international politics a few year later. Indeed, states and other international actors not only soon found the framework useful for tackling novel security threats, but also began to legitimate their anti-terrorism actions with the language. The EU played a big part in this, as it saw R2P as a tool to boost its image, secure Europe against terrorism and gain a more prominent role in global security politics in a new strategic situation.[167] In this climate, the African Union also adopted R2P-like principles,[168] and even the USA found it strategically wise to change its previously cold attitude towards human security and R2P.[169] And most importantly, with the 2005 World Summit approaching, Canada started to tirelessly promote R2P on every possible platform.[170]

The attempts to mainstream human security and responsibility to protect, heavily supported also by the UN Secretary General Kofi Annan,[171] eventually paid off. More than 150 heads of state endorsed the concept by consensus at the 2005 World Summit. This endorsement came with important changes to the concept, however, which rendered it quite different from the radical formulation of the ICISS Report. Indeed, the Summit version of R2P has subsequently been characterised by commentators as 'R2P lite'. While paragraphs 138 and 139 of the World Summit Outcome 'provided the foundation for a new international norm premised on two basic principles: state responsibility and non-indifference', they also redefined R2P by limiting its scope – in stark contrast to the broad definition of the ICISS Report – to the four core crimes of genocide, war crimes, crimes against humanity and ethnic cleansing.[172] Nevertheless, the R2P

[166] Cohen (n 65) 175.

[167] M Kaldor et al, *A Human Security Doctrine for Europe: The Barcelona Report of the Study Group on Europe's Security Capabilities* (Study Group on Europe's Security Capabilities, 2004); S Tadjbakhsh and A Chenoy, *Human Security: Concepts and Implications* (London, Routledge, 2007) 205.

[168] Bellamy, *Responsibility to Protect*, 77–81. See also Glanville, *Sovereignty and the Responsibility to Protect*, 195.

[169] Bellamy (n 155) 81–82.

[170] ibid 71–75.

[171] UNGA, 'Report of the Secretary-General: In Larger Freedom: Towards Development, Security and Human Rights for All' (2005) 59th session, UN Doc A/59/2005.

[172] M Serrano, 'The Responsibility to Protect and Its Critics: Explaining the Consensus' (2011) 3 *Global Responsibility to Protect* 425, 427–29. See also G Marlier and NC Crawford, 'Incomplete and

agenda of the Summit Outcome was not as 'lite' as it might seem at first hand. As Bellamy writes approvingly, the 'admission of responsibility that governments made to their own citizens' opened the door to a wide range of R2P-related measures 'designed to encourage and assist governments in meeting their – now formally acknowledged – responsibilities to their citizens'.[173]

Following the World Summit, R2P was quickly mainstreamed across UN activities, as reflected, for example, in the Summit's follow-up document, 'Implementing the Responsibility to Protect'.[174] This mainstreaming was accompanied by further changes to the concept. Focus was shifted even further away from military intervention and towards more indirect forms of intervention, based on cooperative measures which are supposed to assist and encourage states in fulfilling their responsibility to protect their populations.[175]

The military aspect of R2P made a short comeback in 2011, when the Security Council appealed to the concept in authorising use of force against a non-consenting, functioning member of the UN in its Resolution 1973 on Libya.[176] Yet, Libya – at first hailed as a final breakthrough of R2P – could have finally 'killed' the concept, as it gave further material for Russia, China and many states of the Global South to argue that the concept was nothing other than a rebranding of the notion of humanitarian intervention.[177] Indeed, in late 2012, when the General Assembly finally agreed on a common understanding of human security,[178] consensus was reached only by dissociating human security explicitly from R2P, and by emphasising that human security does not entail coercive actions and must be implemented with full respect of the UN Charter, including territorial integrity and the principle of non-interference.[179] Hence, if the R2P concept is to continue to play a role in world politics, it will likely be in a radically altered form – such as the 'responsibility while protecting' concept, promoted by Brazil, for example.[180]

Imperfect Institutionalisation of Empathy and Altruism in the "Responsibility to Protect" Doctrine' (2013) 5 *Global Responsibility to Protect* 397, 406.

173 Bellamy (n 155) 196.

174 AJ Bellamy, 'Mainstreaming the Responsibility to Protect in the United Nations System: Dilemmas, Challenges and Opportunities' (2013) 5 *Global Responsibility to Protect* 154, 154. See UNGA, 'Implementing the Responsibility to Protect: Report of the Secretary-General' (2009) B Ki-moon, A/63/677, para 68. See also generally M Lehto, 'Slowly but Surely? The Challenge of the Responsibility to Protect' in R Liivoja and J Petman (eds), *International Law-Making: Essays in Honour of Jan Klabbers* (London, Routledge, 2013) 291.

175 Glanville (n 158) 201–02.

176 For all UNSC Resolutions informed by R2P, visit www.globalr2p.org/resources/335.

177 S Hopgood, 'The Last Rites for Humanitarian Intervention' (2014) 6 *Global Responsibility to Protect* 181, 184–90.

178 UNGA, 'Follow-up to Paragraph 143 on Human Security of the 2005 World Summit Outcome' (2012) 66th session, UN Doc A/Res/66/290, Supp 14, 117, para 3.

179 ibid.

180 M Tourinho, O Stuenkel and S Brockmeier, '"Responsibility While Protecting": Reforming R2P Implementation' (2016) 30 *Global Society* 134.

There have therefore been several backlashes against direct humanitarian interventions since the times of the humanitarian occupation missions and the publishing of the ICISS Report. Nevertheless, the main trends regarding state building have remained more or less intact. In fact, one could argue that some of these particular trends have even strengthened as a result of the metamorphosis of the R2P concept. As mentioned, since the publishing of the 2009 'Implementing the Responsibility to Protect' report, there has been a strong emphasis on indirect forms of intervention, based on cooperative measures which are supposed to assist and encourage states in fulfilling their responsibility to protect their populations.[181] In other words, R2P now focuses less on the rights and obligations of intervening states and more on building the capacity of fragile states.

Overall, then, the current trends in the human security and responsibility to protect seem to support the project of redefining state sovereignty and shaping state institutions while protecting their territorial integrity. State borders are as sacred as ever, but there are new 'demands and expectations in relation to the way states treat their own people'.[182] States have to be willing to fight 'the omnipresent enemies of good health and other real threats to human security on a daily basis'[183] in order to protect their population 'from [the] chronic insecurities of hunger, disease, inadequate shelter, crime, unemployment, social confiict and environmental hazard'.[184] Indeed, the main problem of human security and R2P is now 'the weak institutional capacity of some sovereign states' rather than 'the legal barrier of sovereignty itself'. Hence, instead of direct humanitarian interventions, R2P is now focused on 'more indirect forms of intervention associated with international statebuilding', fulfilled through administrative measures that are supposed to tackle issues 'from development to conflict prevention'.[185]

Yet, the vision of the state being built has been a very specific one. As David Chandler writes, the 2009 'Implementing the Responsibility to Protect' report asks the question of 'why one society plunges into mass violence while its neighbours remain relatively stable' and provides an answer by putting forward 'the neoliberal rational choice perspective, which argues that the institutional framework of the state is the key to paths of development or conflict'.[186] At the centre of this framework is the establishment of the rule of law, which is seen as essential to keeping trade routes, global value chains and markets undisturbed, while ensuring foreign investment. In the words of Bellamy,

[181] Glanville (n 158) 201–02.
[182] ICISS (n 152) para 1.33.
[183] ibid para 2.22.
[184] ibid para 2.23.
[185] D Chandler, 'Understanding the Gap between the Promise and Reality of the Responsibility to Protect' in P Cunliffe (ed), *Critical Perspectives on the Responsibility to Protect: Interrogating Theory and Practice*, reprint edn (London, Routledge, 2012) 26–27.
[186] ibid 28.

> there is a broad neo-liberal consensus among the key agencies involved in post-conflict reconstruction (especially the World Bank) which holds that the key to long-term peace lies in rapid processes of democratisation and market liberalisation designed to attract foreign investment and foster economic growth.[187]

These institutional structures are to be built and maintained through indirect international preventive interventions which are coordinated by experts, thus 'reducing social, economic and political problems to technical and administrative questions of institutional governance'. As the underlying assumption goes, 'the more the institutions of the "failing" or the "post-conflict" state are engaged with by international actors, the more secure their sovereignty and their capacity to take up "responsibilities" will be'.[188]

V. HUMANITARIAN GOVERNANCE OF REFUGEES

It could be argued that humanity discourse has been on the decline, or at least has played a less significant role in global governance since the populist backlash. Yet, a field where the humanity discourse still plays a key role – and for good reasons – is the humanitarian governance of refugees.[189]

The world of refugee governance is 'a globalized apparatus: a set of organizations, networks, agents, and financial means distributed across different countries and crisscrossing the world'.[190] There is thus no simple, hierarchical structure in refugee governance, although the UNHCR does play a leading role, outsourcing its operations to numerous NGOs. Over the years, the UNHCR has developed from a refugee organisation into a humanitarian agency which undertakes a wide array of tasks, now including the encampment of internally displaced persons.[191] Another important – albeit different – role is played by the International Organization of Migration (IOM), which has recently been included in the UN family. Operating on behalf of its 172 member states and primarily focused on 'promoting humane and orderly migration for the benefit of all',[192] the IOM has traditionally focused on controlling migration flows, but has recently started to play an increasingly important role in humanitarian governance by managing the camps of internally displaced people in

[187] Bellamy (n 155) 168.

[188] Chandler, 'Understanding the Gap', 29.

[189] On the concept of humanitarian governance, see MN Barnett, 'Humanitarian Governance' (2013) 16 *Annual Review of Political Science* 379, 279.

[190] M Agier, 'Humanity as an Identity and Its Political Effects (A Note on Camps and Humanitarian Government)' (2010) 1 *Humanity: An International Journal of Human Rights, Humanitarianism, and Development* 29, 32.

[191] D Stevens, 'Rights, Needs or Assistance? The Role of the UNHCR in Refugee Protection in the Middle East' (2016) 20 *International Journal of Human Rights* 264, 267.

[192] See the IOM website at www.iom.int/about-iom.

post-crisis situations.[193] Both the UNHCR and the IOM have quite free hands to deal with refugees because not only do states tend to bow to their expertise, but most states are also more than willing to let the organisations deal with issues the states themselves are uncomfortable to address openly.[194]

From a law of humanity perspective, the humanitarian governance of refugees is a conflictual field, divided between humanitarianism and state security, sovereignty as freedom and sovereignty as responsibility.[195] Although the field is permeated with humanity language, it is also possible to view refugee governance from the law of humanity perspective as one of the last bastions where selfish sovereignty still rules. For example, the Syrian refugee case can be seen to highlight the systematic failures in distributing the cost of refuge protection equitably across states.[196] If ever there were a reason to invoke the responsibility to protect concept, one could argue, it would be in the context of the current refugee crisis (even though this might not fit R2P conceptually). But the international community has not been willing to share the burden,[197] which suggests to some commentators a point of collapse in the law of humanity mindset.[198]

In a way, then, refugee protection seems to be a key site of struggle for the law of humanity project. As two law of humanity-minded commentators write,

> the identities and values shared by the world community, among which are international obligations assumed by the States of protecting the juridical reflections of human dignity, ie human rights ... only become effective if one considers the protagonism of the persons (ie the migrants), not of the State, in the migratory process.[199]

This, they argue, entails adopting a human rights-based approach to migration and the humanisation of refugee law. Echoing again the main tenets of the law of humanity project, they advocate for interpretation and soft law as the best tools for this humanisation process.[200]

The complex and conflictual relationship between refugee protection and the ideals of the law of humanity project is also reflected in the work of the most important actors in the field. After a long period of ambivalence towards

[193] J Klabbers, 'Notes on the Ideology of International Organizations Law: The International Organization for Migration, State-Making, and the Market for Migration' (2019) 32 *Leiden Journal of International Law* 383.

[194] M Pallis, 'The Operation of UNHCR's Accountability Mechanisms' (2004) 37 *New York University Journal of International Law and Politics* 869, 910–11; Klabbers, 'Notes on the Ideology of International Organizations Law'.

[195] T Gammeltoft-Hansen, *Access to Asylum: International Refugee Law and the Globalisation of Migration Control*, reprint edn (Cambridge, Cambridge University Press, 2013) 13.

[196] ET Achiume, 'Syria, Cost-Sharing, and the Responsibility to Protect Refugees' (2015) 100 *Minnesota Law Review* 687, 703–04.

[197] ibid.

[198] ibid 707.

[199] L Lyra Jubilut and R de Oliveira Lopes, 'Strategies for the Protection of Migrants through International Law' (2017) 5 *Groningen Journal of International Law* 34, 45.

[200] ibid 50–51.

human rights, the UNHCR started referring to itself as a human rights organisation from the early 1990s onwards.[201] Now the UNHCR's documentation is filled with references to a 'rights-based approach'. Pinning down what exactly is meant by that expression is not easy, however.[202] As one commentator notes, the human rights approach often means little in the field except for functioning as 'a reminder that the delivery of assistance by norm entrepreneurs should have the individual at its centre, that is, his or her human dignity should be paramount'.[203] Refugees and internally displaced persons are rarely encouraged to see themselves as rights holders or to see the UNHCR as an accountable duty bearer, even if basic needs are now increasingly framed as rights.[204] Instead, persons in need are commonly seen as recipients of aid and charity.[205] Moreover, some commentators have warned that rights talk might even be harmful to refugees if it startles states which are already struggling to take care of the basic welfare of their populations.[206]

The complex relation between humanity ideas and refugee protection is further visible in the increasing reliance on indicators as a tool of refugee governance.[207] The UNHCR produces and consumes indicators to map refugee conditions on a country level.[208] The shift to indicators is on a continuum with the more general 1990s shift to managerialist and outcomes-driven results-based approaches which are premised on the assumption that impacts can be measured and results evaluated objectively.[209] Indicators are used for internal programming and restricted summaries are compiled and published in reports aimed at donors and stakeholders.[210] Indicators and other results-based management strategies are also seen as a way of promoting a rights-based approach to migration by increasing participation and empowering 'beneficiaries'. Yet, as critics note, it is far from clear how beneficiaries actually take part in the process and whether indicators truly increase accountability.[211]

When it comes to the IOM, its constitution does not mention a rights-based protection mandate, and the organisation has been criticised for its lack of respect for human rights. Nonetheless, many of the functions of the IOM are humanitarian and its reports tend to make use of human rights language.[212]

[201] KB Sandvik, 'A Legal History: The Emergence of the African Resettlement Candidate in International Refugee Management' (2010) 22 *International Journal of Refugee Law* 20, 44.
[202] Stevens, 'Rights, Needs or Assistance?', 272.
[203] ibid 277.
[204] ibid.
[205] Pallis, 'The Operation of UNHCR's Accountability Mechanisms', 909.
[206] Stevens (n 191) 277–78.
[207] For more on indicators, see sections 7.4.1 and 8.3.1 of this thesis.
[208] E Dunlop, 'Indications of Progress? Assessing the Use of Indicators in UNHCR Operations', UNHCR Research Paper No 214 (2011) 8.
[209] ibid 9.
[210] ibid 12–13.
[211] ibid 26. See also KL Jacobsen and KB Sandvik, 'UNHCR and the Pursuit of International Protection: Accountability through Technology?' (2018) 39 *Third World Quarterly* 1508.
[212] Klabbers (n 193) 394, 398.

Furthermore, the IOM has gradually expanded its role in the coordination of camps for internally displaced people and in crisis management after natural disasters,[213] participating in agenda setting in the context of the 2016 World Humanitarian Summit and the 2016 UN Summit for Refugees and Migrants, for example.[214] It is therefore unquestionable that the IOM is solidifying its role as a major player in the humanitarian field, even if critics argue that the IOM's increasing use of humanity language is primarily an attempt to legitimise and enable its operation in various 'geographically ambiguous' and transnational zones.[215]

Finally, and in glaring contrast to many of its activities, humanity discourse is surprisingly prominent also in the operation of Frontex, the agency in charge of policing the external borders of the European Union.[216] As Aas and Gundhus describe, 'human rights and humanitarian ideals feature prominently in the agency's internal discourse, its training standards and [] its self-presentation'.[217] Indeed, even the security goals of the agency are 'carefully intertwined with the language of human security and the saving of lives'.[218] Furthermore, interviews conducted by the same authors reveal that Frontex officials consider the humane treatment of migrants an important part of their professional identity, although they rarely talk about rights, viewing refugees and migrants more as an object of their help.[219] At the same time, however, the activities of Frontex seem to be characterised by a certain 'lack of "will to knowledge" about migrant mortality' and other unpleasant facts related to attempts to cross Europe's external borders.[220] Indeed, migrant deaths are not systematically counted, nor is there systematic evaluation of the consequences of Frontex operations and diversion practices for migrant security and the right to life. As such, there is, according to Aas and Gundhus, a striking discrepancy 'between the discursive attention paid to human rights and humanitarian ideals and the practical focus on minimizing risk as defined by the objectives of state security'.[221]

It would, however, be a mistake to view the increasing circulation of humanity language and the prevalence of security interests and practices as completely opposite trends in refugee protection. Instead, they seem to be closed intertwined. As the power of humanitarian organisations such as the UNHCR have grown, and their tasks expanded beyond their original mandates, they have

[213] M Bradley, 'The International Organization for Migration (IOM): Gaining Power in the Forced Migration Regime' (2017) 33 *Refuge* 97, 101.

[214] ibid 104.

[215] I Ashutosh and A Mountz, 'Migration Management for the Benefit of Whom? Interrogating the Work of the International Organization for Migration' (2011) 15 *Citizenship Studies* 21, 23.

[216] K Franko Aas and HOI Gundhus, 'Policing Humanitarian Borderlands: Frontex, Human Rights and the Precariousness of Life' (2015) 55 *The British Journal of Criminology* 1.

[217] ibid 4.

[218] ibid 5.

[219] ibid 5–7.

[220] ibid 10.

[221] ibid 13–14.

become increasingly involved in practices of containment and management of those who face 'an uncertain present and an uncertain fate'.[222]

The change in the functions of the UNHCR and other organisations has happened gradually and partly by accident. As the number of refugees has grown in the developing world, more and more refugees have ended up under the responsibility and authority of the UNHCR. In this process, camps originally planned as temporary shelters for refugees have become 'development camps', with schools, churches, hospitals, marketplaces, and so on. Partly because states are unwilling or unable to conduct refugee determinations, or to commit more resources to refugee governance, the UNHCR tends to act as both the gatekeeper and the government of these camps, deciding who is entitled to protection, running and administering the camps, and even wielding judicial and semi-judicial powers.[223]

In its role as a manager for development camps, the UNHCR has also inevitably become involved in 'security, containment, and pre-emptive humanitarian action and assistance'.[224] Indeed, today most asylum seekers do not make it to the Western world but stay indeterminately in camps close to or within their home country.[225] Probably by necessity, the UNHCR has shifted back from resettlement to voluntary repatriation and returnee integration in a world where states are less and less willing to accept migrants and asylum seekers into their territory and where many camps are becoming too large to handle.[226] Under the current policy, the majority of migrants are repatriated, with resettlement now the solution only for 'a small number of carefully screened refugees who need to be moved for security reasons or because of their vulnerability'.[227]

The shift to repatriation has posed a dilemma for the UNHCR: how can it stay relevant while maintaining its humanitarian identity? The solution has been to avoid getting involved in the actual implementation of return while at the same time facilitating the repatriation process and monitoring activities of the implementing authorities[228] In so doing, the UNHCR has started cooperating with the IOM, supporting the expansion of its activities. The end result is that the IOM takes care of the actual return of refugees while the UNHCR facilitates the process, making sure that it respects the 'human rights and human dignity'

[222] Agier, 'Humanity as an Identity and Its Political Effects', 38–39.

[223] Pallis (n 194) 883–86; R Wilde, 'Quis Custodiet Ipsos Custodes: Why and How UNHCR Governance of Development Refugee Camps Should Be Subject to International Human Rights Law Note' (1998) 1 *Yale Human Rights & Development Law Journal* 107, 107–10; L Barnett, 'Global Governance and the Evolution of the International Refugee Regime' (2002) 14 *International Journal of Refugee Law* 238, 251.

[224] Barnett, 'Global Governance and the Evolution', 251.

[225] ibid.

[226] ibid 252; BS Chimni, 'From Resettlement to Involuntary Repatriation: Towards a Critical History of Durable Solutions to Refugee Problems' (2004) 23 *Refugee Survey Quarterly* 55, 55.

[227] Sandvik, 'A Legal History: The Emergence', 41.

[228] A Koch, 'The Politics and Discourse of Migrant Return: The Role of UNHCR and IOM in the Governance of Return' (2014) 40 *Journal of Ethnic and Migration Studies* 905, 915.

of the returned person. Similarly, the UNHCR 'supports the IOM by providing assessments of return projects' compatibility with international human rights law',[229] as well as pre-departure and post-arrival assistance,[230] including the creation of minimum material conditions in the home country of the refugees.[231] The UNHCR and the IOM thus engage in a kind of task sharing which reciprocally legitimises their operations and further blurs the distinction between security interests and humanitarian concerns.[232]

This blurring of borders is also reflected in different practices of classification and regulation. As one commentator notes, the 'UNHCR gathers individual subjects, redistributes them, and finally provides them with a new internationally recognizable identity'.[233] The latest development in the blurring of security and humanitarian concerns is the instigation of the collection of biometric data. Following a piloting period, the UNHCR announced, in December 2010, that biometric data would be collected as a routine feature of its registration processes.[234] Although the UNHCR has stated that it collects the data in order to avoid fraud and make the recognition process smoother, in sharing the data with states and other actors it also enables new forms of intervention to be undertaken in the name of national security.[235] Indeed, for most other actors, the primary purpose of enhanced recognition is to eliminate threats in the form of 'terrorists disguising themselves as refugees', as has already happened, for example, in Senegal, where the government has used the UNHCR's biometrical data to combat what it sees as a terrorist threat emanating from neighbouring Mali.[236] More recently, concerns about governments' potential access to the data has been raised in relation to the Rohingya refugee crisis and in the case of Syrian refugees in Lebanon.[237] As commentators describe, biometric data is used to classify migrants and constitute populations in camps through different techniques of knowing and verifying. The refugees are classified and put through different procedures depending on where they arrive from, but also on the basis of events in their country of origin.[238]

[229] ibid 916–17.

[230] ibid 918.

[231] Barnett (n 223) 252; Chimni, 'From Resettlement to Involuntary Repatriation', 55.

[232] Koch, 'The Politics and Discourse of Migrant Return', 906–07.

[233] F Debrix, 'Space Quest: Surveillance, Governance, and the Panoptic Eye of the United Nations' (1999) 24 *Alternatives: Global, Local, Political* 269, 287–88.

[234] KL Jacobsen, 'On Humanitarian Refugee Biometrics and New Forms of Intervention' (2017) 11 *Journal of Intervention and Statebuilding* 529, 532.

[235] ibid 530–31, 540.

[236] ibid 541–42.

[237] Jacobsen and Sandvik, 'UNHCR and the Pursuit of International Protection: Accountability through Technology?', 7.

[238] LS Newhouse, 'More than Mere Survival: Violence, Humanitarian Governance, and Practical Material Politics in a Kenyan Refugee Camp' (2015) 47 *Environment and Planning A: Economy and Space* 2292, 2296. See also M Duffield, 'The Resilience of the Ruins: Towards a Critique of Digital Humanitarianism' (2016) 4 *Resilience* 147, 161.

The IOM, too, engages in different practices of classification. According to its constitution, the IOM not only ensures the 'orderly flow of migration movements throughout the world', but also provides tailored assistance to states, including identity management and verification services.[239] Most recently, however, the IOM has started to increase its institutional role in the humanitarian field by using its bureaucratic expertise in 'classifying objects and people', and in so doing shifting 'their definition and identity', especially with regard to refugee status determination and the management of internally displaced persons. A key tool for the IOM in this respect has been its Displacement Tracking Matrix. The Matrix is used to categorise people as displaced or not displaced in post-conflict or post-disaster contexts and states, and other organisations have come to depend on these categorisations as well as other quantitative information produced by the IOM. However, according to commentators, this data is far from neutral, as the IOM exercises considerable discretion in its classification and data collection.[240]

Further, commentators have also noted that life in development camps tends to be based on different 'normative principles of classification: child, handicapped, wounded, unsuitable, illiterate, retarded, underdeveloped, etc'.[241] Hence, whilst the right to live is attributed to a universal victim – the generic 'human' – at the level of rhetoric, in practice the right is granted on the basis of belonging to a particular, strictly defined group, such as a refugee child or a displaced person. In order to qualify, a person has to be able to tell a story or show an injury which evidences this belonging. The consequence is that the category of 'refugee' is further 'divided into several distinct subcategories of "vulnerability" which end up creating a hierarchy of misery' within the camp.[242] In a way, then, the refugee system provides one solution to the old question of what to do with the world's surplus population – the undesirables who have no place or voice in this world.[243] Humanitarian governance normalises the migrants in the sense that they are no longer 'free-flowing, wandering, or nomadic individuals', but are 'reorganized and reinserted within the international community as yet another type of calculated distribution'.[244] In this way, humanitarian governance of refugees not only protects the life of the refugees – even though it certainly does crucially important work in this respect – but also sorts 'good refugees' from 'bad apples', in a striking resemblance to the debates on what to do with

[239] Klabbers (n 193) 392–93.

[240] Bradley, 'The International Organization for Migration (IOM)', 104.

[241] Agier (n 190) 32.

[242] ibid 39.

[243] See further M Duffield, 'Human Security: Linking Security and Development in an Age of Terror' in S Klingebiel, *New Interfaces between Security and Development: Changing Concepts and Approaches* (Bonn, German Development Institute (DIE), 2006).

[244] Debrix, 'Space Quest', 287–88.

the poor in the sixteenth century.[245] In so doing, it also makes the difficult mass of migrants governable and allows the smooth functioning of global life.

Some critics have gone so far as to argue that categorisation of refugees serves to maintain a distinction between the centre and the periphery of the global order. According to Chimni, the humanitarian governance of refugees helps establish a system which is focused on containment and the management of internal competition for resources but does nothing to promote international distribution of resources, thus maintaining an unjust international system which manifests in periodic crises and conflicts in the developing world.[246] Fassin, too, argues that there is a clear difference between the Global South, where migrants are confined in camps, and the Global North, where asylum seekers are dealt with on a case-by-case basis. As he writes, the camps in the South are a condition of the detailed selection process in the North

> given that the casuistry involving the respect of human rights for asylum seekers supposes the selection of small numbers made possible by the extensive internment of refugees in poor countries and the strict control of their access to the benefits of the protection of wealthy nations.[247]

In a way, then, humanitarian governance and limited resettlement provides a 'humanitarian alibi' for restrictive asylum policies, enabled by the globalisation of screening and selection.[248]

These critiques provide a bridge to the issue of the relation between the humanitarian governance of refugees and the state. As is the case with most regimes studied in this chapter, that relation seems to be a two-pronged one. On the one hand, the refugee protection regime does little to challenge the importance of the state in global law and politics, and certainly does not bring about the demise of the state. Although authority is redistributed from states to the 'international community', represented in this case by non-governmental and international organisations, the regime nevertheless highlights the centrality of the order of states. The refugee regime's vision of the world is still one where 'the world is divided into a plurality of states in which the human population is segmented, ordered, and governed'.[249] It is this global order that the refugee regime protects in taking care of the world's surplus population.

On the other hand, the regime is also involved in shaping and disciplining the state. The UNHCR is increasingly involved in creating minimum political

[245] See AS Brett, *Changes of State: Nature and the Limits of the City in Early Modern Natural Law*, paperback edn (Princeton, Princeton University Press, 2014). See especially the distinction between vagrants and beggars, on the one hand, and the 'deserving poor' on the other. I thank Martti Koskenniemi for this point.

[246] Chimni (n 226) 71–72.

[247] D Fassin, 'Policing Borders, Producing Boundaries. The Governmentality of Immigration in Dark Times' (2011) 40 *Annual Review of Anthropology* 213, 216–17.

[248] Sandvik (n 201) 46–47.

[249] R Lui, 'The International Government of Refugees' in W Larner and W Walters (eds), *Global Governmentality: Governing International Spaces* (London, Routledge, 2004) 121.

conditions in the developing world, including the conduct of free elections, low-intensity democracy and control over territory, in order to facilitate repatriation. But perhaps more revealing is the case of the IOM. Although the IOM often acts on behalf of states, doing the work that its member states do not want to do, it also effectively shapes states, influencing their policies and practices to an even greater extent than most other organisations do. This it does, for example, by evaluating states' border management regimes and building states' capacities in these practices. Furthermore, it produces different handbooks and sets of 'best practices' and conducts state assessments, evaluating how well the best practices are followed and how many resources states are willing to direct to the control of migration and associated phenomena such as human trafficking. The IOM also extends its influence by training state officials and providing expert advice – advice which states eagerly take heed of, bolstered as it is by the aura of legitimacy deriving from the IOM's expert position and the deep-seated assumption that international organisations produce good. As Klabbers notes, all of these combined produce 'a continuous loop of mutual direction and influence' which at least partly 'makes states' at the same time as it protects them from unwanted migration flows.[250]

VI. OBSERVATIONS

This chapter has analysed a wide range of uses of the humanity discourse in global governance. By way of conclusion, I would like to draw attention to three threads that have run through the chapter. The first two relate to two key assumptions of the law of humanity project – that increased use of humanity rhetoric produces human empowerment and well-being; and that this is connected to the withering or disciplining of the state – whereas the third one, the use of humanity language to push through broadly 'neoliberal' transformations, emerged more spontaneously from the material under scrutiny.

The main element characterising the theoretical humanity discourse is the desire to increase human well-being and empower individuals and peoples. A key assumption of the proponents of the law of humanity project is that this goal can be advanced by increased circulation of the humanity language. For this reason, many of the proponents of the project have concluded, on the basis of an analysis of humanity language in court decisions and official documents, that international law is – or at least was – moving towards a law of humanity direction.

The observations made in this chapter certainly support the empirical argument about increased circulation of the humanity language. It is remarkable how widespread and strong the humanity rhetoric has been in different areas

[250] Klabbers (n 193) 395.

of global governance during the past three decades, as legitimacy of law and politics has been drawn from protecting human life, human rights and human dignity.[251] As Alexander Somek has argued, on both sides of the millennium, authority and power seemed to depend less and less on the free choice of peoples and correct arrangements of checks and balances and more on 'an act of reasonable recognition concerning the supreme value and authority of human dignity and human rights'.[252] In other words, the rhetoric indeed seemed to imply that 'humanity' had become the 'major organizing principle' of international law and global governance, and the vulnerable individual their focus.[253]

At the same time, however, the observations made in this chapter complicate the idea that the increased importance of 'humanity' at the level of discourse would necessarily translate into increased well-being and freedom on the ground. Indeed, many of the outcomes described above are ambiguous and some are even outright inimical to the aims of the law of humanity project. The case of terrorist sanctions is the obvious example, but an analysis of the humanitarian occupation missions also demonstrates that while the missions could be considered a success in the sense of establishing institutions, the right to self-determination of local populations got almost completely steamrolled by international administrators. Similarly, refugee protection can, in saving lives, lead to sometimes harsh disciplinary practices, and the benefits of investment law have sometimes gone into the pockets of a very limited number of individuals.

The developments surrounding the increased use of humanity language can therefore perhaps best be described as the increased importance of what Didier Fassin has called 'biolegitimacy', that is to say, the recognition of life – understood in the sense of simply being alive – as the most fundamental of all values.[254] Crucially, however, Fassin emphasises that whilst biolegitimacy plays a crucial role in the redistribution of authority and power, it does not necessarily lead to human empowerment or even to the kind of maximisation of life which is at the heart of what Foucault called 'biopower'.[255] Indeed, the accomplishments of the increased circulation of humanity language seem to be related mostly to 'the prevention of cruelty and the preservation of bare human life against persecution and atrocities perpetrated by either governments or social groups'.[256]

[251] A Somek, *The Cosmopolitan Constitution* (Oxford, Oxford University Press, 2014). See also S Esmeir, *Juridical Humanity: A Colonial History* (Stanford, Stanford University Press, 2014).
[252] Somek, *The Cosmopolitan Constitution*, 9.
[253] ibid 153–54. See also P Cheah, *Inhuman Conditions: On Cosmopolitanism and Human Rights* (Cambridge, MA, Harvard University Press, 2007) 155–56.
[254] D Fassin, *Humanitarian Reason: A Moral History of the Present* (Berkeley, University of California Press, 2011) 249. See further D Fassin, 'Another Politics of Life Is Possible' (2009) 26 *Theory, Culture & Society* 44; D Fassin, 'Compassion and Repression: The Moral Economy of Immigration Policies in France' (2005) 20 *Cultural Anthropology* 362.
[255] M Foucault, *The History of Sexuality: The Will to Knowledge*, vol 1, new edn (R Hurley trans, London, Penguin, 1998) pt 5.
[256] Somek (n 251) 153–54.

The turn to biolegitimacy and the increasing circulation of humanity language also has important consequences in more mundane matters than the prevention of atrocities. A key characteristic of the turn to biolegitimacy is that it empowers those actors who manage to win struggles over the ownership of the humanity language and the definition of concepts such as human rights, human security and human dignity, or enables actors to present themselves as protecting life more efficiently than their competitors. In this way, the turn to biolegitimacy redistributes authority on the global scale. But what has it empowered different actors to do?

This question leads us to the second key assumption of the law of humanity project, namely that, in order to become the primary actor of global law, the human person must oust the state from its current position. For some, this may entail the diminution of the role of the state,[257] whereas others are more interested in reshaping the state into a trustee, official or fiduciary of humanity.[258] According to the observations made in this chapter, the practice of global governance seems to be more in line with the latter view. When it comes to the state, two trends emerge from the analysis. The first is that the humanity language has been used to pierce the veil of state sovereignty, reconceive sovereignty as responsibility or discipline the state in other ways. For example, in the humanitarian occupation missions, international actors took it upon themselves to 'organise societies in a manner that purports to promote the functioning of domestic institutions and the realisation of the rights of individuals'.[259] Although less intrusive than humanitarian occupation missions, the anti-terrorism campaign was very efficient in convincing states to develop standardised domestic policies which allowed 'the core' – most importantly, the USA – to control what goes on in 'the periphery' and thus 'discipline populations both in the centre and the periphery while appearing to shape only the latter'.[260] International investment law has efficiently disciplined states by making them dependent on foreign investment, and by setting strict standards for gaining that investment, coupled with a completely globalised arbitration system run by a very small elite and heavily weighted towards the interests of the investors. Several measures in international criminal law have attempted to 'disrupt the relationship between the individual and the State and relegate the latter from its status as the primary actor in the international system'.[261] Finally, a very notable recent

[257] R Domingo, *The New Global Law*, reprint edn (Cambridge, Cambridge University Press, 2011) 58; C Barbara, 'International Legal Personality: Panacea or Pandemonium? Theorizing about the Individual and the State in the Era of Globalization' (2007) 12 *Austrian Review of International and European Law* 17.

[258] E Benvenisti, 'Sovereigns as Trustees of Humanity: On the Accountability of States to Foreign Stakeholders' (2013) 107 *American Journal of International Law* 295; J Waldron, 'Are Sovereigns Entitled to the Benefit of the International Rule of Law?' (2011) 22 *European Journal of International Law* 315; Criddle and Fox-Decent, *Fiduciaries of Humanity*.

[259] Stahn (n 61) 755–56.

[260] Scheppele (n 119) 251.

[261] McAuliffe (n 43) 268.

development within human rights law and refugee protection is the increasing use and relevance of indicators and periodic reviews. Indicators – which, importantly, depend on political decisions on what qualifies as worth measuring and what is left outside – shape national governmental decision-making as it is important for many states to perform well in order to boost their reputation and have access to resources.[262]

Yet, while these practices may challenge state sovereignty as traditionally understood, as well as the right to self-determination, they also seem to support the continued existence of states. This is true even for the most extreme practice studied above, namely humanitarian occupation. According to Fox, the practice 'suggests a deep commitment to preserving existing states, but equally to a model of the state as embodied in the human rights and territorial integrity norms'. Despite intervening radically in domestic affairs of states, the aim of all humanitarian occupations has been the 'rehabilitation of a state'.[263] Existing borders have been preserved and populations maintained intact and in particular places – sometimes even with the help of coercive measures.[264] This respect for state borders has been only strengthened through the development of the human security and responsibility to protect concepts in the post-humanitarian occupations political context, in which the focus has shifted from the rights of intervening states to support for fragile ones,[265] the main idea being that human security is to be achieved by building states and their capacities in full respect of territorial integrity.[266] Indeed, the determination to maintain an international order built around existing states is reflected in all areas of global governance. For example, although some have argued that refugees represent the emergence of a deterritorialised politics, the practice of the refugee regime seems to lead in the completely opposite direction. As Robyn Lui has shown, the regime effectively maintains an international order of states where 'the human population is segmented, ordered, and governed' through relations between states and their citizens.[267] Similarly, the human rights system is based completely on the relation between states and their citizens, and the terrorist sanction regime was accomplished only by giving states something they could use for their own purposes.

Indeed, as James Crawford writes, with a nod to Mark Twain, the rumours of the death of the state have been 'much exaggerated'.[268] In contrast to such

[262] KE Davis, B Kingsbury and SE Merry, 'Indicators as a Technology of Global Governance' (2012) 46 *Law & Society Review* 71, 83–84.

[263] Fox (n 57) 7.

[264] ibid 73.

[265] Glanville (n 158) 201–02; Chandler (n 185) 28–29.

[266] UNGA, 'Follow-up to Paragraph 143 on Human Security of the 2005 World Summit Outcome' (2012) 66th session, UN Doc A/Res/66/290, Supp 14, 117, para 3, provisions d–h.

[267] Lui, 'The International Government of Refugees', 121.

[268] J Crawford, 'Sovereignty as a Legal Value' in J Crawford, M Koskenniemi and S Ranganathan (eds), *The Cambridge Companion to International Law* (Cambridge, Cambridge University Press, 2012) 132.

rumours, the analysis above suggests that the international community has shown great determination in maintaining and even reinforcing the state system. But what the increasing relevance of the humanity language has allowed its most successful wielders to do is to shape a very specific type of state, and in doing so contribute to what Anne Orford has called the 'battle for the state', a battle for what states should be like and what goes on within them.[269] Indeed, in most of the examples above, the bolstering of the state has been linked to radical rethinking of the notion of state sovereignty and to different ways of disciplining the state into adopting certain types of institutions, legislation and policies, from terrorist laws to the regulation of markets.

The state being developed through these humanity language-empowered disciplinary practices leads me to my third observation. Unlike the first two, this third observation is not linked to what has been said previously in this book about the law of humanity project, but emerges from the material studied above. The observation is that humanity language has been used to push through broadly neoliberal political, legal and economic transformations in the developing world. Here, again, it is possible to start with the perhaps now historical examples of humanitarian occupations and the occupation of Iraq. As was discussed in more detail above, the occupations involved the creation of some of the most investment-friendly environments in the world: the opening of markets, privatisation, changes in taxation and the complete revamping of the agricultural sectors of the occupied territories, all aimed at the inclusion of domestic markets in global value chains. These changes were made with little regard to historical, political or economical particularities, and in many cases against the explicit wishes of the local population. Furthermore, the political institutional structure was restructured according to the liberal model that is deemed necessary for the smooth operation of economy. All of this was done in the name of human rights and the well-being of the occupied populations.

This emphasis on free markets, global supply chains and investment-friendly environment was soon afterwards adopted in the ICISS Report and subsequent documents on responsibility to protect, and is also visible in other areas analysed in this chapter. Apart from the obvious case of investment law, the promotion of international criminal justice has been marketed as an economically sound investment;[270] refugee governance is linked to the management of the surplus populations which have been left outside the economic system, and the war on terrorism is connected to economics at least through the invasion of

[269] A Orford, 'Food Security, Free Trade, and the Battle for the State' (2015) 11 *Journal of International Law & International Relations* 1; A Orford, 'Theorizing Free Trade' in A Orford and F Hoffmann (eds), *The Oxford Handbook of the Theory of International Law* (Oxford, Oxford University Press, 2016). I will return to Orford's argument in more detail in the next chapter.

[270] 'The Dividends of International Criminal Justice', Address from Carla del Ponte, Prosecutor of the ICTY, at Goldman Sachs, London, 6 October 2005, www.icty.org/x/file/Press/PR_attachments/cdp-goldmansachs-050610-e.htm.

Iraq. Furthermore, recent historical analyses have demonstrated lucidly how the human rights language has been used to further neoliberal policies, especially by disseminating and enforcing the 'morals of the market'.[271]

***

If the central argument of chapter three was that the key concepts of the law of humanity project are analytically indeterminate, and can be used strategically for multiple different purposes, this chapter has suggested that there are nevertheless some consistent patterns in the use of these concepts in the practice of global governance and world politics – or, perhaps more precisely, in the outcomes of those practices. These patterns seem to partly coincide with the aims of the law of humanity project, but also partly deviate from them. For example, although the law of humanity theorists herald the diminishing of the role of the state or the unbundling of state sovereignty, I am quite certain that they would protest against many of the outcomes of the war on terrorism. Moreover, many of the law of humanity theorists do not seem to have very explicit economic aims, and some (although not all) might be very troubled by the possibility that humanity language is used to achieve neoliberal reforms. In that sense, humanity language and the key concepts of the law of humanity seem to have started to live a life of their own, as they have descended from the level of theory into the muddier waters of practice, become embedded in the complex network of power relations that characterises global governance and been used to empower actors who may not share all of the aims of the law of humanity project.

[271] Whyte (n 5); Slobodian, *Globalists: The End of Empire*.

5

Inequality and the Populist Backlash: The Law of Humanity Project at a Crossroads

THE PEAK OF the law of humanity project, which started in the 1990s, did not last long. The dynamics of global governance had already started to change when the war on terrorism occupied the minds of world leaders and policy experts after the 9/11 terrorist attacks. But the real blow to the project came when domestic politics around the world started to shift to a more right-wing, authoritarian direction some years after the 2008 economic crisis. The crisis was responded to by bailing out financial institutions while cutting public services and imposing other austerity measures. Finance and economics continued as usual, and the top one per cent reaped the benefits while the rest bore the burden. In the ensuing climate of despair, accompanied by the so-called refugee crisis, it was not difficult for populist strongmen to manipulate public opinion by tapping into frustrations and fears that had already been bubbling under the surface for some time.

Although there is also left-wing populism, focusing on the elite's failure to solve economic inequalities and different forms of discrimination, the more influential form of populism recently has been the nationalistic right-wing version. While this form of populism, too, draws from disdain for elites and economic inequalities, the brunt of its project is aimed at immigration and the loss of traditional values. Economic issues do play an important role in the right-wing populist rhetoric, to be sure, but the populists typically focus on blaming the ambiguous enemies of globalisation and unnamed elites for the loss of traditional industries and jobs, without questioning the hegemonic economic ideology or the structural forces of capitalism.

The nationalistic right-wing populism has swept across the Europe and North America in particular. In 2016, Donald Trump was elected President of the USA amidst promises to 'Make America Great Again', and in the same year the UK voted for Brexit, following a campaign that attacked not only European elites, but also immigrants from Eastern Europe and the Middle East. These populist victories were part of a continuum with similar events in Poland, where the Law and Justice Party had been surging in popularity for a decade and had managed to win a majority government in 2015; in Hungary, where Victor Orban's Fidesz

Party had already won power in 2010; and in the Nordic countries, where the populist Sweden Democrats, the Danish People's Party and the Finns Party had emerged as serious political contenders. Furthermore, soon after the US election and the Brexit vote, the People's Party became the dominant party in a coalition government in Austria, and the Five Star Movement and the League formed a coalition government in Italy. Vox in Spain, the Party for Freedom in the Netherlands and the Alternative for Germany also did well in elections, as did Marine Le Pen and her National Front in France.

In the Global South, populism has reacted to slightly different phenomena than in the North. At the heart of southern populism has been, among other things, concern over non-integrated informal sectors, the exclusion of the developing world from global decision-making, problems in export, mistrust in political institutions and the unequal global distribution of wealth. Nevertheless, North-style right-wing populism has been gaining ground in the South as well. This is exemplified, for example, in the presidential elections of Roberto Duterte in the Philippines, Jair Bolsonaro in Brazil (both of whom openly admire and mimic Trump) and Narendra Modi in India (who is apparently also a 'close friend' of Trump's). Furthermore, while Mexico's Andrés Manuel López Obrador's campaign seemed to align with Latin American left-wing populism, his policies and rhetoric during his presidency have been on the right side of the populist spectrum.

The rise of populism at the domestic level has been reflected at the international level in the upsurge of anti-internationalist rhetoric and in states withdrawing from international organisations and treaties or simply denouncing different fora of international cooperation. Examples include the USA 'unsigning' the Trans-Pacific Partnership Agreement, withdrawing from the Paris Agreement and blocking the operation of the World Trade Organization's (WTO) Appellate Body; the Russian Federation 'unsigning' the International Criminal Court's Rome Statute and withdrawing from the Energy Charter Treaty; Bolivia, Ecuador, and Venezuela denouncing the International Centre for Settlement of Investment Disputes (ICSID) Convention; Bolivia, Ecuador, Venezuela, South Africa, Indonesia, Italy, Russia and India withdrawing from their bilateral treaties; and the UK withdrawing from the EU. Moreover, as I am writing this chapter, President Trump has just announced that the USA will withdraw from the World Health Organization. As a consequence of these setbacks, there seems to be a wide consensus among international lawyers and international relations theorists across different school of thought that something has changed radically in international law and international relations. Although the very core of the liberal international legal system is unlikely to be shaken, the 'top layers, at least, are at risk of erosion in the current political climate'.[1]

[1] J Crawford, 'The Current Political Discourse Concerning International Law' (2018) 81 *MLR* 1, 21.

Those top layer sediments which have not yet turned into solid rock unfortunately include the developments and victories celebrated by the law of humanity project. Many key values and concepts of the project are at jeopardy as violent right-wing activism and the xenophobic targeting of minorities and refugees have become everyday phenomena, and governments are cutting development assistance and funding of international organisations. Indeed, human rights experts have described populism as 'explicitly antagonistic to all or much of the human rights agenda', and thus posing a challenge to the human rights movement,[2] whereas proponents of global constitution have portrayed it as 'an attack on the three foundational features of the global constitution – democracy, human rights, and the rule of law'.[3] Thus, while, by the mid-1990s, it seemed inevitable that the law of humanity vision would come to play a key role in world affairs and international law, that moment in history seems to have already come to a sudden end. Under the present circumstances, a law of humanity seems a very distant dream.

Yet, it might be too hasty to declare the law of humanity project dead and buried. Although the rhetoric and actions of many governments have become more cautious or even outright hostile towards human rights and other law of humanity concepts, academics and activists still hold on to the law of humanity ideas, and non-state actors still continue their persistent humanitarian work and human rights activism.

For example, Philip Alston has called for human rights actors and scholars to galvanise themselves and revitalise the human rights movement by giving a more important role to social and economic rights while doubling down on the familiar strategies that have worked so well for civil and political rights, namely recognition, institutionalisation and accountability. As Alston writes:

> We need to … start with legislative and other forms of recognition of a right … Next we need to build up specialized institutions which are going to promote the right in ways that are meaningful in that society. Finally, we need to build up accountability mechanisms.[4]

Similarly, Paul Gready defends the importance of human rights work even when success is uncertain and responses are hostile because it is the right thing to do and because moral acts 'leave a trace, sow a seed'.[5] The challenge, as he sees it, lies mainly in communication: the human rights movement ought to spend more

[2] P Alston, 'The Populist Challenge to Human Rights' (2017) 9 *Journal of Human Rights Practice* 1, 1–2.

[3] J Havercroft et al, 'Editorial: Donald Trump as Global Constitutional Breaching Experiment' (2018) 7 *Global Constitutionalism* 1, 4. For an excellent critical review of recent trends in human rights scholarship, see D Scott, 'Human Rights' in J d'Aspermont and J Haskell (eds), *International Law at a Tipping Point: Critique and Commitment* (Cambridge, Cambridge University Press, 2019).

[4] Alston, 'The Populist Challenge to Human Rights', 9.

[5] P Gready, 'Reflections on a Human Rights Decade, Near and Far' (2019) 11 *Journal of Human Rights Practice* 422, 423.

time and energy on being persuasive, on learning how to frame arguments and how to embed facts in compelling narratives about the future of society, and on rethinking solidarities without and within.[6] And while Mark Heywood starts from a critical position, pointing out that capitalists and neoliberals have found that they have 'a self-interest in advancing human rights frameworks',[7] he argues that surrendering the framework would 'leave us much weaker in our fight for equality'.[8] If the human rights covenants have produced disappointing results, this is so, according to Heywood, primarily because the United Nations Treaty Bodies they produced 'have not yet been effectively utilized by civil society to demand their enforcement as global standards'.[9]

In these different ways, scholars call for the recommitment to the human rights movement in stopping the spread of authoritarian populism and protecting the entire global legal order.[10] Furthermore, in places like Syria, where state action has been disappointing at best, and sometimes hostile towards humanitarian non-governmental organisations (NGOs), organisations like Médecins Sans Frontières still continue to provide medical aid where they can envisage their interventions 'as undertaken within a "smooth space of universal human medical relief that knows no boundaries"'.[11]

Thus, although the law of humanity project has no doubt been weakened, it is not dead. Rather, the project has entered a crossroads. If the project is to retain any value under the current circumstances, it must carefully consider external threats, internal weaknesses and past mistakes, before selecting the best path ahead. In particular, although the law of humanity project has not stimulated the backlash, nor is it its target, it is important to consider the ways in which the project is by necessity embedded in a complex web of more general mindsets, practices, forms of expertise and power relations that the backlash is both feeding from and reacting to. Furthermore, the proponents of the project should stop being so shy about considering themselves as wielding power. Failing to do so, the project risks remaining politically irrelevant or even having some of its key concepts hijacked by competing mindsets and projects, some of which are likely to produce outcomes inimical to its aims. But if the law of humanity project succeeds in adjusting itself to this political, material and ideological landscape – not in line with the right-wing populists, of course, but more openly

[6] ibid 431–35.

[7] M Heywood, 'South Africa's Journey from Socialism to Human Rights: The True Confessions of an Errant Socialist' (2019) 11 *Journal of Human Rights Practice* 305, 317.

[8] ibid.

[9] ibid 318.

[10] For a critical discussion, see Scott, 'Human Rights'; L Bonadiman and U Soirila, 'Human Rights, Populism, and the Political Economy of the World' (2019) 37 *Nordic Journal of Human Rights* 301.

[11] C Duncombe and T Dunne, 'After Liberal World Order' (2018) 94 *International Affairs* 25, 39. The authors are referring to F Debrix, 'Deterritorialised Territories, Borderless Borders: The New Geography of International Medical Assistance' (1998) 19 *Third World Quarterly* 827, 831.

and efficiently against them and the forces responsible for their triumph – its key values might provide a valuable counterforce to the currently prevailing trends. For this purpose, this chapter studies the root causes of the populist backlash, the forms of power and knowledge that have produced them, and their relation to the law of humanity project. The chapter concludes by sketching out some possibilities as to how a conversation for creating a more contextualised law of humanity project could start and what issues the project should consider in moving ahead from the crossroads at which it has recently found itself.

I. ON THE ROOT CAUSES OF THE BACKLASH

Trying to understand the relations between the backlash against 'globalism', the rise of populist politics and international law is very difficult. As Anne Orford notes, 'International law and institutions do not represent a coherent project, and it is difficult to diagnose what precisely has fueled populist support for withdrawal from international legal regimes or institutions even within a particular country, let alone globally'.[12] Thus, there are probably almost as many narratives of the backlash as there are scholars who have commented on it. Nevertheless, the most convincing of such narratives tend to emphasise, in one form or another, either the role of cultural values and identity politics or that of material inequality. These narratives are represented perhaps in their most powerful form in international legal discourse in Martti Koskenniemi's 2019 American Society of International Law Annual Grotius Lecture and Orford's comment to it. Furthermore, both Koskenniemi and Orford emphasise a third key element in the backlash, namely the role of expertise.

According to Koskenniemi, the backlash should be understood first and foremost as a reaction to the hegemony of a specific liberal culture and liberal claims of expertise. As Koskenniemi explains, the 1960s witnessed a shift in liberal international thinking. Whereas the focus had previously been on nation states as bearers of autonomy in relation to each other, now the rights and freedoms of individuals within states started to gain a more central place. The focus on individual rights reached its highpoint in the 1990s, as reflected, for example, in Thomas Franck's *The Empowered Self*;[13] and at least to a certain extent in the emergence of the law of humanity project, too. The rise of the 'empowered self' created significant changes in the prevailing culture which had previously been dominated by national, social and religious norms. But most of all, it created

[12] A Orford, 'International Law and the Populist Moment: A Comment on Martti Koskenniemi's Enchanted by the Tools? International Law and Enlightenment' (2019) 35 *American University International Law Review* 427, 429.

[13] TM Franck, *The Empowered Self: Law and Society in an Age of Individualism* (Oxford, Oxford University Press, 1999).

changes in 'status', especially for those white heterosexual men who had not enjoyed great wealth but had nevertheless had a certain position in society simply for the sake of their race, gender and sex. It is this 'status anxiety' produced by 'the emergence of a universal politics of human rights that was deeply intolerant of traditional value and hierarchies', and the subsequent desire to 'take back control', that Koskenniemi sees as a key cause of the backlash.

Closely connected to the issue of status anxiety in Koskenniemi's narrative is that of expertise. The last decades of the twentieth century brought not only the empowerment of the individual and the ensuing culture wars, but also the rise of governance – both in its domestic and global variants.[14] Governance presents itself as rule through expertise. Power is no longer portrayed as a question of politics, but as one of knowledge: 'experts rule because they are experts, because they *know* that climate change is true, that increasing prison sentences have no effect on criminality, and that the greatest to suffer from Brexit are its supporters'.[15] This attitude of knowing better is a red flag for the backlashers, especially when connected to the observation that, in reality, experts continuously disagree amongst themselves. As Koskenniemi has demonstrated in his previous work, the differences between experts are at the heart of the 'fragmentation' of international law: using their own vocabularies, mindsets and ways of seeing the world, a trade expert and a human rights expert would likely decide the same dispute in very different ways.[16] But it is perhaps even more blatant in other forms of science, promoting different scientific models which give different answers to the same questions. As Koskenniemi notes: 'From this the backlashers have drawn the conclusion that there really is no difference between expert "knowledge" and opinion, truth and bias.'[17] And this, again, has allowed the backlashers to argue that experts merely disguise their privileged opinions as truths, so as to exclude the backlashers and other non-elites, and to remove issues from political contestation.

Together, status anxiety and increasing mistrust of experts – especially international experts and other 'globalists' – soon gave birth to increasing challenges to established institutions. While global governance institutions, including the UN and the EU, were engaging in different problem-solving tasks, audiences at

[14] On the role of expertise in global governance and political economy, see D Kennedy, *A World of Struggle: How Power, Law, and Expertise Shape Global Political Economy* (Princeton, Princeton University Press, 2016).

[15] M Koskenniemi, 'Enchanted by the Tools? An Enlightenment Perspective' (2019) 35 *American University International Law Review* 397, 406 (original emphasis).

[16] ILC Study Group, 'Fragmentation of International Law: Difficulties Arising from the Diversification and Expansion of International Law, Finalized by Martti Koskenniemi', UN Doc A/CN.4/L.682 and Add 1 and Corr 1; M Koskenniemi and P Leino, 'Fragmentation of International Law? Postmodern Anxieties' (2002) 15 *Leiden Journal of International Law* 553; M Koskenniemi, 'Hegemonic Regimes' in MA Young (ed), *Regime Interaction in International Law: Facing Fragmentation* (Cambridge, Cambridge University Press, 2011).

[17] Koskenniemi, 'Enchanted by the Tools', 409.

home were experiencing 'austerity, the narrowing down of possibilities of political contestation, and the rise of a new technocracy'.[18] It was easy for populists to take advantage of this situation and push through reactionary political agendas, aimed at restoring a past era when white men had control and all sorts of 'others' did not tell them what to do.[19]

If Koskenniemi emphasises the cultural side of liberalism as a cause of the backlash, Orford focuses on its material side. Although the 1960s and 1990s both play an important role in Orford's account as well, it is less because of the breakthrough of non-conformism related to human rights and more because of 'the turn to international law as a vehicle for protecting the rights of property holders and investors against the risks of redistribution, whether in the form of decolonization in the South or of leftist social policymaking in the North'.[20] This turn was reflected in the establishment of the ICSID system in 1966 and the growing number of detailed bilateral investments treaties (BIT), which focused increasingly on 'the everyday conduct of government regulation and its impact on the profits of foreign investors', and was consolidated during the 1990s in the negotiation of even more BITs and broad-reaching agreements such as the Energy Charter Treaty and the North American Free Trade Agreement (NAFTA).[21] Furthermore, the 1990s witnessed the increasing use of international law 'as a vehicle for entrenching a particular approach to economic policymaking through regional and international economic integration'. In particular, the completion of the Uruguay Rounds negotiations and the birth of the WTO led to 'a significant expansion in the range of activities brought within the scope of the international trade regime' as focus shifted from tariffs to various behind-the-border measures.[22]

According to Orford, it is these economic aspects of liberal internationalism that have been the main target of the backlash – at least when it comes to international law. As she notes, the backlash has taken the form of states withdrawing from the ICSID Convention in an attempt to combat privatisation; termination of BITs, and the reluctance to conclude new ones; withdrawals from the Energy Charter Treaty; attempts to renegotiate NAFTA; Brexit; and the freezing of the WTO Appellate Body. Thus, for Orford, the backlash is a

[18] ibid 405.

[19] ibid.

[20] Orford, 'International Law and the Populist Moment', 432. See also Q Slobodian, *Globalists: The End of Empire and the Birth of Neoliberalism* (Cambridge, MA, Harvard University Press, 2018); J Whyte, *The Morals of the Market: Human Rights and the Rise of Neoliberalism* (London, Verso, 2019).

[21] Orford, 'International Law and the Populist Moment' (n 12) 432–33.

[22] ibid 433. See also A Orford, 'Theorizing Free Trade' in A Orford and F Hoffmann (eds), *The Oxford Handbook of the Theory of International Law* (Oxford, Oxford University Press, 2016); A Lang, *World Trade Law after Neoliberalism: Reimagining the Global Economic Order*, reprint edn (Oxford, Oxford University Press, 2013).

response to the material limits to economic liberalism and failed attempts to tackle issues such as

> how to respond to the people who are routinely dispossessed or displaced to enable new forms of economic liberalization, and how to address the exhaustion of the capacity of the natural world to act as energy resource and waste disposal unit'.[23]

For Orford, then, the populist backlash is a reaction to central problems that need urgent addressing. Unfortunately, however, the backlash has taken a very damaging form in many countries as right-wing populism has been more successful in gaining the attention of the public than other possible forms of populism or resistance.[24] Indeed, not only have the right-wing populists adopted xenophobic policies, but they have also largely failed – or been unwilling – to counter the neoliberal policies that have removed arrangements that are claimed to be necessary for the smooth functioning of markets from political contestation.[25] As commentators point out, right-wing populist parties have in fact adopted strict austerity measures and pursued free movement of capital and privatisation – a fact that is perhaps not that surprising, considering that many of those parties include important members who have been strongly influenced by neoliberal ideas and thinkers, and in some cases are members of neoliberal societies and organisations.[26]

II. A STRUGGLE OF PROJECTS

Although the cultural and economic explanations of the root causes of the rise of authoritarian populism differ somewhat, they do not necessarily contradict one another. Indeed, both Koskenniemi and Orford readily admit that both explanations are at least partly accurate and that their relative weights vary from country to country and context to context. Moreover, the two accounts overlap in important ways, most notably with regard to the role of expertise as one of the root causes of the backlash.

In what follows, then, I am not interested in which account is more 'accurate', but rather in what can be learned from each of them from the perspective of the law of humanity project. There are three key elements that emerge from Koskenniemi's and Orford's narratives of the rise of right-wing populism: the rapid cultural changes partly driven by the human rights revolution; the rise of expert power; and the rise in inequality, especially within states. I suggest that although the law of humanity project is not the main cause of any of these, it is

[23] Orford, 'International Law and the Populist Moment' (n 12) 437.
[24] ibid 440.
[25] Whyte, *The Morals of the Market*, 239–42.
[26] Q Slobodian, 'Neoliberalism's Populist Bastards: A New Political Divide between National Economies' (15 February 2018), www.publicseminar.org/2018/02/neoliberalisms-populist-bastards.

connected to each of them. This is quite obvious with regard to the culture war, as the law of humanity has been proudly part of the human rights revolution and the empowerment of the individual. When it comes to the rise of expertise and inequality, the connection is less immediately clear, but also more interesting. In that regard, I find it significant that the law of humanity project emerged at the same time as two other projects managed to attain a dominant position in global governance. These partly interlinked projects, which managed to turn some of their key ideas into prevalent governance mindsets, are referred to here as 'managerialism' and 'neoliberalism'.

By pointing out that the law of humanity project emerged at the same time as these other projects gained dominant positions, I do not intend to suggest that the law of humanity project would be managerialist or neoliberal in itself. Nor do I argue that the law of humanity project would have helped the other projects attain their position. However, the law of humanity project has had to coexist with these other projects and operate in a world dominated by their ways of thinking. Hence, I am interested in how the law of humanity project has interacted with managerialism and neoliberalism, how the humanity discourse has been impacted by them, and how managerialists and neoliberals have used or even hijacked the humanity language in certain instances.

A. The Law of Humanity Project and Managerialism

While managerialism and neoliberalism gained dominant positions only towards the end of the twentieth century, both of them have their origins in the inter-World War era. The discussion of managerialism started against the background of growing concern over the separation of ownership and control of corporations and the increasing bureaucratisation of the state following World War II.[27] Although managerialism was initially discussed critically, commentators worrying about management of money and services being separated from the interests of the public, it quickly came to be seen as a useful governance mindset and technique.[28] As a practice of governance, it is based on 'a division between the managerial or strategic part of an organization that determines ends, and the operational part of an organization that performs tasks needed to achieve those ends',[29] and operates through policies and directives, supported by

[27] A Orford, 'Book Review Article: International Territorial Administration and the Management of Decolonization' (2010) 59 *International & Comparative Law Quarterly* 227, 245; J Murphy, 'The Rise of Global Managers' in S Dar and B Cooke (eds), *The New Development Management: Critiquing the Dual Modernization* (London, Zed Books, 2013).

[28] A Prasad and P Prasad, 'The Empire of Organizations and the Organization of Empires: Postcolonial Considerations on Theorizing Workplace Resistance' in A Prasad (ed), *Postcolonial Theory and Organizational Analysis: A Critical Engagement* (New York, Palgrave Macmillan, 2003) 97.

[29] Orford, 'Book Review Article', 246.

funding as an incentivising and disciplinary tool. Furthermore, managerialism also relies on auditing, benchmarking and other techniques of governance that guide its subjects into internalising the aims and values of the managers.[30]

While used first to control the employees of corporations, the managerial technique soon came to be used to control entire states and their populations.[31] One of its most recent forms is the New Public Management (NPM) thinking that was developed in the UK, the USA and Australia in the 1980s, and was mainstreamed globally during the 1990s. The NPM approach tries to make public sector governance more 'efficient' by introducing it to ideas and practices transferred from business life. According to the NPM mindset, public sector organisations must change and become more productive in order to fit the new spirit of capitalism and globalisation. Governance must become more flexible and decentralized, and must be based on competition and outcomes, whereas staff are expected to develop proactive and entrepreneurial attitudes. Furthermore, managerial concepts and methods, skills and competences, knowledge and expertise are portrayed as superior to any other concepts, professional competencies or credentials,[32] whereas the legitimacy of governance is increasingly derived from ideas of virtuous or ethical leadership, which is measured by organisational growth, employee motivation and satisfaction, meeting of stakeholders' values, organisational learning and effectiveness.[33]

When I refer to 'managerialism', I also try to capture a complex and heterodox but closely related set of other ideas, practices and techniques of governance which have been in development from the eighteenth century onwards. The NPM mindset reflects most of these elements, but the elements are not limited to the mindset. For example, I associate managerialism with the liberal problem of governing through freedom. Liberalism is based on the notion that those in control should avoid governing 'too much', as free individuals arrive at the optimal solution to their problems. Yet, this causes problems for the consistency of government – a problem which has been solved by subjectivising the free individuals into using their freedom in a disciplined, predictable way through different technologies of the self.[34] Second, managerialism, as I understand it,

[30] SE Merry, *The Seductions of Quantification: Measuring Human Rights, Gender Violence, and Sex Trafficking* (Chicago, University of Chicago Press, 2016); C Shore and S Wright, 'Governing by Numbers: Audit Culture, Rankings and the New World Order' (2015) 23 *Social Anthropology* 22; KE Davis, B Kingsbury and SE Merry, 'Indicators as a Technology of Global Governance' (2012) 46 *Law & Society Review* 71.

[31] Orford, 'Book Review Article' (n 27) 245–46.

[32] T Diefenbach, 'New Public Management in Public Sector Organizations: The Dark Sides of Managerialistic "Enlightenment"' (2009) 87 *Public Administration* 892.

[33] G Vasconcelos Vilaca, 'The Place of Ethical Leadership, Virtues and Narrative in International Organizations' in G Vasconcelos Vilaca and M Varaki (eds), *Ethical Leadership in International Organizations: Concepts, Narratives, Judgment and Assessment* (Cambridge, Cambridge University Press forthcoming).

[34] M Foucault, *Security, Territory, Population: Lectures at the Collège de France, 1977–78* (M Senellart, F Ewald and A Fontana trans, New York, Picador, 2007); N Rose, *Inventing Our Selves: Psychology, Power, and Personhood*, reprint edn (Cambridge, Cambridge University Press, 1998).

shares at least an affinity with the kind of biopolitical governmentality that Michel Foucault described as aiming to maximise the health and productivity of the population, with 'political economy as its major form of knowledge, and apparatuses of security as its essential technical instrument'.[35] Third, it is linked to the strengthening of the executive branch, guided by the idea that that branch must at each moment have such powers as are proportionate to adequately tackle whatever threat they are facing at that moment – a notion that is closely linked to biopolitics in that it is justified to the public through the things that they 'cannot help wanting [such as] their life, their health, their safety'.[36] Finally, managerialism, as I use it here, is connected to the notion that power and authority should belong to whatever actor is best at fulfilling the aims of the administration (such as the protection of the life and health of the population) – an idea which is 'balanced' by the requirement of 'accountability' of those actors for their performance.[37]

At the international level, these broadly managerial ideas and techniques were first tested in the colonial context, as a form of indirect rule of a small number of colonial rulers over the indigenous majority.[38] And soon afterwards, many of these practices were adopted and widely applied by the UN and other international institutions in the governance of the decolonised world.[39] Much like at the domestic level, managerialism intensified in the 1990s as the fall of the Berlin Wall and the end of the Cold War opened 'the door to the governance ethos in the international world', giving the impression that the 'world could be governed like the domestic'.[40] International organisations mushroomed, giving birth to a global governance network which is 'the sum of myriad – literally millions of – control mechanisms driven by different histories, goals, structures, and processes'.[41] Within this network, authority was separated from sovereignty and vested in whatever expert body seemed best fit to tackle a particular problem.[42]

[35] Foucault, *Security, Territory, Population*, 108. See also M Foucault, *The History of Sexuality* (R Hurley trans, New York, Vintage Books, 1988); M Foucault, *'Society Must Be Defended': Lectures at the Collège de France, 1975–76* (M Bertani, A Fontana and D Macey trans, New York, Picador, 2003).

[36] A Somek, *The Cosmopolitan Constitution* (Oxford, Oxford University Press, 2014) 216.

[37] A Orford, *International Authority and the Responsibility to Protect* (Cambridge, Cambridge University Press, 2011) chs 3 and 4.

[38] M Mamdani, *Citizen and Subject: Contemporary Africa and the Legacy of Late Colonialism* (Princeton, Princeton University Press, 1996).

[39] Orford, *International Authority and the Responsibility to Protect*; GF Sinclair, *To Reform the World: International Organizations and the Making of Modern States* (Oxford, Oxford University Press, 2017).

[40] M Koskenniemi, 'Global Governance and Public International Law' (2004) 37 *Kritische Justiz* 241, 248.

[41] J Rosenau, 'Governance in the Twenty-First Century' in R Wilkinson (ed), *The Global Governance Reader* (London, New York, Routledge, 2005) 48.

[42] N Walker, *Intimations of Global Law* (Cambridge, Cambridge University Press, 2014) 13–14; Lawrence S Finkelstein, 'What Is Global Governance' (1995) 1 *Global Governance* 367, 369.

What connects the otherwise separate law of humanity and managerial mindsets is their focus on the protection of human life. Above, I suggested that managerialism could be linked from a Foucauldian perspective to biopolitical managerialism and thus to the maximisation of the life of the population. But even if one were hesitant to make such theoretical leaps, and take a more historical approach, preferring to focus more directly on the questions of authority, accountability, efficiency and productivity that have been at the heart of the post-war discussion of managerialism and the NPM, there is nevertheless a connection between the rise of managerialism and the law of humanity mindset, for, since the 1990s, managerialism at the global level has increasingly focused on questions of humanitarianism, human security and human rights.

This development, as I see it, can be at least partly explained by two interlinked developments that occurred during the twentieth century. The first, more background development is the rise of American social sciences, both in academia and in global governance, and the increasingly significant normative role it was given in grounding technical expertise and the politics of great powers and international organisations.[43] The second, more directly connected to the law of humanity, is the increased relevance of what Didier Fassin has called 'biolegitimacy'. By that term, Fassin refers to the sacredness and power of life – understood in the sense of simply being alive – as the most fundamental of all values and as the source of legitimacy of governance.[44] Indeed, even without making complicated and contestable arguments about the actual empowerment of individuals, about increasing welfare or biopower, it seems that, at the level of discourse and values, the protection and sacredness of life gained an increasingly prevalent role towards the end of the twentieth century. This was also the development that the law of humanity theorists were reacting to and drawing from, as it became commonplace to argue that the international community 'supplants sovereignty with subsidiarity or "humanity" as its major organizing principle [and] places the vulnerable individual at the center of the international order'.[45] Teitel, in particular, seems to have touched upon the ethos of the time when she mapped the rise of an ethical and legal discourse based on human survival.[46]

[43] G Vasconcelos Vilaca, 'Book Review: To Reform the World: International Organizations and the Making of Modern States Written by Guy Fiti Sinclair' (2018) 15 *International Organizations Law Review* 221, 226; Sinclair, *To Reform the World*; Mark Mazower, *Governing the World: The History of an Idea, 1815 to the Present* (New York, Penguin Books, 2013) 285.

[44] D Fassin, *Humanitarian Reason: A Moral History of the Present* (Berkley, University of California Press, 2011) 249. See further D Fassin, 'Another Politics of Life Is Possible' (2009) 26 *Theory, Culture & Society* 44; D Fassin, 'Compassion and Repression: The Moral Economy of Immigration Policies in France' (2005) 20 *Cultural Anthropology* 362.

[45] Somek, *The Cosmopolitan Constitution*, 153–54. See also P Cheah, *Inhuman Conditions: On Cosmopolitanism and Human Rights* (Cambridge, MA, Harvard University Press, 2007).

[46] R Teitel, *Humanity's Law* (Oxford, Oxford University Press, 2011).

The emergence of biolegitimacy as the foundation of governance further amplified managerialism, which was already on the rise in the 1990s. When legitimacy derives from the protection of human life, authority tends to devolve to whatever instance manages to represent itself as the conscience of humanity and convince others that it can protect human life most efficiently. Inherent in this mindset is a compulsion that decisions have to be made quickly, meaning that (expert) decision makers cannot be tied to burdensome procedures or tiresome rules.[47] As one commentator puts it, when human life is made the ultimate value of the international community, 'we cease to ask "why?" questions and start to ask "how?"', for at that point we have 'a vision of global law that transcends the authority of states and peoples'.[48]

Furthermore, in the era of biolegitimacy, global managers became increasingly interested in the protection of life. Behind this was both a genuine determination to protect life and reasons of power and authority. As scholars have noted, the discretion and power of different organisations and networks is increased significantly so long as they are seen to be acting in the name of humanity.[49] Issues of funding have also played a role in this regard. As humanitarian governance has started to attract funders, but the number of humanitarian actors has simultaneously grown exponentially, humanitarian actors have increasingly adopted business-like, managerial practices and mindsets, which are seen to make governance more efficient, attract media attention and correspond to the demands of funders.[50]

As the managerial mindset became increasingly prevalent following the breakthrough of American social science and as international experts started to orient towards humanitarian governance, humanity language started to be increasingly used as part of managerial projects. Thus, although law of humanity theories are not managerial in themselves, the law of humanity project started to converge with managerial ones. One example is the humanitarian occupation missions – in other words, international territorial administration missions which derived their normative foundation from biolegitimacy and employed the humanity language to the extent that some commentators felt they deserved to be separated from previous missions with a new name.[51] As was discussed in the previous chapter, international actors 'took on a dizzying array of tasks' as part of these missions, managing the day-to-day activities of the states, 'from profound matters of policy to mundane custodial functions'.[52] The authority

[47] Orford, 'Book Review Article' (n 27) 234. See also Somek (n 36) 226–28.

[48] S Hopgood, *The Endtimes of Human Rights* (Ithaca, NY, Cornell University Press, 2013) 6–8.

[49] J Klabbers, 'The Life and Times of the Law of International Organizations' (2001) 70 *Nordic Journal of International Law* 287, 288; E Benvenisti, *The Law of Global Governance* (The Hague, Brill-Nijhoff, 2014) 92. See also DW Kennedy, 'New World Order: Yesterday, Today, and Tomorrow' (1994) 4 *Transnational Law & Contemporary Problems* 329.

[50] Duncombe and Dunne, 'After Liberal World Order', 40–41; MN Barnett, 'Humanitarian Governance' (2013) 16 *Annual Review of Political Science* 379.

[51] GH Fox, *Humanitarian Occupation* (Cambridge, Cambridge University Press, 2008).

[52] ibid 72–73.

and powers of these managers were derived from the fulfilment of their technical and humanitarian tasks, including the 'welfare of populations', rather than from any established status or rules of international law, as functions were 'vested in this or that social group or actor, in the way that a manager might vest a task in this or that organizational department'.[53] Moreover, the early managerial techniques, tested in the colonial context, were also put to use as the international actors governed 'through local laws where possible, trumping them with administrative regulations and decrees where necessary to achieve the goals determined centrally', whereas local parliaments and courts were subordinated to administrative rule. Furthermore, international administrators were both spatially and legally separated from the local population in that they lived in separate zones and were subject to special regimes of privileges and immunities.[54]

The convergence of the law of humanity project and managerialism is also visible in the humanitarian governance of refugees, and in particular in the administration of the so-called 'development camps'. In running the camps, humanitarian organisations take care of most functions of the state, based solely on the authority of protecting human life.[55] Moreover, one of the key sources of inspiration of the law of humanity theories, namely the emergence of the responsibility to protect concept, is the result of a merger between biolegitimacy and managerialism. Seeking to safeguard the efficient protection of life and human security of the population, the responsibility to protect concept casts sovereignty as a matter of degree and makes it dependent on efficient fulfilment of certain functions (protection of life). In so doing, it also posits international managers, in the form of the UN and global governance organisations, as the ultimate guarantors of the completion of that task.[56]

The merger of managerialism and humanitarianism is a theme that has also been studied by several legal anthropologists. For example, in her ethnographic study, Lori Allen describes how human rights organisations landed in Palestine in the 1980s and how human rights have since been mainstreamed throughout the society despite most Palestinians having become increasingly cynical of the process. As Allen demonstrates in detail, the revolutionary, activist spirit of human rights actors quickly turned into increasing standardisation and professionalisation as donors sought to regulate the work of human rights organisations. Over time, human rights came to be 'utilized more and more as a technocratic tool, as if "human rights" were a set of skills that could

[53] Orford, 'Book Review Article' (n 27) 243.

[54] ibid 247.

[55] M Pallis, 'The Operation of UNHCR's Accountability Mechanisms' (2004) 37 *New York University Journal of International Law and Politics* 869, 883–86; R Wilde, 'Quis Custodiet Ipsos Custodes: Why and How UNHCR Governance of Development Refugee Camps Should Be Subject to International Human Rights Law Note' (1998) 1 *Yale Human Rights & Development Law Journal* 107, 107–10; L Barnett, 'Global Governance and the Evolution of the International Refugee Regime' (2002) 14 *International Journal of Refugee Law* 238, 251.

[56] Orford, *International Authority and the Responsibility to Protect* (n 37).

be taught and mastered, regardless of any change in political framework'.[57] Strictly standardised statehood, based on human rights, came to be performed for the international audience,[58] despite growing internal discontent amongst Palestinians, who had wished for forms of 'collective liberation and solidarity' which differ starkly from the current market-oriented model.[59]

Finally, another illustrative example of the merger is the rise of indicators and audits. Originally used primarily in business management, indicators have now also pervaded humanitarian governance of refugees and human rights law. As Sally Engle Merry defines them, 'Indicators are statistical measures that are used to consolidate complex data into a simple number of rank that is meaningful to policy makers and the public'.[60] Far from being purely quantitative, indicators often include qualitative information, such as evaluations of legislation and policies (quantified, for example, by counting the number of laws), which is then reduced into a measurable number. Furthermore, many indicators 'are composites of other indicators, a blending and weighting of established indicators into a new bundle'.[61] These indicators are now used, for example, to evaluate a country's or an organisation's efforts to promote and defend human rights and to distribute resources on this basis.[62] The result is the birth of an entire human rights audit culture in which states and organisations render themselves auditable through different forms of self-management which allow the governors to 'withdraw from checking behavior and simply check indictors of performance'.[63]

As Merry notes, the turn to indicators marks an important shift in human rights administration. The burden of assessment can now be claimed to 'rest on the indicator itself, with its agreed-on standards and means of measurement', producing 'an unambiguous and easily replicated field for judgment' and shifting responsibility to the monitored state or organisation. Whereas the practice of human rights treaty bodies has been to persuade states to develop their own indicators, more recently there has been a move towards developing universal indicators for all states.[64] This has direct effects on the distribution of power,

[57] L Allen, *The Rise and Fall of Human Rights: Cynicism and Politics in Occupied Palestine* (Stanford, Stanford University Press, 2013) 3–4.

[58] ibid 12–16.

[59] ibid 17. See also A Von Schnitzler, 'Performing Dignity: Human Rights, Citizenship, and the Techno-politics of Law in South Africa' (2014) 41 *American Ethnologist* 336 for an account of how an access campaign in a poor area of Johannesburg was slowly transformed from a human dignity battle into a question of basic biological needs as it moved up the South-African court system, eventually boiling down to a competition between two foreign experts on how many litres of water a person needs per day.

[60] SE Merry, 'Measuring the World: Indicators, Human Rights, and Global Governance' (2011) 52 *Current Anthropology* 83, 86.

[61] ibid.

[62] Davis et al, 'Indicators as a Technology of Global Governance', 83.

[63] Merry, 'Measuring the World', 88.

[64] ibid.

authority and resources, as indicators are widely used to make decisions and allocate resources, such as development aid. As indicators put emphasis on long-term statistical management of entire populations and their setting requires complex methodological decisions, they shift power from political and judicial leaders to managers.[65]

In all of the examples cited above, there has been a significant shift of power from democratically elected representatives of the state to global managers who derive their authority from technical expertise and the perceived capacity to efficiently protect life and human rights. In many of these instances, however, the local populations viewed this shift of power with scepticism. This is clear in, for example, Allen's account of Palestine, where most of the Palestinians quickly grew cynical of the human rights experts, and started dreaming of a collective project, based on solidarity and welfare. Similarly, the relation between the East Timorese and the United Nations Transitional Administration in East Timor (UNTAET) was very difficult, the locals feeling that their wishes and hopes were disregarded by the international expert administration.[66] And in Europe, too, the widely shared impression that the people are losing sovereignty, as decision-making power is shifted to EU experts, has been a continuous source of discontent. All over the world, then, this perceived loss of power to experts has formed a fertile breeding ground for populism.

Considering the connection between managerialism, humanitarianism and the humanity language, as well as the position that human rights have gained in public discussion during the past three decades, it is perhaps not surprising that many of the backlashes against expertise have been directed at human rights – especially not when the prominent positions of expertise and human rights are connected to the indeterminacy of the rights language. As critical legal scholars have emphasised for decades now, human rights are fundamentally indeterminate and thus capable of supporting various, often competing claims. As was demonstrated in chapters three and four, they can be used to both support war on terror in the name of security and protest against it in the name of privacy and civil liberties; or to protect strong property rights as well as limit them in the name of equality and general welfare. Yet, human rights experts have always seen themselves as able to distinguish 'genuine' human rights concerns from what they perceive as cynical attempts to abuse rights, thus using their expertise to protect some views and interests while rejecting others. This has often seemed baffling or even unfair to outsiders, who have felt that their rights have been ignored. 'In the absence of clear criteria to distinguish "real" from "fake" rights, the human rights camp seems to be merely trying to impose its values on the world' while hiding behind the image of humanitarian neutrality.'[67] This has

[65] ibid 85.

[66] OP Richmond and J Franks, 'Liberal Peacebuilding in Timor Leste: The Emperor's New Clothes?' (2008) 15 *International Peacekeeping* 185, 197.

[67] Koskenniemi (n 15) 415.

made human rights easy prey for the backlashers, who have learned to abuse their indeterminacy and thus present them as nothing more than '*leftist policy in un-political disguise*'.[68] Although such a claim might have rung hollow a decade or two earlier, by the aftermath of the 2008 financial crisis it very much hit its target, as the public had started to view the human rights-speaking Third Way politicians and experts as an elite that spoke of free trade but had nothing more than austerity and growing inequality to offer to most people.

B. The Law of Humanity Project and Neoliberalism

The question of inequality brings us to the second powerful mindset and project that the law of humanity project has had to coexist and interact with, and that has sought to hijack some of its key concepts: namely, neoliberalism. Neoliberal theory was created in continental Europe in the 1930s. Since then, it has developed into different schools, such as the Freiburg school, the Geneva school, the Chicago school and the Cologne school, and has gone from one transformation to another.[69] Furthermore, as the term 'neoliberalism' has become mainstreamed, it has been given – especially by its critics – such different meanings that many have argued that it has become meaningless. Yet, as Quinn Slobodian has argued, labelling neoliberalism helps to see it 'as one body of thought and one mode of governance among others', and hence as a form of regulation, rather than its radical 'other', as it is sometimes presented.[70]

To clarify, then, by 'neoliberalism', I mean a way of thinking and a political, economic, moral and legal project which adopts certain aims of classical liberalism, such as privatisation, deregulation and the idea that 'human well-being can best be advanced by liberating individual entrepreneurial freedoms',[71] but combines them with the very non-classical notion that 'the market does not and cannot take care of itself'.[72] Thus, neoliberals have sought not only to liberalise markets, but to 'encase them, to inoculate capitalism against the threat of democracy, to create a framework to contain often-irrational human behavior, and to reorder the world after empire as a space of competing states in which borders fulfil a necessary function'.[73] Neoliberalism is therefore not opposed to regulation, as is sometimes claimed, but rather is itself a form of regulation, aimed at constituting and maintaining markets, and protecting them from political contestation. Public authorities are not allowed to second-guess market

[68] ibid 416 (original emphasis).
[69] D Plehwe, Q Slobodian and P Mirowski (eds), *Nine Lives of Neoliberalism* (Brooklyn, Verso, 2020).
[70] Slobodian, *Globalists*, 3.
[71] D Harvey, *A Brief History of Neoliberalism* (Oxford, Oxford University Press, 2007) 2.
[72] Slobodian (n 20) 2.
[73] ibid.

signals, but they do play an active role, for example, in guaranteeing the quality and integrity of money, in setting legal and policy structures which protect private property and the enforcement of contracts, and in creating markets where they did not exist before, for example by privatising areas such as water and healthcare, which used to belong to the public sphere.[74] Furthermore, the authorities are supposed to cultivate and enforce 'a moral climate that instils personal responsibility and regards it as just that people are rewarded materially based on how valuable their services are to their fellows'.[75] In the neoliberal society, commercial values are promoted and self-interest rewarded, duties towards others are limited to not harming them and fulfilling market obligations, and redistribution and egalitarian commitments are discouraged or made impossible.[76]

Neoliberalism was tested as a dominant theory of government in Chile in the 1970s and was adopted by countries such as the USA and the UK in the 1980s. By the mid-1990s, it had spread to virtually all corners of the globe.[77] With respect to international and transnational law, the neoliberal way of thinking has guided the attempts of the World Bank, the International Monetary Fund (IMF), the WTO, NAFTA, the EU, other international institutions and central banks to shield the world economy from democratic contestation. It is also reflected in the creation of tax havens, which protect property owners from the redistribution of their wealth, as well as in the insulation of investors from domestic politics and laws.[78] Neoliberalism is also associated with free trade policies, although 'in practice it has largely only been in the developing world, with the turn away from import substitution, that the neoliberal turn has systematically gone in hand with a turn towards unilateral free trade in any doctrinaire sense'.[79] As Andrew Lang has demonstrated, neoliberalism in world trade has been reflected less in the removal of trade barriers than in the interpretation of indeterminate rules in a way that casts some governmental activities as trade barriers, while others are left outside that treatment, and in the delegitimation of collective purpose as a rationale for trade policies or interventions.[80]

The connection between the key concepts of the law of humanity project – most notably human rights – and neoliberalism has been the topic of much academic discussion lately. Law of humanity theories are not neoliberal and many of the law of humanity theorists are probably highly critical of neoliberalism. Yet, as Koskenniemi would surely note, the historically most significant rights

[74] Harvey, *A Brief History of Neoliberalism*, 2.
[75] Whyte (n 20) 10–11.
[76] ibid 10–14.
[77] Harvey (n 71).
[78] Slobodian (n 20) 4.
[79] Lang, *World Trade Law after Neoliberalism*, 2.
[80] Lang (n 22).

struggles have been about the recognition of rights to own property, as reflected recently, for example, in the argument that the right to repatriate profits from the investment can be derived from a right to property. Perhaps drawing from similar observations, several scholars have made a strong connection between human rights and neoliberalism. Wendy Brown, for example, has pointed out the interlinkages between human rights and free trade, and the ways in which the former serves to legitimate the latter,[81] whereas Upendra Baxi and Makau Mutua have done some pioneering work on market-friendly human rights and the disregard of economic powerlessness.[82] And perhaps most prominently, Susan Marks has argued that the human rights discourse has been complicit in the rise of neoliberalism by sweeping the structural foundation of inequality under the carpet,[83] and by concentrating on the protection of property and enclosure.[84]

Others have cautioned against making such strong claims. Samuel Moyn, for example, argues that there is nothing neoliberal in human rights per se, and that proponents of human rights have rarely been sympathetic to neoliberalism. Yet, Moyn, too, makes the case that human rights have been unwitting companions to neoliberalism in that, at the heyday of neoliberalism, they have settled all too easily on sufficiency at the expense of equality (partly due to structural differences between the enforcement of civil and political rights, on the one hand, and economic, social and cultural rights, on the other). Thus, although human rights have proven valuable in poverty reduction – that is to say, in raising the poorest to the level of sufficiency – they have been incapable of addressing the rising wealth gap that is characteristic of contemporary societies in our neoliberal age.[85] Moreover, the individualism of human rights has matched well with neoliberalism's emphasis on property rights, and both human rights champions and neoliberals have shared a certain suspicion of the state – the former as a potential source of political oppression and the latter as a potential threat to the smooth functioning of the economy.

Regardless of where one puts the emphasis in the discussion of the connections between human rights and neoliberalism, then, most commentators would find that some aspects of human rights have been hijacked and used by

[81] W Brown, '"The Most We Can Hope For ...": Human Rights and the Politics of Fatalism' (2004) 103 *South Atlantic Quarterly* 451.

[82] U Baxi, *The Future of Human Rights* (Oxford, Oxford University Press,2008); M Mutua, 'Human Rights and Powerlessness: Pathologies of Choice and Substance Essay Collection: Class-crits: Part I: Thinking through Law's Questions of Class, Economics, and Inequality' (2008) 56 *Buffalo Law Review* 1027.

[83] S Marks, 'Four Human Rights Myths' in D Kinley, W Sadurski and K Walton (eds), *Human Rights: Old Problems, New Possibilities* (Cheltenham, Edward Elgar Publishing, 2014).

[84] S Marks, *A False Tree of Liberty: Human Rights in Radical Thought* (Oxford, Oxford University Press, 2019). See also P O'Connell, 'On the Human Rights Question' (2018) 40 *Human Rights Quarterly* 962.

[85] S Moyn, *Not Enough: Human Rights in an Unequal World* (Cambridge, MA, Belknap Press at Harvard University Press, 2018).

neoliberals in order to be used as tools in different struggles. This argument has been made in great detail in two important recent works. In his *Globalists*, Quinn Slobodian demonstrates how neoliberals have used states and global institutions to insulate the markets against state action, democratic demands for material equality and other possible 'threats'.[86] To accomplish this task, neoliberals found a powerful tool in human rights, which they defined in a quite specific way so that they could be used to protect individual trading, market and capital rights, and to eventually reimagine the project of neoliberal federalism as one of protecting universal liberal human rights. As Slobodian writes, this idea was initially proposed after World Wars II by the International Chamber of Commerce, and was eventually used by academics, politicians and global administrators shortly after the establishment of the WTO to defend it against mounting criticism.[87] For example, Ernst-Ulrich Petersmann reacted to the 1999 Seattle WTO Protest by arguing for the adoption of a human rights framework within the WTO in order to increase its legitimacy, while interpreting human rights in a very particular way, emphasising property rights, limits to governmental exercise of power and non-discriminatory open markets.[88] In so doing, he imagined – along with the director of the WTO, Pascal Lamy, and other influential persons – a global constitutional system in which market citizenship and the individual as an economic actor can knit the global system together from the bottom up,[89] and in which 'trade is human rights in practice'.[90]

In another important recent work, Jessica Whyte has further elaborated on the connection between human rights and neoliberalism.[91] According to Whyte, economic theories are only one aspect of neoliberalism. Equally important have been the attempts to create a 'moral and civilized' society in which individuals are subjugated to market rationality, and to support this model of society with domestic and international institutions that are efficient in protecting markets from mass politics. In order to establish and enforce 'morals of the market', early neoliberals participated actively in the struggle over the conceptualisation of human rights, developing an account of human rights as 'moral and legal support for a liberal market order', and making the case that 'only a liberal market economy could foster human rights'.[92] Although neoliberal

[86] Slobodian (n 20).
[87] ibid 277–78.
[88] EU Petersmann, 'The WTO Constitution and Human Rights' (2000) 3 *Journal of International Economic Law* 19; EU Petersmann, 'From "Negative" to "Positive" Integration in the WTO: Time for "Mainstreaming Human Rights" into WTO Law?' (2000) 37 *CML Rev* 1363; EU Petersmann, 'Human Rights and International Economic Law in the 21st Century. The Need to Clarify Their Interrelationships' (2001) 4 *Journal of International Economic Law* 3.
[89] Slobodian (n 20) 279–80.
[90] P Lamy, 'Lamy Calls for Mindset Change to Align Trade and Human Rights' (13 January 2010), www.wto.org/english/news_e/sppl_e/sppl146_e.htm.
[91] Whyte (n 20).
[92] ibid 18–19.

thinkers rejected any notion of material equality, they embraced the capacity of human rights to protect formal equality and thus counter any attempt at redistribution.[93] And although the neoliberal conception of human rights was, and is, only one amongst many, it has been influential in that NGOs and other actors have adopted the dichotomy, cherished by neoliberals, between civil and commercial society, on the one hand, and state and politics, on the other, casting the first as a realm of freedom and the latter as violent and conflictual.[94]

As the human rights revolution turned out to be a success and biolegitimacy came to guide global governance towards the end of the twentieth century, the strategic importance of humanity language increased significantly. The co-optation of the humanity language to advance neoliberal goals was demonstrated most powerfully in the humanitarian occupation missions in the 1990s and the first years of the new millennium. As was demonstrated in the previous chapter, the missions, legitimated on the basis of the protection of human life, human rights, human dignity and human security, included far-reaching transformations of the target states, so as to meet the requirements of a neoliberal market society. Kosovo, for example, was rapidly transformed through international administration, international expert-led law-making and private sector-led development into a liberal market economy, and its institutions and administration were shaped according to the neoliberal vision.[95] Centralised economic planning was dismantled, socially owned enterprises were privatised, the agricultural sector was integrated into global value chains and industrial restructuring was left to market actors.[96] Similarly, in East Timor, UNTAET entered into a local governance project treaty with the World Bank. The Bank took control over East Timor's economic governance, implementing a neoliberal political and economic transformation project, which preferred a small state, and aimed to develop capitalism, privatise as many sectors as possible, commercialise agriculture and attract foreign investors, who indeed soon overran the country, conducting lucrative deals with UNTAET.[97] And in Iraq, the occupiers declared from the outset that the country would be transformed from a state-owned economy to a 'dynamic' private sector one.[98] The banking sector was opened to foreign ownership, flat tax rates were introduced, tariffs and custom duties

[93] ibid 24.

[94] ibid 29–30, ch 5.

[95] LJ Uberti, 'Neoliberalism and Industrial Policy in Kosovo: The Mining and Metals Industry in the Post-War Transition' (2014) 30 *East European Politics* 482.

[96] M Grasten and N Tzouvala, 'The Political Economy of International Transitional Administration: Regulating Food and Farming in Kosovo and Iraq' (2018) 24 *Contemporary Politics* 588, 594–98.

[97] Richmond and Franks, 'Liberal Peacebuilding in Timor Leste, 197; A Orford, *Reading Humanitarian Intervention: Human Rights and the Use of Force in International Law*, reissue edn (Cambridge, Cambridge University Press, 2007) 135–36.

[98] Cited in GH Fox, 'The Occupation of Iraq' (Social Science Research Network, 2004), SSRN Scholarly Paper ID 595163, 24–25, www.papers.ssrn.com/abstract=595163.

were suspended, business was opened to foreign investors, bankruptcy laws were changed to encourage risk-taking, intellectual property laws were strengthened, a new stock exchange was established and agriculture was commercialised and absorbed into global value chains.[99]

In addition to these large-scale projects, there are also numerous humanitarian NGOs – 'with a strong belief in the holy trinity of the global market economy, promoting liberal democracy and human rights'[100] – which utilise the humanity language to push through broadly neoliberal reforms in the developing world. Many of these NGOs work in shaping and supporting the institutions of fragile states, while at the same time subjecting themselves to the market logic in competing for limited financial resources provided by donors.[101] To take again the case of Palestine as an example, Lori Allen describes the disappointment of many Palestinians that the state being built under the tutelage of human rights organisations and public and private donors is characterised by a market-oriented mindset instead of collective care. As Allen writes, the international managers conceptualise citizens as consumers and human rights as a market-driven industry – a vision which clashes with the common Palestinian dream of 'collective liberation and solidarity'.[102] Indeed, as commentators note, human rights and humanitarian NGOs, financed by international donors, 'were among the first sectors in Palestinian society to embrace neoliberalism', and 'have acted as an important conduit of its development paradigm', as well as 'an "anti-politics machine" that has depoliticized Palestinian society, sustained the occupation, and initiated the long march toward neoliberal hegemony that has found its most elaborate manifestation to date in the [Palestinian Authority's] statehood plan'.[103]

Although the value of neoliberal theory and the outcomes of the neoliberal turn can be debated, it seems incontestable that the neoliberal age has seen a sharp rise in economic inequality, especially within states. Neoliberal policies and legislation have included massive tax cuts for the rich, privatisation, deregulation and attacks on trade unions, and these reforms have been extended to all corners of the world through international organisations and other global governance organisations. Furthermore, the increasingly important role of rent and financialisation has granted the rich increasing control over money, which is

[99] Fox, 'The Occupation of Iraq'; N Tzouvala, 'Food for the Global Market: The Neoliberal Reconstruction of Agriculture in Occupied Iraq (2003–2004) and the Role of International Law' (2017) 17 *Global Jurist*; 'The Political Economy of International Transitional Administration: Regulating Food and Farming in Kosovo and Iraq' (2018) 24 *Contemporary Politics* 588.

[100] F Johansson, 'The Question of Power: A View from a Critical Insider' in L Doutje and L van Troost (eds), *Debating the Endtimes of Human Rights: Activism and Institutions in a Neo-Westphalian World* (Amsterdam, Strategic Studies Project, 2014).

[101] Duncombe and Dunne (n 11) 40–41; Barnett, 'Humanitarian Governance'.

[102] Allen, *The Rise and Fall of Human Rights*, 17.

[103] R Khalidi and S Samour, 'Neoliberalism as Liberation: The Statehood Program and the Remaking of the Palestinian National Movement' (2011) 40 *Journal of Palestine Studies* 6, 20.

used less and less to invest in the production of goods and services and more to invest in rent and interest harvesting and capital gains.[104] With the growing role of finance, the world has become increasingly unequal, and is growing more so every day. As Thomas Piketty famously demonstrated, this is the 'central contradiction of capitalism': as the rate of return on capital grows higher than the rate of income/growth, 'wealth accumulated in the past grows more rapidly than output and wages', entrepreneurs become rentiers and the economic gap between those who own and those who earn only through labour grows larger and larger.[105] Indeed, since the breakthrough of neoliberalism in the 1980s, the top 0.1 per cent has captured as much growth as the bottom half of the world adult population. Today, the top 10 per cent own more than 70 per cent of the total wealth, while the bottom 50 per cent own less than 2 per cent, according to data collected from the USA, Europe and China, and it is estimated that the contrast would be even more arresting if data from the rest of the world were included.[106] Furthermore, every crisis seems to further entrench this trend, as has been evidenced most recently by the COVID-19 crisis, during which the wealth of the richest persons in the world has increased significantly, while the rest have suffered.[107]

The rising inequalities have provided fertile feeding ground for populists. As inequalities have been steadily growing and unemployment and individual debt have been steadily rising, more and more people have started to lose faith in the 'old' leaders and institutions, and are searching for scapegoats and alternatives. The final straw was the 2008 economic crisis, as people saw the responsible financial institutions bailed out while they had to bear the burden in the form of austerity measures, personal insolvency and so on. In this situation, right-wing populists managed to capture many people's minds, even though the populists often operate without a sophisticated understanding of the economy and have been unable or unwilling to tackle the root causes of underlying mindsets behind the growing inequality gap, settling for throwing vague accusations towards 'elites', 'experts' and other political parties.

III. PATHS AHEAD FROM THE CROSSROADS

If it wishes to be efficient in fulfilling its aims of increasing welfare and human empowerment, and to be able to counter the root causes of the populist backlash, the law of humanity project needs to find more methods to tackle the

[104] Harvey (n 71); G Monbiot, *How Did We Get Into This Mess?: Politics, Equality, Nature*, reprint edn (London, Verso, 2017); A Sayer, *Why We Can't Afford the Rich*, reprint edn (Bristol, Policy Press, 2015).

[105] T Piketty, *Capital in the Twenty-First Century*, reprint edn (A Goldhammer trans, Cambridge, MA, Belknap Press at Harvard University Press, 2017) 571.

[106] World Inequality Report 2018, www.wir2018.wid.world/files/download/wir2018-summary-english.pdf.

[107] See, eg www.inequality.org/great-divide/billionaire-bonanza-2020.

trends of rising inequality and people being left out of the decision-making, which are characteristic of the neoliberal and managerial era. This task is particularly pertinent yet difficult, as the law of humanity project has by necessity been embedded within a complex web of power relations and forms of knowledge, dominated by the neoliberal and managerial mindsets. Although the law of humanity theories are neither managerialist nor neoliberal, the project blossomed during their heyday and has had to coexist with them. It has therefore been unavoidable that the humanity language has intersected with, and sometimes even been hijacked by, the managerialist and neoliberal projects in the messy practice of global governance.

This has been enabled not only by the fact that, without a clear institutional and scientific discourse of its own, the beautiful ideas of the law of humanity project have been easy to absorb into the frameworks and models of the governance machinery, dominated by very specific strands of social science and economics,[108] but also by the other fact that, despite their key differences, the law of humanity theory shares with managerialism and neoliberalism certain ideas and ways of thinking, most importantly the urge to discipline the state.

Indeed, from the perspective of all three projects, the sovereign state is a potential source of chaos, coercion and violence, and is thus regarded with suspicion. For the law of humanity project, the disciplining of the state is necessary for a shift towards a more human-centred global legal system. For the managerialists, the state – which consists of a number of practices, ways of doing things, rationales, programmes and techniques that have gradually taken over[109] – is an important tool of governance but is always susceptible to adopting the wrong forms of knowledge and practices, and is thus in need of constant shaping and reining in. Finally, what differentiates neoliberalism most clearly from classical liberalism is that neoliberals have understood that markets are not natural but need to be produced and maintained through laws and institutions. The neoliberal project needs the state, for the state remains the most efficient actor in the maintenance of markets, the surrounding institutional and legal structure, and the morals of the market.[110] The state, with its police and regulatory power, is therefore a necessary tool for the insulation of markets against political contestation.[111] But this means that the state must be strictly limited in other ways in order to avoid becoming a vehicle of mass politics.[112] Strong yet limited, the state must use its strength to resist organised interests and guarantee property

[108] I thank Guilherme Vasconcelos Vilaça for this point.

[109] M Foucault, *The Birth of Biopolitics: Lectures at the Collège de France, 1978–1979* (M Senellart trans, New York, Picador, 2010) 77.

[110] Whyte (n 20).

[111] Slobodian (n 20).

[112] Harvey (n 71) 2.

rights and the uninhibited operation of the market in all possible ways.[113] It must have the right institutions and laws to safeguard the boundaries of imperium and dominium,[114] and must be able to beat people into submission to the market logic, thus replacing the dangerous sovereignty of the people with the sovereignty of the markets.[115]

The fact that the humanity language has occasionally been used by managerialists and neoliberalism is not the fault of law of humanity theories, nor an inherent weakness of the project per se. But taking account of these realities is necessary in order to choose the best path at the crossroads where the project now finds itself. The need to rethink the project is emphasised especially by the fact that many of its key values, such as global cooperation, international solidarity and the protection of human rights, seem to be some of the primary victims of the backlash, whereas neoliberalism has so far been left unscathed, apart from some states withdrawing from BITs and international economic cooperation – minor casualties which are unlikely to touch the key causes of global material inequality, such as finance capitalism. In fact, while attacking the 'globalist' agenda and replacing humanitarianism with xenophobic policies, most of the new authoritarian and populist leaders have embraced austerity measures and other neoliberal ideas, and have been willing to use hard disciplinary measures in order to ensure the smooth functioning of the economy.[116]

In what follows, then, I seek to start a discussion on what an updated law of humanity project, tailored for the era of neoliberalism, managerialism and populism, could look like. I argue that such an updated project needs to be more aware of the networks of power it is embedded in, oppose itself more directly against neoliberalism, seek to make itself more useful and visible for persons and groups engaged in grassroot level struggles, and find enhanced techniques for addressing issues of material inequality. I suggest that this entails at least four closely interlinked steps.

A. A Struggles Perspective to Concepts

First, as a general point, and at the level of theory, the law of humanity project needs to be more sensitive to the ways in which concepts are objects of

[113] N Tzouvala, 'The Ordo-Liberal Origins of Modern International Investment Law: Constructing Competition on a Global Scale' in JD Haskell and A Rasulov (eds), *New Voices and New Perspectives in International Economic Law: New Voices, New Perspectives* (Springer, 2020) 37. For an example of how such a state is produced, see A Orford and J Beard, 'Making the State Safe for the Market: The World Bank's World Development Report 1997 Critique and Comment' (1998) 22 *Melbourne University Law Review* 195.

[114] Slobodian (n 20) 13.

[115] Whyte (n 20).

[116] ibid 239–42; Slobodian, 'Neoliberalism's Populist Bastards'.

struggle and tools of power. Many of the law of humanity theories seem to belong – perhaps unwittingly – to the venerable tradition of thought that seeks to define concepts and then instantiate them. What this approach tends to miss, however, is the point that the meaning of a concept in the social world is not about its reference, but its use.[117] The meanings of concepts change as a consequence of both situational and more long-term struggles over their meaning and ownership,[118] and these changes also alter behaviour with concrete political outcomes in the 'real' world.[119] Thus, mere references to humanity language should not be seen as 'progress' in itself. In addition to documenting references to law of humanity concepts, more attention should be paid to what is done with the concepts at the ground level and by whom,[120] while keeping in mind that the interests of those invoking the humanity language are not necessarily the same as a large part of the 'humanity' they represent, nor is 'the strength of the official human rights organizations and institutions … necessarily an index of the state of humanity itself'.[121]

Indeed, it has been part of the managerial and neoliberal strategies to 'neutralise' humanity language, while using it to veil what are quintessentially political projects.[122] Thus, there is a need to let go of the idea of depoliticisation of the law of humanity concepts. Having accepted that the concepts are often used politically, they can be used to address growing material inequality. Indeed, it seems that a growing number of human rights scholars and activists have come to realise that the effective protection of human rights demands that a stronger stance be taken against 'free markets' in favour of more effective forms of redistribution from the rich to the poor.[123] In the words of Paul O'Connell, in 'the contemporary era of austerity and commodification', struggles for water, food, healthcare and housing demand 'a rejection of the logic of the market, of the basic impulse of the capitalist system'.[124] Thus, the proponents of the law of humanity project should develop increasingly sophisticated methods to detect and address the ways in which the law of humanity concepts are appropriated to facilitate market fundamentalism.

[117] F Kratochwil, 'Has the "Rule of Law" Become a "Rule of Lawyers"? An Inquiry into the Use and Abuse of an Ancient Topos in Contemporary Debates' in G Palombella and N Walker (eds), *Relocating the Rule of Law* (Oxford, Hart Publishing, 2009) 195.

[118] K Palonen, 'An Application of Conceptual History to Itself: From Method to Theory in Reinhart Koselleck's Begriffsgeschifte' (1997) 1 *Finnish Yearbook of Political Thought* 36, 64–65.

[119] T Ball, J Farr and RL Hanson, 'Editors' Introduction' in T Ball, J Farr and RL Hanson (eds), *Political Innovation and Conceptual Change* (Cambridge, Cambridge University Press, 1989).

[120] F Kratochwil, 'Leaving Sovereignty Behind? An Inquiry into the Politics of Post-Modernity' in R Falk, M Juergensmeyer and V Popovski (eds), *Legality and Legitimacy in Global Affairs* (Oxford, Oxford University Press, 2012) 131.

[121] Whyte (n 20) 235–36.

[122] ibid 239–42.

[123] R Dudai, 'Human Rights in the Populist Era: Mourn then (Re)Organize' (2017) 9 *Journal of Human Rights Practice* 16, 19.

[124] O'Connell, 'On the Human Rights Question', 988.

B. Engagement with Grassroot Struggles

Second, in line with the aims of taking a stronger stance against market fundamentalism, making humanity language more politically relevant and enabling it to regain its legitimacy in the eyes of the people, there is a need for the law of humanity project to engage more with concrete struggles at the grassroot level. This engagement could take several forms.

For one, the law of humanity project could think about techniques of translation that would help connect the needs and insights of grassroot activists with the mechanisms of international institutions.[125] As human rights scholars such as Ron Dudai have noted, there is a significant difference between diplomatic forums such as Geneva and local activism, and an intensifying need to reconnect the two so that human rights are deployed not in abstract discussions, but to campaign against very concrete injustices. If the law of humanity project wants to become better equipped to combat the most destructive forms of economic globalisation, it could seek ways 'to work with those activists seeking to envision and work towards alternate, non-exploitative ways of being'.[126] The most important struggles for equality and welfare are often quite different from the more governmental, judicial uses of the humanity language, described in most accounts of the humanisation of international law. Many of the most successful grassroot movements are heterogeneous and flexible in character and are impossible to characterize, for example, as human rights movements, despite them occasionally taking advantage of humanity language.[127] As Balakrishnan Rajagopal describes, many of the movements use human rights in a very place-based, contextual way, often constituting 'another kind of human rights, aimed at building radical alternatives to the received models of markets and democracy'.[128] For these movements, humanity language is 'a partial, fragmentary, and a sometimes useful tool of mobilization – not by any means a sole language of resistance and emancipation for oppressed social majorities around the world'.[129] Furthermore, subaltern resistance is primarily political and may involve combining humanity language and non-legal, unfortunately sometimes even illegal, forms of resistance.[130] While it might be unrealistic and perhaps

[125] Scott (n 3).

[126] A Orford, 'Contesting Globalization: A Feminist Perspective on the Future of Human Rights Symposium: International Human Rights at Fifty: A Symposium to Commemmorate the 50th Anniversary of the Universal Declaration of Human Rights' (1998) 8 *Transnational Law & Contemporary Problems* 171, 198.

[127] B Rajagopal, *International Law from Below: Development, Social Movements and Third World Resistance* (Cambridge, Cambridge University Press, 2003) 167.

[128] ibid 170.

[129] ibid 232.

[130] B de Sousa Santos and CA Rodríguez-Garavito, 'Law, Politics, and the Subaltern in Counter-Hegemonic Globalization' in B de Sousa Santos and CA Rodríguez-Garavito (eds), *Law and Globalization from Below: Towards a Cosmopolitan Legality* (Cambridge, Cambridge University Press, 2005) 15–16.

even unproductive to ask the proponents of the law of humanity project to take direct part in such activities, the project could play a role in translating these struggles 'up' to the institutional languages it is more familiar with and to translate some global issues 'down' to the grassroot level, connecting them to local battles.[131]

Another way for the law of humanity project to increase its practical relevance could be to pay more attention to the materiality of humanitarian and human rights practices: 'how these practices are facilitated, how long they take, how much they cost, where that money comes from, and who is or is not able to access it'.[132] As David Scott writes, thinking about humanitarian and human rights actions as a supply chain, where 'energy (and money) are entered at one end with the hope of some tangible outcome at the other', may help identify the opportunities and limitations of the work, as well as the 'pressure points and "chokeholds" that can be analyzed, targeted, and struggled over'.[133] Forging connections between critical scholarship and grassroot activism, the law of humanity project could bring to light constraints and opportunities of human rights and humanitarian work, provide a better understanding of when and how humanity language is hijacked by neoliberal and managerial projects, find ways to resist those practices and become more effective in fighting against structural injustice. Furthermore, increased understanding of the chokeholds of the system might help address the internal disillusionment that, according to Dudai, derives from human rights proponents' increasing frustration with the inability of human rights institutions to 'deliver the goods'.[134]

Finally, a more practically relevant and political approach to human rights and humanitarianism also entails increased willingness to enter into 'debates with experts in areas from security to education, health to housing, environment to agriculture, all areas where governance takes place'. Many critics would argue that the increased use of law of humanity concepts has so far mostly failed to create more inclusive and equal policies or to help in global redistribution of wealth.[135] This could be at least partly because of two issues. On the one hand, expertise in human rights, human security or human dignity does not involve expertise in anything specific, but consists mainly of some rather general preferences. And on the other hand, the law of humanity project and mainstream

[131] For an analysis of how such translation operates and what pitfalls it may meet, see SE Merry, *Human Rights and Gender Violence: Translating International Law into Local Justice* (Chicago, University of Chicago Press, 2006).

[132] Scott (n 3).

[133] Scott (n 3). See also more generally the IGLP Law and Global Production Working Group, 'The Role of Law in Global Value Chains: A Research Manifesto' (2016) 4 *London Review of International Law* 57.

[134] Dudai, 'Human Rights in the Populist Era', 17.

[135] Moyn, *Not Enough*; Whyte (n 20) 239–42; S Marks, 'Four Human Rights Myths' in D Kinley, W Sadurski and K Walton (eds), *Human Rights: Old Problems, New Possibilities* (Cheltenham, Edward Elgar Publishing, 2014).

human rights movements have been too shy to outline the actual policies that the law of humanity project supports, and hence to answer questions such as what exactly should be done to achieve better healthcare and social security, how to combat unemployment or climate change, and what contribution the law of humanity project can make in this regard. To become effective, and produce social effects, the rather broad preferences of the law of humanity project must be turned into economic, development, agricultural, labour and security policies, determined in debates with experts.[136]

C. Sovereignty, Global Actors and the Battle for the State

Third, addressing the root causes of the populist backlash, and in particular the growing inequality gap, demands increased perception and flexibility in identifying which actors are exercising power, from national to international and from public to private. Much of the law of humanity literature seems to be heavily influenced by the post-Cold War human rights ethos, literature and practice that is characterised by the 'enthusiasm for treating states as the principal violators of rights'.[137] Even when root causes are examined, the inquiry typically ends at the level where blame can be put on state vulnerabilities or bad leadership.[138] Thus, humanitarian crises and individual violations are seen to be caused by government actors, leading to the need to constrain or abandon state sovereignty and enable collective international action for the protection of those in need. Influenced by this mindset, some law of humanity theorists make the case that states have traditionally been the main violators of human rights. Others worry that states are becoming incapable of effectively protecting the human rights of their citizens in the face of increasing globalisation.[139] Still others take a more theoretical stance, and argue that our fixation on the state hinders the progress of international law and its development towards a global law of humanity.[140] In any case, most see the diminishing or altering role of the state as an inherently progressive phenomenon.

Thus, in the semantic field within which the law of humanity project is embedded, the concept of humanity – typically represented by international organisations and NGOs – seems to be presented as being in opposition to the state.[141] Furthermore, the humanity/state binary can be seen as a zero-sum game

[136] Here I draw from an unpublished paper by M Koskenniemi.

[137] Orford, 'Contesting Globalization', 177.

[138] S Marks, 'Human Rights and Root Causes' (2011) 74 *MLR* 57.

[139] E Benvenisti, 'Sovereigns as Trustees of Humanity: On the Accountability of States to Foreign Stakeholders' (2013) 107 *The American Journal of International Law* 295, 295.

[140] R Domingo, *The New Global Law*, reprint edn (Cambridge, Cambridge University Press, 2011) 58; C Barbara, 'International Legal Personality: Panacea or Pandemonium? Theorizing about the Individual and the State in the Era of Globalization' (2007) 12 *Austrian Review of International and European Law* 17, 45–47.

[141] See Kratochwil, 'Leaving Sovereignty Behind?', 129.

where increasing the power of one requires the reduction of that of the other. Consequently, the two sides of the binary are charged with different types of energy: positive in the case of humanity and international organisations, and negative in the case of the state. This is the outcome of associating humanity with such allied concepts as democracy, cosmopolitanism and progression, whereas state sovereignty is associated with concepts such as tyranny, nationalism and conservatism. The effect is further enhanced by the simplification of social reality: for example, by highlighting the human rights violations committed by domestic governments and hence moving attention away from global structural issues to individual atrocities;[142] or by downplaying the role of the state in ensuring the material conditions of human life and thus protecting human rights.

Such a view is, however, problematic for at least two interconnected reasons. First, the binary misses the positive aspects of statehood and the negative aspects of international organisations. This becomes visible if the aforementioned frozen binaries are 'melted'.[143] It is certainly true that state sovereignty has often been abused as an apology by states that mistreat parts of their population. Nevertheless, this tendency to view state sovereignty predominantly through its dark side has the problem of neglecting the other side of the coin. The bright side of statehood has been described by Martti Koskenniemi as enabling 'collective life as a *project*'.[144] This project does not have to be based on any kind of nationalism or idea of natural, organic communities. By contrast, what is to be defended is precisely the 'wonderful artificiality of the state'.[145] The state provides 'a set of institutions or practices in which the forms of collective life are constantly imagined, debated, criticized and reformed, over and again'. The project that Koskenniemi envisions is therefore not one of essence, but one of becoming. It is about different versions of 'what domestic democracy and international governance *ought to be*',[146] and about carving space for such discussion in the first place.

On the other side of the binary, humanity is usually seen to be represented by international institutions which tend to be viewed predominantly through their bright side, obscuring the fact that they, too, can enable abuse and human rights violations. This they can do through direct actions, or by influencing domestic policies of states. Perhaps the clearest example of this are the structural

[142] Orford, *Reading Humanitarian Intervention* (n 97) 82, 85.

[143] K Palonen, 'Rhetorical and Temporal Perspectives on Conceptual Change: Theses on Quentin Skinner and Reinhart Koselleck' (1999) 3 *Finnish Yearbook of Political Thought* 41.

[144] M Koskenniemi, 'Conclusion: Vocabularies of Sovereignty – Powers of a Paradox' in H Kalmo and Q Skinner (eds), *Sovereignty in Fragments: The Past, Present and Future of a Contested Concept*, reprint edn (Cambridge, Cambridge University Press, 2014) 241 (original emphasis).

[145] M Koskenniemi, 'The Wonderful Artificiality of States' (1994) 88 *American Society of International Law Proceedings* 22.

[146] M Koskenniemi, 'It's Not the Cases, It's the System' (2017) 18 *Journal of Investment & Trade* 343, 351.

adjustment and shock therapy programmes that the World Bank and the IMF have demanded of states in exchange for loans and other resources. Demanding that states privatise public sector activities, liberalise investment and financial sectors, impose austerity measures that target, for example, healthcare, integrate agriculture to global value chains, focus on export at the expense of local markets, limit social securities and implement political, economic and legal reforms that facilitate change towards capitalism, the World Bank and the IMF have created conditions that have led, and continue to lead, to human rights violations. Not only do these changes hinder self-determination and political participation by shifting decision-making power from democratic fora to international experts, giving the latter control over such central questions of human life as labour, education, healthcare and social security, but they also significantly constrain states' possibility to hold on to their obligations to guarantee economic, social and cultural rights. As states are forced to prioritise the market logic over access to education, food or health, or to privatise and cut their expenses, the least advantaged members of their population risk becoming marginalised and deprived of essential services. This may further produce a climate where violations of civil and political rights are likely to increase and produce civil unrest as the gap between ordinary citizens and the protected foreign investors grows disproportionately.[147]

Similarly, the WTO's focus on behind the border measures constrains the possibility for states and their populations to decide on their political, economic and social projects, and may lead to human rights violations, for example by privileging the property interests of transnational corporations over the welfare and rights of local populations.[148] Thus, international institutions shape the economic, legal and political systems of many states, and through such actions may also impact human rights, human security and human dignity.

The point here is not that state sovereignty is somehow 'good' or sacred, or that the international community is 'bad'. Such a reading would mean simply switching the charges of the concepts from positive to negative, or vice versa, without challenging the binaries themselves. Indeed, it would be close to what the populists have attempted – although it does not seem that the populists would have managed or even sought to alter these dichotomies or their conceptual associations, most populists celebrating quite openly nationalism, conservatism and even xenophobia.

Rather, my case is for a more complex and contextual analysis. This leads to my second reason as to why the state versus humanity binary is so troublesome, which is that viewing the world through such a binary may obscure the

[147] Orford, 'Contesting Globalization' (n 126) 179–82.

[148] A Orford, 'Beyond Harmonization: Trade, Human Rights and the Economy of Sacrifice' (2005) 18 *Leiden Journal of International Law* 179; Orford, 'Theorizing Free Trade'; Orford, 'Contesting Globalization' (n 126) 182–88; Lang (n 22).

complex connections between different actors and mindsets in world politics, and veil how power actually operates in global governance and how it impacts the interests of the law of humanity project. In particular, such a rigid approach underestimates the extent to which globalisation has reshaped sovereignty and how it is attributed across the global order. Sovereignty does not have to be exercised only by states, but can also be exercised through international institutions and fluid global networks. As Hardt and Negri have argued, previous dichotomies between rulers and ruled, core and periphery, have become blurred – or deterritorialised and reterritorialised – in today's world.[149] In particular, sovereignty has been disseminated both on the global level and within states. Instead of clear dichotomies, today we have new types of hierarchies, 'constituted and sustained by more complex patterns and logics, which are obscured, and hence reinforced, where globalization is elided with neo-imperialism'.[150] Indeed, in today's functionally fragmented world, what we call 'the state' is probably best seen as a heterogeneous assemblage of different global governmental mindsets. Koskenniemi writes:

> Try to find out the national position on a matter and you will hear different answer depending on whom you ask: the policy of the Ministry of Finance, declared in Washington, is not identical with that of the Ministry of the Environment, declared in Geneva.

This is because the national representatives have internalised the position and views of their corresponding global truth regime.[151]

One method for teasing out these subtle operations of power is to follow Anne Orford in viewing international law as a 'battle for the state'. As Orford writes, international law is not only about the relations between states or between international organisations and states, but is just as often 'about enabling particular kinds of administration by one group of people over another, about entrenching particular state forms and not others, about securing particular vital systems of resource exploitation, and about constituting property relations'. Hence, even if the role of the state as a sovereign actor would have diminished, as some theorists have argued, it would still remain at the heart of international law as the target of measures aimed at rooting 'particular forms of the state'.[152] As Orford describes, towards the end of the twentieth century, this disciplining of the state 'became "a joint enterprise" carried out "by economists, international lawyers,

[149] M Hardt and A Negri, *Empire* (Cambridge, MA, Harvard University Press, 2001).

[150] S Marks, 'Empire's Law: The Earl A Snyder Lecture in International Law' (2003) 10 *Indiana Journal of Global Legal Studies* 449, 463–64.

[151] M Koskenniemi, 'The Fate of Public International Law: Between Technique and Politics' (2007) 70 *MLR* 1.

[152] A Orford, 'Food Security, Free Trade, and the Battle for the State' (2015) 11 *Journal of International Law & International Relations* 1, 23–24.

and rational-choice political scientists" with a particular focus upon informing doctrinal scholarship and institutional design through diagnosing "substantive problems" and proposing legal solutions'.[153]

There are, of course, many participants in this 'battle for the state'. In the interwar period, the state being built through international law, and in particular through the International Labour Organization's standard-setting and technical assistance, was a welfare state with a strong emphasis on full employment. Similarly, the post-colonial state in the making after the Second World War was a centralised, administrative-welfare one, as Keynesianism emerged as the prevalent economic idea in the post-war period, and was combined with ideas of modernisation and biopolitics.[154] More recently, however, the dominant force in the battle has been neoliberalism, the influence of which is also reflected in the managerialist NPM approach.

The success and outcomes of the neoliberal disciplining and shaping of the state are reflected in various phenomena described in this chapter, from structural adjustment programmes and shock therapy to humanitarian occupations and the human rights reforms in Palestine. Furthermore, it is reflected in such 'mundane' (although fundamentally important) issues as agriculture and food security. As Orford describes, the food security discourse is dominated by the view that food security is best protected by liberalising trade in agriculture, intensifying agricultural industrialisation and removing state support for domestic farming.[155] Consequently, it is held that food security is best protected by the 'international community', represented by international organisations, whereas states are supposed to play a very specific – important but limited – role in maintaining markets.[156] Particularly since the creation of the WTO, writes Orford, 'pressure has increasingly been brought to bear on states to allow a free market in agricultural products, abandon state support for agricultural producers, and abolish measures that restrict international movement in foodstuffs'.[157] Indeed, many agricultural agreements are more than just trade agreements: they are best seen as governance agreements, having as much to do with the proper limits and capacities of the state as with their treatment of foreign and domestic producers. For example, the WTO's Agreement on Agriculture aims to limit the state's ability to protect its population by way of 'discriminatory' support or by restricting the export of foodstuffs. Hence, whilst it certainly deals with

[153] ibid 26–27.

[154] Sinclair (n 39) pts I and II; GF Sinclair, 'Forging Modern States with Imperfect Tools: United Nations Technical Assistance for Public Administration in Decolonized States' (2020) 11 *Humanity: An International Journal of Human Rights, Humanitarianism, and Development* 54; L Eslava and S Pahuja, 'The State and International Law: A Reading from the Global South' (2020) 11 *Humanity: An International Journal of Human Rights, Humanitarianism, and Development* 118.

[155] Orford, 'Food Security, Free Trade, and the Battle for the State', 13.

[156] ibid 9–10.

[157] ibid 6.

trade, it also deals with the role of the state more generally as well as its relation to its population.[158] Furthermore, many trade agreements limit the state's ability to regulate food production through food safety regulations, environmental production or labelling requirements.[159] These trade agreements, as well as different development projects, are extremely efficient in disciplining states into adopting the neoliberal market model, since many countries depend on credit and loans from the World Bank, the IMF and other institutions.

Trade and agricultural agreements are not anomalies in this regard. Indeed, so successful has the mindset been in shaping states that some commentators have argued that market fundamentalism has already become the internal 'organising principle' of many states which now play little role beyond guaranteeing the health and growth of the economy.[160] Yet, the outcomes seem questionable at best. When it comes to food security, for example, millions of people remain undernourished, despite the fact that the world already produces more than enough food to feed its entire population.[161] Furthermore, inequality is growing within states, providing a fertile breeding ground for authoritarian populism.

Hence, the law of humanity project needs to rethink its contribution to the battle for the state. As neoliberals have understood, the state is still the most important actor in governance, regulation and social reproduction. Therefore, the solution cannot be to abandon the state, or to leave it to the neoliberals, but rather to revive it as a site of solidarity, as a provider of social and economic security, and as a collective project of becoming.[162] Furthermore, this approach should be combined with a contextualised global outlook and an analysis of how a wide variety of actors from states to transnational corporations and international institutions contribute to human rights violations and increasing inequality. Indeed, an increasing focus on the battle for the state is incomplete without developing ways to hold non-state actors accountable for acting through the state. Hence, there is a need to develop forms of human rights, human security and human dignity protection that are 'sufficiently subtle to deal with situations where state functions are privatized in order to limit accountability for the effects of particular activities, or where actions are carried out covertly or in private'.[163]

[158] ibid 59–60.

[159] ibid 64.

[160] S Singh, 'The Fundamental Rights of States in Neoliberal Times' (2015) 4 *Cambridge Journal of International and Comparative Law* 461, 465. See also W Brown, *Edgework: Critical Essays on Knowledge and Politics* (Princeton, Princeton University Press, 2005) 42.

[161] Orford, 'Food Security, Free Trade, and the Battle for the State' (n 152) 12. See also N Wald and DP Hill, '"Rescaling" Alternative Food Systems: From Food Security to Food Sovereignty' (2016) 33 *Agriculture and Human Values* 203, 207.

[162] S Pahuja and J Baskin, 'Never Waste a Crisis: A Practical Guide?' (*Critical Legal Thinking blog*, 20 March 2020), www.criticallegalthinking.com/2020/03/20/never-waste-a-crisis-a-practical-guide.

[163] Orford, 'Contesting Globalization' (n 126) 196–97.

D. Will to Power

Finally, more active participation in political struggles and the reclaiming of the state demands increased willingness to grasp and wield power. Law of humanity theorists and human rights people have often been reluctant to think of themselves as men and women of power, perhaps because of the notion that power corrupts.[164] Thus, they have been content to have humanity language appear in court decisions or policy documents. Yet, as this book has tried to demonstrate, that language can be used for countless different purposes, some of them inimical to the aims of the law of humanity project. Thus, unless the project is willing to state its political goals and policy preferences more clearly and in more detail, engage openly in the expert discussions beyond general human rights policies and take oppositional positions if need be, it risks becoming a rather weak adversary, if not a tool, for whatever power or mindset manages to rise to a hegemonic position. Hence, the fourth and final step in rethinking the law of humanity project must be to accept and grasp power, wherever possible. If the proponents of the project are serious about their aim of increasing the welfare of human beings worldwide, they must be braver in presenting their view of a better world and taking concrete steps towards it.

[164] I refer again to an unpublished paper by M Koskenniemi.

6

Conclusion

MUCH HAS CHANGED between the birth of the law of humanity project and the present. Enthusiasm of a new world order and an emerging law of humanity, characteristic of the 1990s and the beginning of the new millennium, has changed to shock and dismay as a consequence of the rise of reactionary, authoritarian politics around the world and the ensuing unilateralism and isolationism. The law of humanity project has therefore reached a crossroads at which it must reconsider some of its underlying assumptions and strategies, and carefully select the best way forward. In this, the populist backlash, while a significant threat, may also help spur the reorientation of the project by exposing certain weaknesses and blind spots that have pestered the law of humanity project from the beginning but have been difficult to unveil until now.

This book has described the law of humanity project as a cluster of loosely connected theoretical and practical attempts to either describe a structural shift in international law – from a field built around sovereign states to a global law built around the individual and the interests of humanity – or to actively push international law in that direction. As the book has argued, the different streams of the project are united by their focus on the individual, the attempt to radically alter or diminish the role of the state and the trust they put on concepts such as human rights, human security and human dignity as a conduit for revolutionising how international law is perceived, interpreted and practised.

One of the book's main points of critique against the law of humanity project has been that its proponents make a mistake in assuming that increased references to the aforementioned concepts or the increased use of the humanity language necessarily lead to the changes or produce the outcomes that they assume and desire. There are few, if any, concepts which have been considered, during the past few decades, as sacred as that of humanity, which seems to have become the foundation of authority in our contemporary times.[1] References to 'humanity' have brought discussions to a close and permitted actions which

[1] J Bartelson, *Sovereignty as Symbolic Form* (Abingdon, Routledge, 2014) 4. See also A Supiot, *Homo Juridicus: On the Anthropological Function of the Law* (S Brown trans, New York, Verso, 2007) 187; D Fassin, *Humanitarian Reason: A Moral History of the Present* (Berkeley, University of California Press, 2011).

would have been considered controversial under different circumstances.[2] Yet there has been less consensus on what exactly humanity refers to in specific circumstances, beyond the simple meaning of the totality of human beings. We are likely to have different ideas about how best to protect humanity or what kinds of actions might go against its 'dignity'. Moreover, as contemporary debates in bioethics demonstrate, we cannot even agree on where its borders should be drawn – fortunately. The concept of humanity is therefore an incredibly powerful tool for those who can speak in its name. Because of is simultaneous weight and indeterminacy, it is easy for those who get to define its meaning to use it to realise their special interests.[3] Thus, the law of humanity concepts can be used for multiple purposes, even ones that are opposed to the aims of the project.

For this reason, this book has provided an analysis of the use of the humanity language in the practice of global governance. Although the observations from such a wide range of areas as human rights law, foreign investment, international criminal law, international territorial administration, global security law and humanitarian governance of refugees are of course diverse and fragmented, there are certain trends that emerged quite strongly from the studied material. Although the observations confirmed the law of humanity theorists' claim that the interests of humanity and the vulnerable individual became the major organising principle and source of legitimacy of global governance in the 1990s and the first decade of the new millennium, they also challenged the assumption that the increased relevance of the humanity discourse would have necessarily translated into increased well-being and freedom. The primary outcome of the use of humanity language seems to have been the disciplining of the state and the shift of decision-making power to the 'international community', represented by international organisations, non-governmental organisations, international tribunals, investors, transnational corporations and sometimes even occupying states. In many cases, the disciplining of the state has taken the form of broadly neoliberal political, legal and economic transformations, including the creation of some of the most investment-friendly environments in the world, the opening of markets, privatisation, changes in taxation, the complete revamping of the agricultural sectors of the occupied territories with the aim of including of domestic markets in global value chains, and the shielding of these policies, rules and institutions from political contestation.

'Whoever invokes humanity wants to cheat', the nineteenth-century French anarchist thinker Pierre-Joseph Proudhon once stated.[4] However, I do not think

[2] I Feldman and M Ticktin, 'Introduction: Government and Humanity' in I Feldman and M Ticktin (eds), *In the Name of Humanity: The Government of Threat and Care* (Durham, NC, Duke University Press, 2010) 1.

[3] M Koskenniemi, 'International Law in Europe: Between Tradition and Renewal' (2005) 16 *European Journal of International Law* 113, 116.

[4] The statement is now often linked to Carl Schmitt. See C Schmitt, *The Concept of the Political: Expanded Edition*, enlarged edn (G Schwab trans, Chicago, University of Chicago Press, 2007) 54.

that this statement applies to the proponents of the law of humanity project. Rather, they have shown great determination in improving the lives of individuals and peoples around the globe. But, as Proudhon would have predicted, the proponents may have underestimated the indeterminacy of the concepts they rely on, the ways in which they can be used to further multiple interests and the fact that there are myriad participants in the battle over the ownership of the concepts – some of which may have entered the struggle with less pure intentions (at least from the law of humanity perspective).[5] Indeed, the shift of power from the people and democratic institutions to international experts in the humanitarian occupation missions, the ensuing shock therapy capitalism, the use of human rights and human dignity language to support the possibility of investors to repatriate profits and the association of humanity concepts with the war on terrorism are all likely to give many law of humanity proponents pause for thought. And while these instances are not attributable to the law of humanity project, this book has suggested that, in presenting a kind of success story where each invocation of humanity is a further step towards an emerging law of humanity, the narrative about an emerging law of humanity has helped provide legitimacy to competing projects such as managerialism and neoliberalism, especially when they have managed to hijack some of the law of humanity concepts. In this way, the law of humanity project has inadvertently helped to sustain such relations and structures of power as are inimical to its stated aims, unwelcomed by the law of humanity theorists and difficult to justify through the humanity rhetoric.

If these observations are correct, then it follows that, should it fail to address the blind spots and weaknesses which have allowed external forces to utilise its key concepts for their own ends, the law of humanity project risks being reduced more or less to an ideology, obscuring social reality and helping sustain such relations and structures of power as are inimical to its aims – that is to say, those that are most likely unwelcomed by the law of humanity theorists and that are difficult to justify through the humanity rhetoric.[6] This it can do in several ways. For one, it can serve to legitimate different actions, for example, by reinforcing the image that those actions are conducted for the benefit of local populations or humanity at large.[7] In so doing, it may provide a false sense of legitimacy to measures that turn out to be economically exploitative or anti-democratic. The

[5] For example, radical right-wing transnational non-governmental organisations have recently managed to successfully employ human rights language, winning supporters especially among young adults, and challenging established human rights organisations. See A Schneiker, 'The New Defenders of Human Rights? How Radical Right-Wing TNGOs Are Using the Human Rights Discourse to Promote Their Ideas' (2019) 33 *Global Society* 149.

[6] Here I am inspired by S Marks, *The Riddle of All Constitutions: International Law, Democracy, and the Critique of Ideology* (Oxford, Oxford University Press, 2001). See also W Rech, 'Ideology' in J d'Aspermont and S Singh (eds), *Concepts for International Law: Contributions to Disciplinary Thought* (Cheltenham, Edward Elgar Publishing, 2019).

[7] Marks, *The Riddle of All Constitutions*, 19.

humanity discourse may also sustain unfair power relations through dissimulation, by obscuring and masking social reality.[8] Here I have in mind the way in which the narrative that all uses of humanity language contribute to a humanisation of international law obscures the strategic uses of the language and the difficult political questions related to many of those uses. Another possible way in which ideology can sustain relations of power is unification, by which Susan Marks means the way in which 'social relations come to appear coherent and harmonious, and cleavages are made to seem non-existent, or, at any rate, irrelevant'.[9] This is again visible, in my opinion, in the progress story in which all uses of humanity language analysed are absorbed into one narrative and assumed to benefit the interests of humanity. Then there is the closely related process of progressive narration of every invocation of 'humanity' in international legal practice or global governance as a small victory in itself and yet another step in the path towards law of humanity, irrespective of what the exact consequences might be. Finally, the previous chapter discussed at some length the ways in which the theories of law of humanity might mask the operation of power by constructing almost ironclad binaries which make the international legal order seem like a zero-sum game between two opposing forces – humanity and state sovereignty – the first of which is presented in a positive light and the latter in a negative one.

The problem with these narratives and imaginative geographies is that they tend to obscure the conflicts of interest at the background of many invocations of 'humanity' and the complex concrete outcomes of those invocations. In particular, the narratives brush over struggles over the meaning and ownership of those concepts and the ways in which they are used strategically to achieve very concrete goals and to legitimate ideological change.[10] At the moment, it would be especially important to pay more attention, first, to the use of humanity language to support neoliberal ends, and second, to the causal connection between neoliberal policies, inequality and the rise of authoritarian politics. Indeed, as hinted above, it now seems uncontestable that there has been at least an indirect link between concepts such as human rights and the shift of power from the people to global experts,[11] on the one hand, and the intensification of

[8] ibid 20.

[9] ibid.

[10] K Palonen, 'Rhetorical and Temporal Perspectives on Conceptual Change: Theses on Quentin Skinner and Reinhart Koselleck' (1999) 3 *Finnish Yearbook of Political Thought* 41, 47.

[11] A Orford, *International Authority and the Responsibility to Protect* (Cambridge, Cambridge University Press, 2011); A Orford, *Reading Humanitarian Intervention: Human Rights and the Use of Force in International Law*, reissue edn (Cambridge, Cambridge University Press, 2007); M Koskenniemi, 'Human Rights Mainstreaming as a Strategy for Institutional Power' (2010) 1 *Humanity: An International Journal of Human Rights, Humanitarianism, and Development* 47; M Koskenniemi, 'Enchanted by the Tools? An Enlightenment Perspective' (2019) 35 *American University International Law Review* 397; C Douzinas, *Human Rights and Empire: The Political Philosophy of Cosmopolitanism*, new edn (London, Routledge-Cavendish, 2007); S Hopgood, *The Endtimes of Human Rights* (Ithaca, NY, Cornell University Press, 2013).

unfair economic policies, on the other.[12] These connections should be of utmost interest to the project, for not only do the diminishing democratic power of the people and the growing material inequality fly against its core aims, but they have also fed the rise of its current nemesis, right-wing authoritarianism, by providing a fertile breeding ground for extremist movements to triumph. And although the law of humanity project cannot be blamed for those policies, recent studies have demonstrated that neoliberals have managed to use humanity language to provide legitimacy to their project,[13] while the humanity language and the human rights institution have at the same provided a convenient target and scapegoat for the populist backlashers, who have left neoliberal policies mostly intact. Indeed, most of the populist backlashers have not really challenged the basic tenets of neoliberalism, but rather have transformed it into 'nationalist neoliberalism', which is not as radically different from its previous forms as would be easy to assume – perhaps because conservative moral values and extreme measures for the encasement of markets have been part of the neoliberal project from the very beginning.[14] Although such core tenets of liberalism as non-discrimination and formal equality have been eroded, private property, the possessive individual and selfish wealth accumulation are still celebrated, commons are still privatised, taxes are cut for the wealthy and large corporations, and any attempts at democratic control of the markets are strongly resisted.[15]

After two triumphant decades, followed by the shock of the populist backlash, the law of humanity project finds itself at a crossroads. The fundamental values of the project can provide an important counterforce to the authoritarian trends of our time, but this requires self-reflection, some creative rethinking of the project and the unsettling of the imaginative geography that has guided it during the past few decades. In order to retain its value in our complex political landscape, the project must take a more explicit stance against the neoliberal and authoritarian ideologies, while avoiding the lure of managerialism. To succeed in this task, the project must gain a better understanding of that very system it aims to transform, see and reveal the connections between rights and markets,[16]

[12] J Whyte, *The Morals of the Market: Human Rights and the Rise of Neoliberalism* (London, Verso, 2019); Q Slobodian, *Globalists: The End of Empire and the Birth of Neoliberalism* (Cambridge, MA, Harvard University Press, 2018); S Marks, 'Four Human Rights Myths' in D Kinley, W Sadurski and K Walton (eds), *Human Rights: Old Problems, New Possibilities* (Cheltenham, Edward Elgar Publishing, 2014); S Moyn, *Not Enough: Human Rights in an Unequal World* (Cambridge, MA, Belknap Press at Harvard University Press, 2018); P O'Connell, 'On Reconciling Irreconcilables: Neo-Liberal Globalisation and Human Rights' (2007) 7 *Human Rights Law Review* 483; P O'Connell, 'On the Human Rights Question' (2018) 40 *Human Rights Quarterly* 962.

[13] Whyte, *The Morals of the Market: Human Rights and the Rise of Neoliberalism*; Slobodian, *Globalists: The End of Empire and the Birth of Neoliberalism*; T Kochi, *Global Justice and Social Conflict: The Foundations of Liberal Order and International Law* (Abingdon, Routledge, 2019).

[14] Whyte (n 12); Slobodian (n 12).

[15] T Kochi, 'The End of Global Constitutionalism and Rise of Antidemocratic Politics' (2020) 34 *Global Society* 487, 500.

[16] Amy Kapczynski, 'What Comes after Not Enough?' (*Law and Political Economy blog*), www.lpeproject.org/blog/what-comes-after-not-enough.

and adopt egalitarian legal and political strategies that attempt to disrupt and displace neoliberalism. In this regard, the populist backlash can be not only a significant threat, but also a possibility. The new adversary in the form of right-wing populists has already prompted a process of rethinking within associated projects, such as the human rights movement, and filled them with new energy.[17] Furthermore, the backlash has helped to expose some of the blind spots of the law of humanity project and may also help to reorient it more clearly against policies, practices, structures and mindsets that produce material inequality.

The indeterminacy of the law of humanity concepts may actually turn out to be an asset in this reorientation.[18] As has been argued by several scholars, it is precisely due to its universal and formal yet indeterminate nature that the humanity language can be used as a tool for protest and to give voice and universal language to the excluded.[19] Most recently, Susan Marks has delved into the rights discussion in sixteenth- to eighteenth-century England to unearth a forgotten tradition of human rights thought. Contrasting the views of forsaken thinkers such as Thomas Spence to the eventually more successful tradition of rights, which has been used primarily to support property rights and other civil and political rights, Marks argues that it is possible to use the concept of rights in a more radical way. Indeed, as Spence conceived them, the rights of man were about revealing and transforming conditions of oppression, and about subsistence, as opposed to property and enclosure. While universal, they were rights of particular people in particular places, focused on articulating social-systemic injustice and addressing the gap between our shared humanity and real inequalities.[20]

As this book has suggested, a discussion of such an updated, radicalised law of humanity project, more in line with Marks's reading of Spence's conception of rights, could perhaps start with four steps. First, those theorising or describing a shift towards the law of humanity project must adopt a struggles perspective to the use of law of humanity concepts. They must focus more on what is done by the concepts and by whom, as well as on who benefits and who loses. In particular, they must play closer attention to the co-optation of the humanity language by neoliberal and managerial projects and the links between neoliberal social and economic policies, inequality and the rise of authoritarian politics.

[17] P Alston, 'The Populist Challenge to Human Rights' (2017) 9 *Journal of Human Rights Practice* 1.

[18] That said, it should be noted that that very same indeterminacy has also allowed radical right-wing organisations to employ humanity language. See Schneiker, 'The New Defenders of Human Rights?'.

[19] See, eg C Douzinas, *The End of Human Rights* (Oxford, Hart Publishing, 2000); Koskenniemi, 'Human Rights Mainstreaming as a Strategy for Institutional Power'; M Koskenniemi, 'Human Rights, Politics, and Love' (2001) 2001 *Mennesker & Rettigheter* 33; J Rancière, 'Who Is the Subject of the Rights of Man?' (2004) 103 *South Atlantic Quarterly* 297.

[20] S Marks, *A False Tree of Liberty: Human Rights in Radical Thought* (Oxford, Oxford University Press, 2019).

Second, the law of humanity project must find ways to connect with grassroots struggles against local injustices while keeping in mind global structural issues. The battle against nationalist backlashers and the most destructive forms of capitalism is equally about narratives and material practices, the imaginary and the structures. In order to win back the streets and politics, the law of humanity project must find methods for working with different actors, from environmentalists to labour unions, who are better equipped to deal with some of the issues that have contributed to the current situation.[21] In order to succeed in this, the proponents of the law of humanity project must avoid hegemonising the imagination and resources of grassroots movements and complement rather than foreclose other strategies of resistance.[22]

Third, the law of humanity project must let go of the binary that casts sovereignty against humanity and states against international organisations, and find improved methods for identifying which actors are exercising power, from national to international and from public to private. Focusing on disciplining the state while seeking to improve the power of international organisations risks abandoning the state to the neoliberals, who have been the dominant force in the battle for the state for the past few decades, and missing how some actions and policies of international organisations have drastically undermined the fulfilment of social and economic rights in several states. Equally avoiding the opposite, authoritarian pull of sanctifying state sovereignty while putting all the blame on international organisations, the struggle for a more equal world must be fought simultaneously at the level of states and international organisations.

Finally, typically shy of perceiving themselves as women and men of power, the proponents of the law of humanity project must be increasingly willing to grasp power and openly use it to further their political projects. They must be able to present a clearer, more detailed image of their ideal world and combine that ideal with concrete proposals for reaching it. In order to do so, they must learn to engage with experts and decision-makers on specific policy goals and technical questions.[23] Indeed, one way the human rights movement can take over the current wave of new nationalism is to offer more credible and tangible answers to the questions that have fed that wave, including rising inequality and the erosion of social bonds and welfare.

Although tackling contemporary challenges and threats demands the proponents of the law of humanity project to go outside their comfort zone and move

[21] L Bonadiman and U Soirila, 'Human Rights, Populism, and the Political Economy of the World' (2019) 37 *Nordic Journal of Human Rights* 301.

[22] D Kennedy, 'International Human Rights Movement: Part of the Problem? Boundaries in the Field of Human Rights' (2002) 15 *Harvard Human Rights Journal* 101; W Brown, '"The Most We Can Hope For …": Human Rights and the Politics of Fatalism' (2004) 103 *South Atlantic Quarterly* 451; D Scott, 'Human Rights' in J d'Aspermont and J Haskell (eds), *International Law at a Tipping Point: Critique and Commitment* (Cambridge, Cambridge University Press, 2019).

[23] Koskenniemi, 'Enchanted by the Tools'.

beyond humanity language, the law of humanity concepts can nevertheless play an important role in the process. Human rights and human security, focused on socio-economic rights, and human dignity, understood as equality, can help to ground the technical discussions, policies and politics on the forgotten notion of solidarity.[24] In this way the concepts can be used to disrupt the market fundamentalist thinking based on individual rights and competition, and reveal the social struggles at the heart of law. If the unfortunate fate of the law of humanity project has been to be 'pulled into the mainstream' and to thus constantly risk becoming 'part of the problem',[25] as the humanity language has become the routine language of global governance, in the current political context the project has the possibility to become part of the resistance. It is important to seize this opportunity.

[24] E Christodoulidis, 'Social Rights Constitutionalism: An Antagonistic Endorsement' (2017) 44 *Journal of Law and Society* 123; Bonadiman and Soirila, 'Human Rights, Populism, and the Political Economy of the World'.

[25] Here I am referring to Kennedy, 'International Human Rights Movement'; M Koskenniemi, 'The Pull of the Mainstream' (1989) 88 *Michigan Law Review* 1946.

Bibliography

Aas, KF and Gundhus, HOI, 'Policing Humanitarian Borderlands: Frontex, Human Rights and the Precariousness of Life' (2015) 55 *British Journal of Criminology* 1.

Achiume, ET, 'Syria, Cost-Sharing, and the Responsibility to Protect Refugees' (2015) 100 *Minnesota Law Review* 687.

Acquaviva, G, 'Human Rights Violations before International Tribunals: Reflections on Responsibility of International Organizations' (2007) 20 *Leiden Journal of International Law* 613.

Agamben, G, *Homo Sacer: Sovereign Power and Bare Life* (Stanford, Stanford University Press s, 1998).

Agamben, G, *What Is an Apparatus?: And Other Essays* (Stanford, Stanford University Press, 2009).

Agamben, G, *The Kingdom and the Glory: For a Theological Genealogy of Economy and Government/(Homo Sacer II, 2)* (L Chiesa and M Mandarini trans, Stanford, Stanford University Press, 2011).

Agier, M, 'Humanity as an Identity and Its Political Effects (A Note on Camps and Humanitarian Government)' (2010) 1 *Humanity* 29.

Alkire, S, 'A Conceptual Framework for Human Security', Working Paper 2 (Oxford, CRISE, 2003).

Alkire, S, 'A Vital Core That Must Be Treated with the Same Gravitas as Traditional Security Threats' (2004) 35 *Security Dialogue* 359.

Allen, L, *The Rise and Fall of Human Rights: Cynicism and Politics in Occupied Palestine* (Stanford, Stanford University Press, 2013).

Alston, P (ed), *Non-State Actors and Human Rights* (Oxford, Oxford University Press, 2005).

Alston, P, 'The Populist Challenge to Human Rights' (2017) 9 *Journal of Human Rights Practice* 1.

Alvarez, JE, 'Hegemonic International Law Revisited' (2003) 97 *American Journal of International Law* 873.

Amnéus, D, *Responsibility Protect by Military Means – Emerging Norms on Humanitarian Intervention?* (Stockholm, Department of Law, Stockholm University, 2008).

Andorno, R, 'Human Dignity and Human Rights as a Common Ground for a Global Bioethics' (2009) 34 *Journal of Medicine & Philosophy* 223.

Ashutosh, I and Mountz, A, 'Migration Management for the Benefit of Whom? Interrogating the Work of the International Organization for Migration' (2011) 15 *Citizenship Studies* 21.

Axworthy, L, 'Human Security and Global Governance: Putting People First' (2001) 7 *Global Governance* 19.

Axworthy, L, 'A New Scientific Field and Policy Lens' (2004) 35 *Security Dialogue* 348.

Baer, S, 'Dignity, Liberty, Equality: A Fundamental Rights Triangle of Constitutionalism' (2009) 59 *University of Toronto Law Journal* 417.

Bagaric, M and Allan, J, 'The Vacuous Concept of Dignity' (2006) 5 *Journal of Human Rights* 257.

Ball, T, Farr, J and Hanson, RL, 'Editors' Introduction' in T Ball, J Farr and RL Hanson (eds), *Political Innovation and Conceptual Change* (Cambridge, Cambridge University Press, 1989).

Banchoff, T, 'Religion and the Global Politics of Human Dignity: The Catholic Church and Beyond' in MP Lagon and AC Arend (eds), *Human Dignity and the Future of Global Institutions* (Washington, Georgetown University Press, 2014).

Barak, A, *Human Dignity: The Constitutional Value and the Constitutional Right* (Cambridge, Cambridge University Press, 2015).

Barbara, C, 'International Legal Personality: Panacea or Pandemonium? Theorizing about the Individual and the State in the Era of Globalization' (2007) 12 *Austrian Review of International and European Law* 17.

Barnett, L, 'Global Governance and the Evolution of the International Refugee Regime' (2002) 14 *International Journal of Refugee Law* 238.
Barnett, MN, 'Humanitarian Governance' (2013) 16 *Annual Review of Political Science* 379.
Barroso, LR, 'Here, There, and Everywhere: Human Dignity in Contemporary Law and in the Transnational Discourse' (2012) 35 *Boston College International & Comparative Law Review* 331.
Bartelson, J, *Sovereignty as Symbolic Form* (New York, Routledge, 2014).
Bauer, JR and Bell, DA (eds), *The East Asian Challenge for Human Rights* (Cambridge, Cambridge University Press, 1999).
Baughen, S, 'Customary International Law and Its Horizontal Effect: Human Rights Litigation between Non-State Actors' (2015) 67 *Rutgers Law Review* 89.
Baxi, U, *The Future of Human Rights* (Oxford, Oxford University Press, 2008).
Beitz, CR, *The Idea of Human Rights* (Oxford, Oxford University Press, 2011).
Bellamy, AJ, *Responsibility to Protect* (Cambridge, Polity, 2009).
Bellamy, AJ, 'Mainstreaming the Responsibility to Protect in the United Nations System: Dilemmas, Challenges and Opportunities' (2013) 5 *Global Responsibility to Protect* 154.
Bellamy, AJ and McDonald, M, '"The Utility of Human Security": Which Humans? What Security? A Reply to Thomas & Tow' (2002) 33 *Security Dialogue* 373.
Benvenisti, E, *The International Law of Occupation*, 2nd edn (Oxford, Oxford University Press, 2012).
Benvenisti, E, 'Sovereigns as Trustees of Humanity: On the Accountability of States to Foreign Stakeholders' (2013) 107 *American Journal of International Law* 295.
Benvenisti, E, *The Law of Global Governance* (The Hague, Brill-Nijhoff, 2014).
Besson, S, 'Human Rights and Constitutional Law' in R Cruft, SM Liao and M Renzo, *Philosophical Foundations of Human Rights* (Oxford, Oxford University Press, 2015).
Bhuta, N, 'The Antinomies of Transformative Occupation' (2005) 16 *European Journal of International Law* 721.
Bianchi, A, 'Immunity versus Human Rights: The Pinochet Case' (1999) 10 *European Journal of International Law* 237.
Bianchi, A, 'Human Rights and the Magic of Jus Cogens' (2008) 19 *European Journal of International Law* 491.
Bianchi, A, *International Law Theories: An Inquiry into Different Ways of Thinking* (Oxford, Oxford University Press, 2016).
Bikundo, E, 'Humanity's Exemplary Justice: From Hostis to Hostia Humani Generis' in B van Beers, L Corrias and WG Werner (eds), *Humanity across International Law and Biolaw* (Cambridge, Cambridge University Press, 2014).
Bonadiman, L and Soirila, U, 'Human Rights, Populism, and the Political Economy of the World' (2019) 37 *Nordic Journal of Human Rights* 301.
Bradley, M, 'The International Organization for Migration (IOM): Gaining Power in the Forced Migration Regime' (2017) 33 *Refuge* 97.
Breslin, S and Christou, G, 'Has the Human Security Agenda Come of Age? Definitions, Discourses and Debates' (2015) 21 *Contemporary Politics* 1.
Brett, AS, *Changes of State: Nature and the Limits of the City in Early Modern Natural Law*, paperback edn (Princeton, Princeton University Press, 2014).
Brown, W, '"The Most We Can Hope For …": Human Rights and the Politics of Fatalism' (2004) 103 *South Atlantic Quarterly* 451.
Brown, W, *Edgework: Critical Essays on Knowledge And Politics* (Princeton, Princeton University Press, 2005).
Brown, W, *Undoing the Demos: Neoliberalism's Stealth Revolution*, reprint edn (Cambridge, MA, Zone Books – MIT Press, 2017).
Brown, W, *In the Ruins of Neoliberalism* (New York, Columbia University Press, 2019).
Browne, C, 'The End of Immanent Critique?' (2008) 11 *European Journal of Social Theory* 5.

Buchanan, A, 'Human Rights and the Legitimacy of the International Order' (2008) 14 *Legal Theory* 39.
Buchanan, A, 'Moral Status and Human Enhancement' (2009) 37 *Philosophy & Public Affairs* 346.
Buchanan, A, *The Heart of Human Rights* (Oxford, Oxford University Press, 2014).
Buchanan, A, 'Why International Legal Human Rights?' in R Cruft, SM Liao and M Renzo, *Philosophical Foundations of Human Rights* (Oxford, Oxford University Press, 2015).
Butler, J, *The Psychic Life of Power: Theories in Subjection* (Stanford, Stanford University Press, 1997).
Byk, C, 'Is Human Dignity a Useless Concept? Legal Perspectives' in M Düwell et al, *The Cambridge Handbook of Human Dignity: Interdisciplinary Perspectives* (Cambridge, Cambridge University Press, 2014).
Cançado Trindade, AA, *International Law for Humankind* (Leiden, Brill Academic Publishers, 2010).
Cassese, A, *International Law*, 2nd edn (Oxford, Oxford University Press, 2003).
Cassese, A, *Realizing Utopia: The Future of International Law* (Oxford, Oxford University Press, 2012).
Cassese, S, *Research Handbook on Global Administrative Law* (Cheltenham, Edward Elgar Publishing, 2017).
Chandler, D, 'Review Essay: Human Security: The Dog That Didn't Bark' (2008) 39 *Security Dialogue* 427.
Chandler, D, 'Understanding the Gap between the Promise and Reality of the Responsibility to Protect' in P Cunliffe (ed), *Critical Perspectives on the Responsibility to Protect: Interrogating Theory and Practice*, reprint (New York, Routledge, 2012).
Cheah, P, *Inhuman Conditions: On Cosmopolitanism and Human Rights* (Cambridge, MA, Harvard University Press, 2007).
Cheng, T-H, 'Power, Authority and International Investment Law' (2004) 20 *American University International Law Review* 465.
Chimni, BS, 'From Resettlement to Involuntary Repatriation: Towards a Critical History of Durable Solutions to Refugee Problems' (2004) 23 *Refugee Survey Quarterly* 55.
Christodoulidis, E, 'Social Rights Constitutionalism: An Antagonistic Endorsement' (2017) 44 *Journal of Law and Society* 123.
Clapham, A, *Human Rights Obligations of Non-State Actors* (Oxford, Oxford University Press, 2006).
Cohen, JL, *Globalization and Sovereignty: Rethinking Legality, Legitimacy, and Constitutionalism* (Cambridge, Cambridge University Press, 2012).
Commission on Human Security, *Human Security Now* (2003).
Connolly, WE, *Why I Am Not a Secularist* (Minneapolis, University of Minnesota Press, 1999).
Corrias, L, 'The Inhuman Stain: Representing Humanity in International Criminal Law' in B van Beers, L Corrias and WG Werner (eds), *Humanity across International Law and Biolaw* (Cambridge, Cambridge University Press, 2014).
Corrias, LDA and Gordon, GM, 'Judging in the Name of Humanity International Criminal Tribunals and the Representation of a Global Public' (2015) 13 *Journal of International Criminal Justice* 97.
Cowan, JK and Billaud, J, 'Between Learning and Schooling: The Politics of Human Rights Monitoring at the Universal Periodic Review' (2015) 36 *Third World Quarterly* 1175.
Craven, M, 'Statehood, Self-Determination, and Recognition' in Malcolm Evans (ed), *International Law*, 4th edn (Oxford, Oxford University Press, 2014).
Crawford, J, 'Sovereignty as a Legal Value' in J Crawford, M Koskenniemi and S Ranganathan (eds), *The Cambridge Companion to International Law* (Cambridge, Cambridge University Press, 2012).
Crawford, J, 'The Current Political Discourse Concerning International Law' (2018) 81 *MLR* 1.
Crawford, JR, *The Creation of States in International Law*, 2nd edn (Oxford, Oxford University Press, 2007).

Criddle, EJ and Fox-Decent, E, *Fiduciaries of Humanity: How International Law Constitutes Authority* (Oxford, Oxford University Press, 2016).
Cruft, R, Liao, SM and Renzo, M, 'The Philosophical Foundations of Human Rights: An Overview' in R Cruft, SM Liao and M Renzo (eds), *Philosophical Foundations of Human Rights* (Oxford, Oxford University Press, 2015).
Daly, E, *Dignity Rights. Courts, Constitutions, and the Worth of the Human Person* (Philadelphia, University of Pennsylvania Press, 2013).
Davis, KE, Kingsbury, B and Merry, SE, 'Indicators as a Technology of Global Governance' (2012) 46 *Law & Society Review* 71.
De Schutter, O, 'Human Rights and the Rise of International Organizations: The Logic of Sliding Scales in the Law of International Responsibility', CRIDHO Working Paper 2010/4 (Univeristé catholique de Louvain, 2010).
Debrix, F, 'Deterritorialised Territories, Borderless Borders: The New Geography of International Medical Assistance' (1998) 19 *Third World Quarterly* 827.
Debrix, F, 'Space Quest: Surveillance, Governance, and the Panoptic Eye of the United Nations' (1999) 24 *Alternatives: Global, Local, Political* 269.
Deleuze, G, *Bergsonism*, reissue edn (Cambridge, MA, MIT Press, 1991).
Delmas-Marty, M, *Towards a Truly Common Law: Europe as a Laboratory for Legal Pluralism* (N Norberg trans, Cambridge, Cambridge University Press, 2002).
Delmas-Marty, M, 'The Imaginative Forces of Law' (2003) 2 *Chinese Journal of International Law* 623.
Delmas-Marty, M, *Ordering Pluralism: A Conceptual Framework for Understanding the Transnational Legal World* (N Norberg trans, Oxford, Hart Publishing, 2009).
Delmas-Marty, M, *Résister, responsabiliser, anticiper: ou comment humaniser la mondialisation* (Paris, Le Seuil, 2013).
Delmas-Marty, M, *Aux quatre vents du monde. Petit guide de navigation sur l'océan de la mondialisation* (Paris, Le Seuil, 2016).
Deng, FM et al, *Sovereignty as Responsibility: Conflict Management in Africa* (FM Deng ed, Washington, Brookings Institution Press, 1996).
Derrida, J, *Dissemination* (B Johnson trans, Chicago, University of Chicago Press, 1983).
Diefenbach, T, 'New Public Management in Public Sector Organizations: The Dark Sides of Managerialistic "Enlightenment"' (2009) 87 *Public Administration* 892.
Domingo, R, *The New Global Law*, reprint edn (Cambridge, Cambridge University Press, 2011).
Donnelly, J, *Universal Human Rights in Theory and Practice*, 2nd edn (Ithaca, NY, Cornell University Press, 2002).
Douzinas, C, *The End of Human Rights* (Oxford, Hart Publishing, 2000).
Douzinas, C, 'Identity, Recognition, Rights or What Can Hegel Teach Us about Human Rights?' (2002) 29 *Journal of Law and Society* 379.
Douzinas, C, 'The End(s) of Human Rights' (2002) 26 *Melbourne University Law Review* 445.
Douzinas, C, *Human Rights and Empire: The Political Philosophy of Cosmopolitanism*, new edn (New York, Routledge-Cavendish, 2007).
Douzinas, C, 'The Paradoxes of Human Rights' (2013) 20 *Constellations* 51.
Dudai, R, 'Human Rights in the Populist Era: Mourn then (Re)Organize' (2017) 9 *Journal of Human Rights Practice* 16.
Duff, A, 'Authority and Responsibility in International Criminal Law' in S Besson and J Tasioulas (eds), *The Philosophy of International Law* (Oxford, Oxford University Press, 2010).
Duffield, M, 'Human Security: Linking Security and Development in an Age of Terror' in S Klingebiel, *New Interfaces between Security and Development: Changing Concepts and Approaches* (Bonn, German Development Institute (DIE), 2006).
Duffield, M, *Development, Security and Unending War* (Cambridge, Polity, 2007).
Duffield, M, 'The Resilience of the Ruins: Towards a Critique of Digital Humanitarianism' (2016) 4 *Resilience* 147.

Duffield, M and Waddell, N, 'Securing Humans in a Dangerous World' (2006) 43 *International Politics* 1.

Duncombe, C and Dunne, T, 'After Liberal World Order' (2018) 94 *International Affairs* 25.

Dunlop, E, 'Indications of Progress? Assessing the Use of Indicators in UNHCR Operations', UNHCR Research Paper No 214 (2011).

Dupré, C, *The Age of Dignity: Human Rights and Constitutionalism in Europe* (Oxford, Hart Publishing, 2015).

Dupuy, P-M, 'The Constitutional Dimension of the Charter of the United Nations Revisited' (1997) 1 *Max Planck Yearbook of United Nations Law Online*, http://booksandjournals.brillonline.com/content/journals/10.1163/187574197x00038.

Dupuy, P-M, 'The Danger of Fragmentation or Unification of the International Legal System and the International Court of Justice Symposium Issue: The Proliferation of International Tribunals: Piecing Together the Puzzle' (1998) 31 *New York University Journal of International Law and Politics* 791.

Dupuy, P-M, 'Some Reflections on Contemporary International Law and the Appeal to Universal Values: A Response to Martti Koskenniemi' (2005) 16 *European Journal of International Law* 131.

Dupuy, P-M, '2000–2020: Twenty Years Later, Where Are We in Terms of the Unity of International Law?' (2020) 9 *Cambridge International Law Journal* 6.

Dworkin, R, *Life's Dominion: An Argument about Abortion, Euthanasia, and Individual Freedom* (New York, Vintage Books, 1993).

Elliott, L, 'Human Security/Environmental Security' (2015) 21 *Contemporary Politics* 11.

Eslava, L and Pahuja, S, 'The State and International Law: A Reading from the Global South' (2020) 11 *Humanity: An International Journal of Human Rights, Humanitarianism, and Development* 118.

Esmeir, S, *Juridical Humanity: A Colonial History* (Stanford, Stanford University Press, 2014).

Fassin, D, 'Compassion and Repression: The Moral Economy of Immigration Policies in France' (2005) 20 *Cultural Anthropology* 362.

Fassin, D, 'Another Politics of Life Is Possible' (2009) 26 *Theory, Culture & Society* 44.

Fassin, D, 'Policing Borders, Producing Boundaries. The Governmentality of Immigration in Dark Times' (2011) 40 *Annual Review of Anthropology* 213.

Fassin, D, *Humanitarian Reason: A Moral History of the Present* (Berkeley, University of California Press, 2011).

Feichtner, I, 'Realizing Utopia through the Practice of International Law' (2012) 23 *European Journal of International Law* 1143.

Feldman, I and Ticktin, M, 'Introduction: Government and Humanity' in Ilana Feldman and Miriam Ticktin (eds), *In the Name of Humanity: The Government of Threat and Care* (Durham, NC, Duke University Press, 2010).

Finkelstein, LS, 'What Is Global Governance' (1995) 1 *Global Governance* 367.

Fischer-Lescano, A and Teubner, G, 'Regime-Collisions: The Vain Search for Legal Unity in the Fragmentation of Global Law' (2003) 25 *Michigan Journal of International Law* 999.

Fitzpatrick, J, 'Speaking Law to Power: The War against Terrorism and Human Rights' (2003) 14 *European Journal of International Law* 241.

Foot, R, 'The United Nations, Counter Terrorism, and Human Rights: Institutional Adaptation and Embedded Ideas' (2007) 29 *Human Rights Quarterly* 489.

Foucault, M, *The History of Sexuality* (R Hurley trans, New York, Vintage Books, 1988).

Foucault, M, *The History of Sexuality: The Will to Knowledge: The Will to Knowledge v 1*, new edn (R Hurley trans, London, Penguin 1998).

Foucault, M, *'Society Must Be Defended': Lectures at the Collège de France, 1975–76* (M Bertani, A Fontana and D Macey trans, London, Picador, 2003).

Foucault, M, *Security, Territory, Population: Lectures at the Collège de France, 1977–78* (M Senellart, F Ewald and A Fontana trans, London, Picador, 2007).

Foucault, M, *The Birth of Biopolitics: Lectures at the Collège de France, 1978–1979* (M Senellart trans, London, Picador, 2010).

Fox, GH, 'The Occupation of Iraq' (Social Science Research Network, 2004) SSRN Scholarly Paper ID 595163, www.papers.ssrn.com/abstract=595163.

Fox, GH, *Humanitarian Occupation*, 1 edn (Cambridge, Cambridge University Press, 2008).

Fox-Decent, E and Criddle, EJ, 'The Fiduciary Constitution of Human Rights' (2009) 15 *Legal Theory* 301.

Francechet, A, 'Global Legalism and Human Security' in SJ MacLean, DR Black and TM Shaw (eds), *A Decade of Human Security: Global Governance and New Multilateralisms* (Farnham, Ashgate Publishing, 2006).

Franck, TM, *The Empowered Self: Law and Society in an Age of Individualism* (Oxford, Oxford University Press, 1999).

Frankenberg, G, 'Human Rights and the Belief in a Just World' (2014) 12 *International Journal of Constitutional Law* 35.

Fukuyama, F, *Our Posthuman Future: Consequences of the Biotechnology Revolution*, reprint edn (London, Picador, 2003).

Gaja, G, 'The Position of Individuals in International Law: An ILC Perspective' (2010) 21 *European Journal of International Law* 11.

Gammeltoft-Hansen, T, *Access to Asylum: International Refugee Law and the Globalisation of Migration Control*, reprint edn (Cambridge, Cambridge University Press, 2013).

Gewirth, A, *The Community of Rights* (Chicago, University of Chicago Press, 1998).

Glanville, L, *Sovereignty and the Responsibility to Protect: A New History* (Chicago, University of Chicago Press, 2013).

Gold, AS and Miller, PB (eds), *Philosophical Foundations of Fiduciary Law* (Oxford, Oxford University Press, 2014).

Granik, M, 'The Human Rights Dialogue: Foundationalism Reconsidered' (2013) 60 *Theoria: A Journal of Social & Political Theory* 1.

Grasten, M and Tzouvala, N, 'The Political Economy of International Transitional Administration: Regulating Food and Farming in Kosovo and Iraq' (2018) 24 *Contemporary Politics* 588.

Gready, P, 'Reflections on a Human Rights Decade, Near and Far' (2019) 11 *Journal of Human Rights Practice* 422.

Griffin, J, *On Human Rights* (Oxford, Oxford University Press, 2009).

Gutmann, A, 'Introduction' in M Ignatieff, *Human Rights as Politics and Idolatry* (A Gutmann ed, Princeton, Princeton University Press, 2003).

Habermas, J, 'The Concept of Human Dignity and the Realistic Utopia of Human Rights' (2010) 41 *Metaphilosophy* 464.

Hampson, FO, 'A Concept in Need of a Global Policy Response' (2004) 35 *Security Dialogue* 349.

Hardt, M and Negri, A, *Empire* (Cambridge, MA, Harvard University Press, 2001).

Harlow, C, 'Global Administrative Law: The Quest for Principles and Values' (2006) 17 *European Journal of International Law* 187.

Harvey, D, *The New Imperialism* (Oxford, Oxford University Press, 2005).

Harvey, D, *A Brief History of Neoliberalism* (Oxford, Oxford University Press, 2007).

Hassan, O, 'Political Security: From the 1990s to the Arab Spring' (2015) 21 *Contemporary Politics* 86.

Havercroft, J et al, 'Editorial: Donald Trump as Global Constitutional Breaching Experiment' (2018) 7 *Global Constitutionalism* 1.

Hennette-Vauchez, S, 'When Ambivalent Principles Prevail: Leads for Explaining Western Legal Orders' Infatuation with the Human Dignity Principle' (2007) 10 *Legal Ethics* 193.

Hennette-Vauchez, S, 'A Human Dignitas – Remnants of the Ancient Legal Concept in Contemporary Dignity Jurisprudence' (2011) 9 *International Journal of Constitutional Law* 32.

Hennette-Vauchez, S, 'Human Dignity in French Law' in M Düwell et al (eds), *The Cambridge Handbook of Human Dignity: Interdisciplinary Perspectives* (Cambridge, Cambridge University Press, 2014).

Herzog, D, 'Aristocratic Dignity?' in M Dan-Cohen and J Waldron (eds), *Dignity, Rank, and Rights* (Oxford, Oxford University Press, 2012).

Heywood, M, 'South Africa's Journey from Socialism to Human Rights: The True Confessions of an Errant Socialist' (2019) 11 *Journal of Human Rights Practice* 305.

Higgins, R, *Problems and Process: International Law and How We Use It*, new edn (Oxford, Oxford University Press, 1995).

Hobsbawm, E, *Age of Extremes: The Short Twentieth Century, 1914–1991*, new edn (London, Abacus 1995).

Hoffman, P, 'Human Rights and Terrorism' (2004) 26 *Human Rights Quarterly* 932.

Hopgood, S, *The Endtimes of Human Rights* (New York, Cornell University Press, 2013).

Hopgood, S, 'The Last Rites for Humanitarian Intervention' (2014) 6 *Global Responsibility to Protect* 181.

Howse, R and Teitel, R, 'Does Humanity-Law Require (or Imply) a Progressive Theory or History? (And Other Questions for Martti Koskenniemi)' (2013) 27 *Temple International & Comparative Law Journal* 377.

ICISS, *The Responsibility to Protect: The Report of the International Commission on Intervention and State Sovereignty*, pap/cdr edn (Ottawa, IDRC Books, 2002).

Ignatieff, M, *Human Rights as Politics and Idolatry* (A Gutmann ed, Princeton, Princeton University Press, 2003).

ILC Study Group, 'Fragmentation of International Law: Difficulties Arising from the Diversification and Expansion of International Law, Finalized by Martti Koskenniemi', UN Doc A/CN.4/L.682 and Add 1 and Corr 1.

Jacobsen, KL, 'On Humanitarian Refugee Biometrics and New Forms of Intervention' (2017) 11 *Journal of Intervention and Statebuilding* 529.

Jacobsen, KL and Sandvik, KB, 'UNHCR and the Pursuit of International Protection: Accountability through Technology?' (2018) 39 *Third World Quarterly* 1508.

Johansson, F, 'The Question of Power: A View from a Critical Insider' in L Doutje and L van Troost (eds), *Debating the Endtimes of Human Rights: Activism and Institutions in a Neo-Westphalian World* (Amsterdam, Strategic Studies Project, 2014).

Johns, F, 'Guantánamo Bay and the Annihilation of the Exception' (2005) 16 *European Journal of International Law* 613.

Jouannet, E, 'A Century of French International Law Scholarship' (2009) 61 *Maine Law Review* 83.

Jouannet, E, *The Liberal-Welfarist Law of Nations: A History of International Law* (C Sutcliffe trans, Cambridge, Cambridge University Press, 2012).

Jubilut, LL and de Oliveira Lopes, R, 'Strategies for the Protection of Migrants through International Law' (2017) 5 *Groningen Journal of International Law* 34.

Kaldor, M et al, *A Human Security Doctrine for Europe: The Barcelona Report of the Study Group on Europe's Security Capabilities* (Study Group on Europe's Security Capabilities, 2004).

Kant, I, *Toward Perpetual Peace and Other Writings on Politics, Peace, and History* (P Kleingeld ed, DL Colclasure trans, New Haven, Yale University Press, 2006).

Keck, ME and Sikkink, K, *Activists beyond Borders: Advocacy Networks in International Politics* (New York, Cornell University Press, 1998).

Kendall, S and Nouwen, S, 'Representational Practices at the International Criminal Court: The Gap between Juridified and Abstract Victimhood' (2013) 76 *Law & Contemporary Problems* 235.

Kennedy, D, *International Legal Structures* (Baden-Baden, Nomos Publishers, 1987).

Kennedy, D, 'International Human Rights Movement: Part of the Problem? Boundaries in the Field of Human Rights' (2002) 15 *Harvard Human Rights Journal* 101.

Kennedy, D, *A World of Struggle: How Power, Law, and Expertise Shape Global Political Economy* (Princeton, Princeton University Press, 2016).

Kennedy, DW, 'New World Order: Yesterday, Today, and Tomorrow' (1994) 4 *Transnational Law & Contemporary Problems* 329.

Keohane, RO, 'Political Authority after Intervention: Gradations in Sovereignty' in JL Holzgrefe and RO Keohane (eds), *Humanitarian Intervention: Ethical, Legal and Political Dilemmas* (Cambridge, Cambridge University Press, 2003).

Khalidi, R and Samour, S, 'Neoliberalism as Liberation: The Statehood Program and the Remaking of the Palestinian National Movement' (2011) 40 *Journal of Palestine Studies* 6.

Kingsbury, B, 'The Concept of "Law" in Global Administrative Law' (2009) 20 *European Journal of International Law* 23.

Kingsbury, B, Krisch, N and Stewart, RB, 'The Emergence of Global Administrative Law' (2005) 68 *Law and Contemporary Problems* 15.

Kjeldgaard-Pedersen, A, *The International Legal Personality of the Individual* (Oxford, Oxford University Press, 2018).

Klabbers, J, 'The Life and Times of the Law of International Organizations' (2001) 70 *Nordic Journal of International Law* 287.

Klabbers, J, 'Redemption Song? Human Rights versus Community-Building in East Timor' (2003) 16 *Leiden Journal of International Law* 367.

Klabbers, J, 'The Concept of Legal Personality' (2005) 11 *Jus Gentium* 35.

Klabbers, J, 'Notes on the Ideology of International Organizations Law: The International Organization for Migration, State-Making, and the Market for Migration' (2019) 32 *Leiden Journal of International Law* 383.

Klabbers, J, Peters, A and Ulfstein, G, *The Constitutionalization of International Law* (Oxford, Oxford University Press, 2011).

Klingebiel, S, 'New Interfaces between Security and Development: Introduction' in Stephan Klingebiel, *New Interfaces between Security and Development: Changing Concepts and Approaches* (Bonn, German Development Institute (DIE), 2006).

Knox, JH, 'Horizontal Human Rights Law' (2008) 102 *American Journal of International Law* 1.

Koch, A, 'The Politics and Discourse of Migrant Return: The Role of UNHCR and IOM in the Governance of Return' (2014) 40 *Journal of Ethnic and Migration Studies* 905.

Kochi, T, *Global Justice and Social Conflict: The Foundations of Liberal Order and International Law* (New York, Routledge, 2019).

Kochi, T, 'The End of Global Constitutionalism and Rise of Antidemocratic Politics' (2020) 34 *Global Society* 487.

Korhonen, O, Gras, J and Creutz, K, *International Post-Conflict Situations: New Challenges for Co-operative Governance* (Helsinki, Erik Castrén Institute of International Law and Human Rights, 2006).

Koskenniemi, M, 'The Pull of the Mainstream' (1989) 88 *Michigan Law Review* 1946.

Koskenniemi, M, 'The Wonderful Artificiality of States' (1994) 88 *American Society of International Law Proceedings* 22.

Koskenniemi, M, 'The Police in the Temple Order, Justice and the UN: A Dialectical View' (1995) 6 *European Journal of International Law* 325.

Koskenniemi, M, 'The Effect of Rights on Political Culture' in P Alston, MR Bustelo and J Heenan (eds), *The EU and Human Rights* (Oxford, Oxford University Press, 1999).

Koskenniemi, M, 'Human Rights, Politics, and Love' (2001) 2001 *Mennesker & Rettigheter* 33.

Koskenniemi, M, *The Gentle Civilizer of Nations: The Rise and Fall of International Law, 1870–1960* (Cambridge, Cambridge University Press, 2002).

Koskenniemi, M, 'Global Governance and Public International Law' (2004) 37 *Kritische Justiz* 241.

Koskenniemi, M, 'International Law and Hegemony: A Reconfiguration' (2004) 17 *Cambridge Review of International Affairs* 197.

Koskenniemi, M, *From Apology to Utopia the Structure of International Legal Argument* (Cambridge, Cambridge University Press, 2005).

Koskenniemi, M, 'International Law in Europe: Between Tradition and Renewal' (2005) 16 *European Journal of International Law* 113.

Koskenniemi, M, 'The Fate of Public International Law: Between Technique and Politics' (2007) 70 *MLR* 1.

Koskenniemi, M, 'Human Rights Mainstreaming as a Strategy for Institutional Power' (2010) 1 *Humanity: An International Journal of Human Rights, Humanitarianism, and Development* 47.

Koskenniemi, M, 'Hegemonic Regimes' in MA Young (ed), *Regime Interaction in International Law: Facing Fragmentation* (Cambridge, Cambridge University Press, 2011).

Koskenniemi, M, 'Between Coordination and Constitution: International Law as a German Discipline' (2011) 15 *Redescriptions: Political Thought, Conceptual History and Feminist Theory* 45.

Koskenniemi, M, 'Conclusion: Vocabularies of Sovereignty – Powers of a Paradox' in H Kalmo and Q Skinner (eds), *Sovereignty in Fragments: The Past, Present and Future of a Contested Concept*, reprint edn (Cambridge, Cambridge University Press, 2014).

Koskenniemi, M, 'It's Not the Cases, It's the System' (2017) 18 *Journal of Investment & Trade* 343.

Koskenniemi, M, 'Enchanted by the Tools? An Enlightenment Perspective' (2019) 35 *American University International Law Review* 397.

Koskenniemi, M and Leino, P, 'Fragmentation of International Law? Postmodern Anxieties' (2002) 15 *Leiden Journal of International Law* 553.

Krasner, SD, *Sovereignty* (Princeton, Princeton University Press, 1999).

Kratochwil, F, 'Has the "Rule of Law" Become a "Rule of Lawyers"? An Inquiry into the Use and Abuse of an Ancient Topos in Contemporary Debates' in G Palombella and N Walker (eds), *Relocating the Rule of Law* (Oxford, Hart Publishing, 2009).

Kratochwil, F, 'Leaving Sovereignty Behind? And Inquiry into the Politics of Post-Modernity' in R Falk, M Juergensmeyer and V Popovski (eds), *Legality and Legitimacy in Global Affairs* (Oxford, Oxford University Press, 2012).

Krause, K, 'The Key to a Powerful Agenda, if Properly Delimited' (2004) 35 *Security Dialogue* 367.

Krever, T, 'International Criminal Law: An Ideology Critique' (2013) 26 *Leiden Journal of International Law* 701.

Krever, T, 'Dispensing Global Justice' [2014] *New Left Review* 67.

Lagon, MP and Arend, AC, 'Constructing a Dialogue on Dignity: The Path Ahead' in MP Lagon and AC Arend (eds), *Human Dignity and the Future of Global Institutions* (Washington, Georgetown University Press, 2014).

Lagon, MP and Arend, AC, 'Introduction: Human Dignity in a Neomedieval World' in MP Lagon and AC Arend (eds), *Human Dignity and the Future of Global Institutions* (Washington, Georgetown University Press, 2014).

Lang, A, *World Trade Law after Neoliberalism: Reimagining the Global Economic Order*, reprint edn (Oxford, Oxford University Press, 2013).

Larrinaga, MD and Doucet, MG, 'Sovereign Power and the Biopolitics of Human Security' (2008) 39 *Security Dialogue* 517.

Le Bris, C, *L'humanité Saisie Par Le Droit International Public* (Paris, LGDJ Lextenso éditions, 2012).

Leaning, J, 'Psychosocial Well-Being over Time' (2004) 35 *Security Dialogue* 354.

Lehto, M, 'Slowly but Surely? The Challenge of the Responsibility to Protect' in R Liivoja and J Petman (eds), *International Law-Making: Essays in Honour of Jan Klabbers* (New York, Routledge, 2013).

Leib, EJ and Galoob, SR, 'Fiduciary Political Theory: A Critique Essay' (2015) 125 *Yale Law Journal* 1820.

Lisk, F, Šehović, AB and Sekalala, S, 'Health and Human Security: A Wrinkle in Time or a New Paradigm?' (2015) 21 *Contemporary Politics* 25.

Luban, D, 'A Theory of Crimes against Humanity' (2004) 29 *Yale Journal of International Law* 85.

Lui, R, 'The International Government of Refugees' in W Larner and W Walters (eds), *Global Governmentality: Governing International Spaces* (New York, Routledge, 2004).

Macfarlane, SN, 'A Useful Concept That Risks Losing Its Political Salience' (2004) 35 *Security Dialogue* 368.

MacFarlane, SN and Khong, YF, *Human Security and the UN: A Critical History* (Bloomington, Indiana University Press, 2006).

Mack, A, 'A Signifier of Shared Values' (2004) 35 *Security Dialogue* 366.

Macklem, P, *The Sovereignty of Human Rights* (Oxford, Oxford University Press, 2015).
Macklin, R, 'Dignity Is a Useless Concept' (2003) 327 *British Medical Journal* 1419.
Macleod, C, 'Towards a Philosophical Account of Crimes Against Humanity' (2010) 21 *European Journal of International Law* 281.
Mamdani, M, *Citizen and Subject: Contemporary Africa and the Legacy of Late Colonialism* (Princeton, Princeton University Press, 1996).
Mamdani, M, 'Responsibility to Protect or Right to Punish?' (2010) 4 *Journal of Intervention and Statebuilding* 53.
Manner, G, 'The Object Theory of the Individual in International Law' (1952) 46 *American Journal of International Law* 428.
Marhia, N, 'Some Humans Are More Human than Others: Troubling the "Human" in Human Security from a Critical Feminist Perspective' (2013) 44 *Security Dialogue* 19.
Marks, S, *The Riddle of All Constitutions: International Law, Democracy, and the Critique of Ideology* (Oxford, Oxford University Press, 2001).
Marks, S, 'Empire's Law: The Earl A Snyder Lecture in International Law' (2003) 10 *Indiana Journal of Global Legal Studies* 449.
Marks, S, 'False Contingency' (2009) 62 *Current Legal Problems* 1.
Marks, S, 'Human Rights and Root Causes' (2011) 74 *MLR* 57.
Marks, S, 'Four Human Rights Myths' in D Kinley, W Sadurski and K Walton (eds), *Human Rights: Old Problems, New Possibilities* (Cheltenham, Edward Elgar Publishing, 2014).
Marks, S, *A False Tree of Liberty: Human Rights in Radical Thought* (Oxford, Oxford University Press, 2019).
Marlier, G and Crawford, NC, 'Incomplete and Imperfect Institutionalisation of Empathy and Altruism in the "Responsibility to Protect" Doctrine' (2013) 5 *Global Responsibility to Protect* 397.
Mazower, M, *Governing the World: The History of an Idea, 1815 to the Present* (London, Penguin Books, 2013).
McAuliffe, P, 'From Watchdog to Workhorse: Explaining the Emergence of the ICC's Burden-Sharing Policy as an Example of Creeping Cosmopolitanism' (2014) 13 *Chinese Journal of International Law* 259.
McCrudden, C, 'Human Dignity and Judicial Interpretation of Human Rights' (2008) 19 *European Journal of International Law* 655.
McDougal, MS, Lasswell, HD and Chen, L, *Human Rights and World Public Order: The Basic Policies of an International Law of Human Dignity* (New Haven, Yale University Press, 1977).
McMahan, J, '"Our Fellow Creatures"' (2005) 9 *Journal of Ethics* 353.
Mégret, F, 'Apology of Utopia; Some Thoughts on Koskenniemian Themes, with Particular Emphasis on Massively Institutionalized International Human Rights Law' (2013) 27 *Temple International & Comparative Law Journal* 455.
Mégret, F, 'What Sort of Global Justice Is "International Criminal Justice"?' (2015) 13 *Journal of International Criminal Justice* 77.
Meron, T, 'The Humanization of Humanitarian Law' (2000) 94 *American Journal of International Law* 239.
Meron, T, *The Humanization of International Law* (Boston, MA, Brill Academic Publishers, 2006).
Merry, SE, *Human Rights and Gender Violence: Translating International Law into Local Justice* (Chicago, University of Chicago Press, 2006).
Merry, SE, 'Measuring the World: Indicators, Human Rights, and Global Governance' (2011) 52 *Current Anthropology* S83.
Merry, SE, *The Seductions of Quantification: Measuring Human Rights, Gender Violence, and Sex Trafficking* (Chicago, University of Chicago Press, 2016).
Milanovic, M, *Extraterritorial Application of Human Rights Treaties: Law, Principles, and Policy* (Oxford, Oxford University Press, 2011).

Milanovic, M, 'On Realistic Utopias and Other Oxymorons: An Essay on Antonio Cassese's Last Book' (2012) 23 *European Journal of International Law* 1033.

Miles, K, 'International Investment Law and Universality: Histories of Shape-Shifting Part I: General Part' (2014) 3 *Cambridge Journal of International and Comparative Law* 986.

Miller, PB and Gold, AS (eds), *Contract, Status, and Fiduciary Law* (Oxford, Oxford University Press, 2016).

Mofidi, M and Eckert, AE, 'Unlawful Combatants or Prisoners of War: The Law and Politics of Labels' (2003) 36 *Cornell International Law Journal* 59.

Möllers, C, 'The Triple Dilemma of Human Dignity: A Case Study' in C McCrudden (ed), *Understanding Human Dignity*, Proceedings of the British Academy Vol 192 (Oxford, Oxford University Press/British Academy, 2013).

Monbiot, G, *How Did We Get Into This Mess?: Politics, Equality, Nature*, reprint edn (London, Verso, 2017).

Moyn, S, *The Last Utopia: Human Rights in History* (Cambridge, MA, Belknap Press of Harvard University Press, 2012).

Moyn, S, *Not Enough: Human Rights in an Unequal World* (Cambridge, MA, Belknap Press of Harvard University Press, 2018).

Murphy, J, 'The Rise of Global Managers' in S Dar and B Cooke (eds), *The New Development Management: Critiquing the Dual Modernization* (London, Zed Books, 2013).

Mutua, M, 'Human Rights and Powerlessness: Pathologies of Choice and Substance Essay Collection: Classcrits: Part I: Thinking through Law's Questions of Class, Economics, and Inequality' (2008) 56 *Buffalo Law Review* 1027.

Newhouse, LS, 'More than Mere Survival: Violence, Humanitarian Governance, and Practical Material Politics in a Kenyan Refugee Camp' (2015) 47 *Environment and Planning A: Economy and Space* 2292.

Niemelä, P, *The Politics of Responsibility to Protect: Problems and Prospects* (Helsinki, The Erik Castrén Institute of International Law and Human Rights, 2008).

Nijman, JE, *The Concept of International Legal Personality: An Inquiry into the History and Theory of International Law* (The Hague, Asser Press, 2004).

Nussbaum, MC, *Sex and Social Justice* (Oxford, Oxford University Press, 2000).

Nussbaum, MC, *Women and Human Development: The Capabilities Approach* (Cambridge, Cambridge University Press, 2001).

Nussbaum, MC, *Creating Capabilities: The Human Development Approach* (Cambridge, MA, Harvard University Press, 2011).

Oberlietner, G, 'Human Security: A Challenge to International Law' (2005) 11 *Global Governance* 185.

O'Connell P, 'On Reconciling Irreconcilables: Neo-Liberal Globalisation and Human Rights' (2007) 7 *Human Rights Law Review* 483.

O'Connell P, 'On the Human Rights Question' (2018) 40 *Human Rights Quarterly* 962.

Ohmae, K, *The End of the Nation State: The Rise of Regional Economies* (New York, Free Press, 1996).

Orford, A, 'Contesting Globalization: A Feminist Perspective on the Future of Human Rights Symposium: International Human Rights at Fifty: A Symposium to Commemorate the 50th Anniversary of the Universal Declaration of Human Rights' (1998) 8 *Transnational Law & Contemporary Problems* 171.

Orford, A, 'Beyond Harmonization: Trade, Human Rights and the Economy of Sacrifice' (2005) 18 *Leiden Journal of International Law* 179.

Orford, A, *Reading Humanitarian Intervention: Human Rights and the Use of Force in International Law*, reissue edn (Cambridge, Cambridge University Press, 2007).

Orford, A, 'Book Review Article: International Territorial Administration and the Management of Decolonization' (2010) 59 *International & Comparative Law Quarterly* 227.

Orford, A, *International Authority and the Responsibility to Protect* (Cambridge, Cambridge University Press, 2011).

Orford, A, 'Food Security, Free Trade, and the Battle for the State' (2015) 11 *Journal of International Law & International Relations* 1.

Orford, A, 'Theorizing Free Trade' in A Orford and F Hoffmann (eds), *The Oxford Handbook of the Theory of International Law* (Oxford, Oxford University Press, 2016).

Orford, A, 'International Law and the Populist Moment: A Comment on Martti Koskenniemi's Enchanted by the Tools? International Law and Enlightenment' (2019) 35 *American University International Law Review* 427.

Orford, A and Beard, J, 'Making the State Safe for the Market: The World Bank's World Development Report 1997 Critique and Comment' (1998) 22 *Melbourne University Law Review* 195.

Osiatynski, W, *Human Rights and Their Limits* (Cambridge, Cambridge University Press, 2009).

Owen, T, 'Human Security – Conflict, Critique and Consensus: Colloquium Remarks and a Proposal for a Threshold-Based Definition' (2004) 35 *Security Dialogue* 373.

Pallis, M, 'The Operation of UNHCR's Accountability Mechanisms' (2004) 37 *New York University Journal of International Law and Politics* 869.

Palonen, K, 'An Application of Conceptual History to Itself: From Method to Theory in Reinhart Kosellecks's Begriffsgeschifte' (1997) 1 *Finnish Yearbook of Political Thought* 36.

Palonen, K, 'Rhetorical and Temporal Perspectives on Conceptual Change: Theses on Quentin Skinner and Reinhart Koselleck' (1999) 3 *Finnish Yearbook of Political Thought* 41.

Pandolfi, M, 'From Paradox to Paradigm: The Permanent State of Emergency in the Balkans' in D Fassin and M Pandolfi (eds), *Contemporary States of Emergency: The Politics of Military and Humanitarian Interventions* (New York, Zone Books, 2010).

Paris, R, 'Human Security: Paradigm Shift or Hot Air?' (2001) 26 *International Security* 87.

Paris, R, *At War's End: Building Peace after Civil Conflict* (Cambridge, Cambridge University Press, 2004).

Parlett, K, *The Individual in the International Legal System: Continuity and Change in International Law*, reprint edn (Cambridge, Cambridge University Press, 2013).

Peters, A, 'The Merits of Global Constitutionalism' (2009) 16 *Indiana Journal of Global Legal Studies* 397.

Peters, A, 'Humanity as the A and Ω of Sovereignty' (2009) 20 *European Journal of International Law* 513.

Peters, A, *Beyond Human Rights: The Legal Status of the Individual in International Law* (J Huston trans, Cambridge, Cambridge University Press, 2016).

Petersmann, E-U, 'The WTO Constitution and Human Rights' (2000) 3 *Journal of International Economic Law* 19.

Petersmann, E-U, 'From "Negative" to "Positive" Integration in the WTO: Time for "Mainstreaming Human Rights" into WTO Law?' (2000) 37 *CML Rev* 1363.

Petersmann, E-U, 'Human Rights and International Economic Law in the 21st Century. The Need to Clarify Their Interrelationships' (2001) 4 *Journal of International Economic Law* 3.

Petersmann, E-U, 'Time for a United Nations "Global Compact" for Integrating Human Rights into the Law of Worldwide Organizations: Lessons from European Integration' (2002) 13 *European Journal of International Law* 621.

Petersmann, E-U, 'Constitutional Theories of International Economic Adjudication and Investor-State Arbitration' in P-M Dupuy, E-U Petersmann and F Francioni (eds), *Human Rights in International Investment Law and Arbitration* (Oxford, Oxford University Press, 2009).

Petersmann, E-U, 'Introduction and Summary: "Administration of Justice" in International Investment Law and Adjudication?' in P-M Dupuy, E-U Petersmann and F Francioni (eds), *Human Rights in International Investment Law and Arbitration* (Oxford, Oxford University Press, 2009).

Petman, J, 'Deformalization of International Organizations Law' in J Klabbers and A Wallendahl (eds), *Research Handbook on the Law of International Organizations* (Cheltenham, Edward Elgar Publishing, 2012).

Phillips, A, *The Politics of the Human* (Cambridge, Cambridge University Press, 2015).

Piketty, T, *Capital in the Twenty-First Century*, reprint edn (A Goldhammer trans, Cambridge, MA, Belknap Press of Harvard University Press, 2017).

Plehwe, D, Slobodian, Q and Mirowski, P (eds), *Nine Lives of Neoliberalism* (New York, Verso 2020).

Portmann, R, *Legal Personality in International Law* (Cambridge, Cambridge University Press, 2010).

Prasad, A and Prasad, P, 'The Empire of Organizations and the Organization of Empires: Postcolonial Considerations on Theorizing Workplace Resistance' in A Prasad (ed), *Postcolonial Theory and Organizational Analysis: A Critical Engagement*, 2003 edn (London, Palgrave Macmillan 2003).

Rajagopal, B, *International Law from Below: Development, Social Movements and Third World Resistance* (Cambridge, Cambridge University Press, 2003).

Rancière, J, *Disagreement: Politics and Philosophy* (Minneapolis, University of Minnesota Press, 1999).

Rancière, J, 'Who Is the Subject of the Rights of Man?' (2004) 103 *South Atlantic Quarterly* 297.

Rave, DT, 'Politicians as Fiduciaries' (2012) 126 *Harvard Law Review* 671.

Rawls, J, *The Law of Peoples*, new edn (Cambridge, MA, Harvard University Press, 2001).

Raz, J, 'Human Rights in the Emerging World Order' (2010) 1 *Transnational Legal Theory* 31.

Rech, W, 'Ideology' in J d'Aspermont and S Singh (eds), *Concepts for International Law: Contributions to Disciplinary Thought* (Cheltenham, Edward Elgar Publishing, 2019).

Renzo, M, 'Human Needs, Human Rights' in R Cruft, SM Liao and M Renzo (eds), *Philosophical Foundations of Human Rights* (Oxford, Oxford University Press, 2015).

Rhodes, RAW, *Network Governance and the Differentiated Polity: Selected Essays*, vol 1 (Oxford, Oxford University Press, 2017).

Richardson, B and Nunes, J, 'What Can Security Do for Food? Lessons from Brazil' (2015) 21 *Contemporary Politics* 70.

Richmond, OP and Franks, J, 'Liberal Peacebuilding in Timor Leste: The Emperor's New Clothes?' (2008) 15 *International Peacekeeping* 185.

Roach, SC, *Politicizing the International Criminal Court: The Convergence of Politics, Ethics, and Law* (Lanham, MD, Rowman & Littlefield Publishers, 2006).

Robertson, G, *Crimes against Humanity: The Struggle for Global Justice* (London, Penguin 2012).

Rorty, R, 'Human Rights, Rationality and Sentimentality' in O Savić and B Krug (ed), *The Politics of Human Rights* (London, Verso, 1999).

Rose, N, *Inventing Our Selves: Psychology, Power, and Personhood*, reprint edn (Cambridge, Cambridge University Press, 1998).

Rosen, M, *Dignity: Its History and Meaning* (Cambridge, MA, Harvard University Press, 2012).

Rosenau, J, 'Governance in the Twenty-First Century' in R Wilkinson (ed), *The Global Governance Reader* (New York, Routledge, 2005).

Roznai, Y, 'The Insecurity of Human Security' (2014) 32 *Wisconsin International Law Journal* 95.

Ruffert, M, 'Administration of Kosovo and East-Timor by the International Community Shorter Articles, Comments and Notes' (2001) 50 *International and Comparative Law Quarterly* 613.

Ruiz Fabri, H, 'Enhancing the Rhetoric of Jus Cogens' (2012) 23 *European Journal of International Law* 1049.

Sandvik, KB, 'A Legal History: The Emergence of the African Resettlement Candidate in International Refugee Management' (2010) 22 *International Journal of Refugee Law* 20.

Santos, B de S and Rodríguez-Garavito, CA, 'Law, Politics, and the Subaltern in Counter-Hegemonic Globalization' in B de Sousa Santos and CA Rodríguez-Garavito (eds), *Law and Globalization from Below: Towards a Cosmopolitan Legality* (Cambridge, Cambridge University Press, 2005).

Sayer, A, *Why We Can't Afford the Rich*, reprint edn (Bristol, Policy Press, 2015).

Schachter, O, 'Human Dignity as a Normative Concept' (1983) 77 *American Journal of International Law* 848.

Schaefer, B, 'Human Rights: Problems with the Foundationless Approach' (2005) 31 *Social Theory & Practice* 27.

Scheinin, M, 'Law and Security: Facing the Dilemmas', EUI Working Paper 58 (2009), http://cadmus.eui.eu//handle/1814/12233.

Scheppele, KL, 'Empire of Security and the Security of Empire' (2013) 27 *Temple International & Comparative Law Journal* 241.

Schmitt, C, *Leviathan in the State Theory of Thomas Hobbes: Meaning and Failure of a Political Symbol* (Westport, CT, Greenwood Press, 1996).

Schmitt, C, *The Concept of the Political*, enlarged edn (G Schwab trans, Chicago, University of Chicago Press, 2007).

Schneiker, A, 'The New Defenders of Human Rights? How Radical Right-Wing TNGOs Are Using the Human Rights Discourse to Promote Their Ideas' (2019) 33 *Global Society* 149.

Scott, D, 'Human Rights' in J d'Aspermont and J Haskell (eds), *International Law at a Tipping Point: Critique and Commitment* (Cambridge, Cambridge University Press, 2019).

Serrano, M, 'The Responsibility to Protect and Its Critics: Explaining the Consensus' (2011) 3 *Global Responsibility to Protect* 425.

Shawki, N, 'Responsibility to Protect: The Evolution of an International Norm' (2011) 3 *Global Responsibility to Protect* 172.

Shore, C and Wright, S, 'Governing by Numbers: Audit Culture, Rankings and the New World Order' (2015) 23 *Social Anthropology* 22.

Sinclair, GF, *To Reform the World: International Organizations and the Making of Modern States* (Oxford, Oxford University Press, 2017).

Sinclair, GF, 'Forging Modern States with Imperfect Tools: United Nations Technical Assistance for Public Administration in Decolonized States' (2020) 11 *Humanity: An International Journal of Human Rights, Humanitarianism, and Development* 54.

Singer, P, *Animal Liberation*, 2nd edn (Bournemouth, Pimlico, 1995).

Singh, S, 'The Fundamental Rights of States in Neoliberal Times' (2015) 4 *Cambridge Journal of International and Comparative Law* 461.

Slaughter, A-M, *A New World Order*, new edn (Princeton, Princeton University Press, 2005).

Slaughter, JR, 'However Incompletely, Human' in C Douzinas and C Gearty (eds), *The Meanings of Rights: The Philosophy and Social Theory of Human Rights* (Cambridge, Cambridge University Press, 2014).

Slobodian, Q, *Globalists: The End of Empire and the Birth of Neoliberalism* (Cambridge, MA, Harvard University Press, 2018).

Soirila, U, 'Human Dignity Mediated: Personhood, Humanity, and the Logic of Property in Law and Bioethics' in A Griffiths, S Mustasaari and A Mäki-Petajä-Leinonen (eds), *Subjectivity, Citizenship and Belonging in Law: Identities and Intersections* (Abingdon, Routledge, 2016).

Soirila, U, 'Othering through Human Dignity' (2018) 15 *No Foundations: An Interdisciplinary Journal of Law and Justice* 127.

Somek, A, *The Cosmopolitan Constitution* (Oxford, Oxford University Press, 2014).

Stahn, C, *The Law and Practice of International Territorial Administration: Versailles to Iraq and Beyond*, reissue edn (Cambridge, Cambridge University Press, 2010).

Stevens, D, 'Rights, Needs or Assistance? The Role of the UNHCR in Refugee Protection in the Middle East' (2016) 20 *International Journal of Human Rights* 264.

Stone Sweet, A and Grisel, F, 'Transnational Investment Arbitration: From Delegation to Constitutionalization?' in P-M Dupuy, E-U Petersmann and F Francioni (eds), *Human Rights in International Investment Law and Arbitration* (Oxford, Oxford University Press, 2009).

Strange, S, *The Retreat of the State: The Diffusion of Power in the World Economy* (Cambridge, Cambridge University Press, 1996).

Supiot, A, *Homo Juridicus: On the Anthropological Function of the Law* (S Brown trans, New York, Verso 2007).

Szasz, PC, 'The Security Council Starts Legislating' (2002) 96 *American Journal of International Law* 901.

Tadjbakhsh, S and Chenoy, A, *Human Security: Concepts and Implications* (New York, Routledge, 2007).

Tallgren, I, 'The Sensibility and Sense of International Criminal Law' (2002) 13 *European Journal of International Law* 561.

Tallgren, I, 'The Voice of the International: Who Is Speaking?' (2015) 13 *Journal of International Criminal Justice* 135.

Tang, SM, 'Rethinking Economic Security in a Globalized World' (2015) 21 *Contemporary Politics* 40.

Tasioulas, J, 'Towards a Philosophy of Human Rights' (2012) 65 *Current Legal Problems* 1.

Teitel, R, *Humanity's Law* (Oxford, Oxford University Press, 2011).

The IGLP Law and Global Production Working Group, 'The Role of Law in Global Value Chains: A Research Manifesto' (2016) 4 *London Review of International Law* 57.

Thomas, C, 'Global Governance, Development and Human Security: Exploring the Links' (2001) 22 *Third World Quarterly* 159.

Thomas, N and Tow, WT, 'The Utility of Human Security: Sovereignty and Humanitarian Intervention' (2002) 33 *Security Dialogue* 177.

Tigerstrom, B von, *Human Security and International Law: Prospects and Problems* (Oxford, Hart Publishing, 2007).

Tourinho, M, Stuenkel, O and Brockmeier, S, '"Responsibility While Protecting": Reforming R2P Implementation' (2016) 30 *Global Society* 134.

Tutuianu, S, *Towards Global Justice: Sovereignty in an Interdependent World*, 2013 edn (The Hague, TMC Asser Press, 2012).

Tzevelekos, VP, 'Revisiting the Humanisation of International Law: Limits and Potential: Obligations Erga Omnes, Hierarchy of Rules and the Principle of Due Diligence as the Basis for Further Humanisation' (2013) 6 *Erasmus Law Review* 62.

Tzevelekos, VP and Lixinski, L, 'Towards a Humanized International "Constitution"?' (2016) 29 *Leiden Journal of International Law* 343.

Tzouvala, N, 'Food for the Global Market: The Neoliberal Reconstruction of Agriculture in Occupied Iraq (2003–2004) and the Role of International Law' (2017) 17 *Global Jurist*.

Tzouvala, N, 'The Ordo-Liberal Origins of Modern International Investment Law: Constructing Competition on a Global Scale' in JD Haskell and A Rasulov (eds), *New Voices and New Perspectives in International Economic Law: New Voices, New Perspectives* (Springer, 2020).

Uberti, LJ, 'Neoliberalism and Industrial Policy in Kosovo: The Mining and Metals Industry in the Post-War Transition' (2014) 30 *East European Politics* 482.

United Nations Development Programme, *Human Development Report 1994*, 5th edn (Oxford, Oxford University Press, 1994).

Urueña, R, *No Citizens Here: Global Subjects and Participation in International Law* (Helsinki, Helsinki University Printing House, 2010).

Urueña, R, 'Deciding What Is Humane: Towards a Critical Reading of Humanity as a Normative Standard in International Law' in B van Beers, L Corrias and WG Werner (eds), *Humanity across International Law and Biolaw* (Cambridge, Cambridge University Press, 2014).

Vasconcelos Vilaca, G, 'The Place of Ethical Leadership, Virtues and Narrative in International Organizations' in G Vasconcelos Vilaca and M Varaki (eds), *Ethical Leadership in International Organizations: Concepts, Narratives, Judgment and Assessment* (Cambridge, Cambridge University Press, forthcoming).

Vasconcelos Vilaca, G, 'Book Review: To Reform the World: International Organizations and the Making of Modern States Written by Guy Fiti Sinclair' (2018) 15 *International Organizations Law Review* 221.

Vattel, E de, *The Law of Nations* (Indianapolis, Liberty Fund, 2008).

Verdirame, PG, *The UN and Human Rights: Who Guards the Guardians?* (Cambridge, Cambridge University Press, 2011).

Villalpando, S, 'The Legal Dimension of the International Community: How Community Interests Are Protected in International Law' (2010) 21 *European Journal of International Law* 387.

Von Schnitzler, A, 'Performing Dignity: Human Rights, Citizenship, and the Techno-politics of Law in South Africa' (2014) 41 *American Ethnologist* 336.

Wählisch, M, 'Human Security: Concept and Evolution in the United Nations' (2014) 18 *Max Planck Yearbook of United Nations Law Online* 1.

Wald, N and Hill, DP, '"Rescaling" Alternative Food Systems: From Food Security to Food Sovereignty' (2016) 33 *Agriculture and Human Values* 203.

Waldron, J, 'Are Sovereigns Entitled to the Benefit of the International Rule of Law?' (2011) 22 *European Journal of International Law* 315.

Waldron, J, *Dignity, Rank, and Rights* (Oxford, Oxford University Press, 2012).

Walker, N, *Intimations of Global Law* (Cambridge, Cambridge University Press, 2014).

Wellman, C, *Real Rights* (Oxford, Oxford University Press, 1997).

Welsh, JM, 'Norm Contestation and the Responsibility to Protect' (2013) 5 *Global Responsibility to Protect* 365.

Wet, E de, 'The International Constitutional Order' (2006) 55 *International and Comparative Law Quarterly* 51.

Whyte, J, *The Morals of the Market: Human Rights and the Rise of Neoliberalism* (London, Verso, 2019).

Wilde, R, 'Quis Custodiet Ipsos Custodes: Why and How UNHCR Governance of Development Refugee Camps Should Be Subject to International Human Rights Law Note' (1998) 1 *Yale Human Rights & Development Law Journal* 107.

Wilde, R, *International Territorial Administration: How Trusteeship and the Civilizing Mission Never Went Away* (Oxford, Oxford University Press, 2010).

Wilt, H van der, 'Crimes against Humanity: A Category Hors Concours in (International) Criminal Law?' in B van Beers, L Corrias and WG Werner (eds), *Humanity across International Law and Biolaw* (Cambridge, Cambridge University Press, 2014).

Winslow, D and Eriksen, TH, 'A Broad Concept That Encourages Interdisciplinary Thinking' (2004) 35 *Security Dialogue* 361.

Yoo, J, 'Iraqi Reconstruction and the Law of Occupation' (2004) 11 *UC Davis Journal of International Law & Policy* 7.

Index

www.ingramcontent.com/pod-product-compliance
Lightning Source LLC
Chambersburg PA
CBHW071351220926
51613CB00008B/51
* 9 7 8 1 5 0 9 9 3 8 9 1 9 *